Workers' Inquiry and Global Class Struggle

Wildcat: Workers' Movements and Global Capitalism

Series Editors:
Immanuel Ness (City University of New York)
Malehoko Tshoaedi (University of Johannesburg)
Peter Cole (Western Illinois University)
Raquel Varela (Instituto de História Contemporânea (IHC) of Universidade Nova de Lisboa, Lisbon New University)
Kate Alexander (University of Johannesburg)
Tim Pringle (SOAS, University of London)

Workers' movements are a common and recurring feature in contemporary capitalism. The same militancy that inspired the mass labour movements of the twentieth century continues to define worker struggles that proliferate throughout the world today.

For more than a century, labour unions have mobilised to represent the political-economic interests of workers by uncovering the abuses of capitalism, establishing wage standards, improving oppressive working conditions, and bargaining with employers and the state. Since the 1970s, organised labour has declined in size and influence as the global power and influence of capital has expanded dramatically. The world over, existing unions are in a condition of fracture and turbulence in response to neoliberalism, financialisation, and the reappearance of rapacious forms of imperialism. New and modernised unions are adapting to conditions and creating class-conscious workers' movement rooted in militancy and solidarity. Ironically, while the power of organised labour contracts, working-class militancy and resistance persists and is growing in the Global South.

Wildcat publishes ambitious and innovative works on the history and political economy of workers' movements and is a forum for debate on pivotal movements and labour struggles. The series applies a broad definition of the labour movement to include workers in and out of unions, and seeks works that examine proletarianisation and class formation; mass production; gender, affective and reproductive labour; imperialism and workers; syndicalism and independent unions, and labour and Leftist social and political movements.

Also available:

Choke Points:
Logistics Workers Disrupting the Global Supply Chain
Edited by Jake Alimahomed-Wilson and Immanuel Ness

Just Work?
Migrant Workers' Struggles Today
Edited by Aziz Choudry and Mondli Hlatshwayo

Wobblies of the World:
A Global History of the IWW
Edited by Peter Cole, David Struthers and Kenyon Zimmer

Southern Insurgency:
The Coming of the Global Working Class
Immanuel Ness

The Spirit of Marikana:
The Rise of Insurgent Trade Unionism in South Africa
Luke Sinwell with Siphiwe Mbatha

Solidarity:Latin America and the US Left in the Era of Human Rights
Steve Striffler

Working the Phones:
Control and Resistance in Call Centres
Jamie Woodcock

The Cost of Free Shipping:
Amazon in the Global Economy
Edited by Jake Alimahomed-Wilson and Ellen Reese

Workers' Inquiry and Global Class Struggle

Strategies, Tactics, Objectives

Edited by Robert Ovetz

First published 2020 by Pluto Press
345 Archway Road, London N6 5AA

www.plutobooks.com

British Library Cataloguing in Publication Data
A catalogue record for this book is available from the British Library

ISBN   978 0 7453 4084 5   Hardback
ISBN   978 0 7453 4086 9   Paperback
ISBN   978 1 7868 0644 4   PDF eBook
ISBN   978 1 7868 0646 8   Kindle eBook
ISBN   978 1 7868 0645 1   EPUB eBook

This book is printed on paper suitable for recycling and made from fully managed
and sustained forest sources. Logging, pulping and manufacturing processes are
expected to conform to the environmental standards of the country of origin.

Typeset by Stanford DTP Services, Northampton, England

Simultaneously printed in the United Kingdom and United States of America

Contents

List of Figures and Tables

Acknowledgments

This book would not have been realized without the unwavering support of my friend and colleague Manny Ness, who encouraged me to assemble it even before I was done with the never-ending edits and revisions of my first book. It began as a series of curated articles for *The Journal of Labor and Society*, for which Manny is the co-editor. I am forever grateful for his support and encouragement, and for his invitation to publish this book as part of the Pluto Wildcat series which he edits. I am also deeply grateful to David Shulman at Pluto, for his enthusiasm for my work and interest in publishing the book. If this were not already enough to celebrate, the first time we met, David asked me what book I planned to write next and then asked me to begin writing it so he could also consider it for Pluto. This book is in excellent company.

I am truly grateful to all the authors who answered the original call for the journal series and the book. It has been a great pleasure to work with each of you.

I wish to thank my colleagues in the Political Science department at San José State University for their unwavering support. Professor Karthika Sasikumar invited me to present my research at a departmental colloquium and answer many probing questions that helped me clarify my research and analysis. Professor Melinda Jackson supported all my travel requests to present my work around the world. My chapter on credible strike threats was made possible by the support of two College of Social Sciences grants, one to conduct the research with the help of my talented Research Assistant Gabriela Crowley, and one for Elio Scudieri of Cinematic Mirror to build https://strikethreats.org to continue my research. For that I am forever grateful.

This book would also be impossible without my partner Darshana's boundless love and brilliant mind. My daughter Nisa's incredible patience, caring, perceptiveness, and passion for challenging my ideas has made producing this book all the more pressing. I hope

someday again to be able to get to five points. They both remind me
daily that it is about both love and struggle.

My deepest gratitude goes out to all of the people, known and
unknown, who have organized, struggled, and fought to make this a
better world by moving us ever closer to getting beyond capitalism.
They have inspired me to keep up the fight.

For my teacher, mentor, and friend Harry Cleaver.

"But who are we? We have no names, no family. Every one of us is poor and powerless. And yet together, we can overthrow an empire."

— High Sparrow, *Game of Thrones*, "Home" (Season 6, Episode 2)

Introduction

Robert Ovetz

"You need to take your enemy's side if you're going to see things the way they do. And you need to see things the way they do if you're going to anticipate their actions, respond effectively, and beat them."

—Tyrion Lannister, *Game of Thrones*, "Beyond the Wall"
(Season 7, Episode 6)

There is little doubt that the global working class is on the retreat and has been for a very long time. Confronted with the strategy of neoliberalism, the balance of power is heavily tilted towards capital. Despite decades of hand-wringing, investigations, reforms, and consolidations and reorganizations of unions, despair has deepened and the assault on workers continues unabated around the world.

The rationale for capital's assault, however, has been almost entirely unexamined. If the level of repression is an expression of the level of the threat, as the novelist Eduardo Galeano once asserted in his classic book *Open Veins of Latin America* (1997), then the threat of global class struggle is clearly apparent to capital even if it has been overlooked by union leaders, labor scholars, and working-class militants.[1] As Jamie Woodcock has reminded us, "between the placid workplace and the all-out strike there are a range of practices—some collective, others individual—that are worthy of sustained attention" (2016: 99). Capitalism has been in crisis during the entire period of neoliberalism. Is it merely a crisis of its own making or does the working class have a role to play in it?

This book is an addition to a growing body of work by workers and scholars that attempts not only to identify, investigate, and analyze new forms of worker cooperation, self-organization, and struggle, but also to examine the strategies, tactics, objectives, and organiza-

1

tional forms undertaken by these workers and the possibilities for circulating their struggles across borders and unleashing a new cycle of global class struggle.[2] To achieve this it is critical that we conduct what are called "workers' inquiries" into the current class composition in as many strategic countries and sectors as possible. This will help shed light and heat on the current global power of capital and the necessary tactics, strategies, objectives, and organizational forms that workers can and are using to counter and disrupt that power. As a step towards carrying out a global workers' inquiry this book offers inquiries from nine countries, representing in total about 70 percent of the global population on four continents.

WORKERS' INQUIRY: NO POLITICS WITHOUT INQUIRY

In 1995, the independent working-class scholar Ed Emery issued a call to form a Network for Research and Action to carry out workers' inquiries around the world. Emery's idea was inspired by Karl Marx's 101-question survey published in *La Revue socialiste* in 1880. Too late in his life to continue the effort, Marx sought to "undertake a serious inquiry into the position of the French working class" to obtain "an *exact and positive* knowledge of the conditions in which the working class—the class to whom the future belongs—works and moves." His questions broached issues ranging from the workplace to community and government, ending with an open-ended 101st question allowing the worker to include "general remarks." Marx reportedly never received a response (Marx 1880).

Inspired by Marx's survey, Emery (1995) argued that the working class should closely study the current class composition before launching into a new round of struggle. As he put it, there should be "no politics without inquiry," since "the new class composition is more or less a mystery to us (and to capital, and to itself) because it is still in the process of formation." For Emery, as for the Italian, French, and American autonomist Marxists who rediscovered and reinvigorated Marx's project from the 1950s to the 1970s, there should be no struggle before we know who we are, the conditions under which we work, how capital is organized, its weaknesses and choke points, as well as our sources of strength, power, and leverage. "Before we can make politics," Emery makes clear, "we have to understand that class composition. This requires us to study it. Analyse it. We do this through a process of inquiry. Hence: No Politics Without Inquiry."

This book is a response to Emery's call for a workers' inquiry into the global composition of class struggle. Its limited scope of nine countries on four continents is meant to be a starting point for examining a class composition "eternally in flux," as Emery reminds us, at this particular point in which "periodically consolidating nodes of class power" appear, are defeated or succeed, and are then attacked, decomposed, and recreated. The book is intended to be a part of a larger project of carrying out a global workers' inquiry into the global class struggle that can be further developed and contributed to.

A workers' inquiry is an invaluable methodology for investigating the class composition at a particular point in time, in a specific workplace, industry, country, or, in its most challenging form which has yet to be attempted, at the planetary scale. Virtually forgotten ever since Marx published his original call, the workers' inquiry was unearthed simultaneously by the Johnson-Forest Tendency (and later the *Zerowork* journal) in the US, *Socialisme ou Barberie* in France, and *Quaderni Rossi*, *Classe Operaia* and other Italian publications in the 1960s and '70s. It was soon all but forgotten—with the exception of *Midnight Notes* in the US in the 1970s and '80s and the book *Hotlines* in Germany in the 1990s—until the resurgence in the past few years of interest in militant worker self-organization. While these efforts carried out inquiries into specific workplaces, industries, and countries, analysis on a global level has only just begun. Such a global workers' inquiry is long overdue and unavoidable today as capital moves almost frictionlessly across national borders, fleeing workers in one country while propelling itself towards those in other countries.

There are others working along the same lines, seeking to document and examine workers' strategies, tactics, and objectives in struggle. Among them is Immanuel Ness, who identifies new forms of self-organization displaying innovative tactics and strategies that either bypass or are antagonistic to the bureaucratization, institutionalization, and corporatism of the existing class-collaborationist unions and social democratic parties. The tactic of "contract unionism," Ness argues, has tied unions to the state and capital as a mechanism for suppressing and defeating the strategy of working-class militancy (2014: 269–78).[3]

There are also others carrying out complementary studies of worker self-organized struggles against both capital and contract unions, including Azzellini and Kraft (2018), Dutta, Nowak, and Birke (2018), and Atzeni and Ness (2018). I myself published a historical workers' inquiry from above, examining these very questions in relation to workers in the US during the tumultuous period 1877 to 1921 (Ovetz 2019). Sinwell and Mbatha (2016) have provided a potent examination of the challenge to contract unionism by self-organized Marikana miners in South Africa, while Ness and Azzellini (2011) have documented the continuing emphasis on workers' control as a persistently relevant strategy and objective of working-class militancy. Ngwane, Sinwell, and Ness (2017) further tie this militancy to struggles in both waged and unwaged workplaces and to workers' communities.

The most important text in this emerging series on self-organized workers' movements is Alimahomed-Wilson and Ness's *Choke Points*, which investigates workers' attempts to disrupt key nodes in the global capital accumulation process to assert their demands, shift the balance of power back in their favor, and extract concessions and victories. "Logistics," they observe, "remains the crucial site for increasing working-class power today." Workers are increasingly able to apply their leverage to make the supply chain "unmanageable" because of their global interlinkages. "These workers, although connected in the global supply chain, largely remain divided across region, nation state, industry, and job sector. In light of this, linking these global struggles remains an important task in developing strategies of resistance" (Alimahomed-Wilson and Ness 2018: 2–4). *Choke Points* is no less than a series of workers' inquiries into the current technical composition of capital and the possibilities for recomposing working-class power so as to disrupt the global capital accumulation process and extract concessions that will move the struggle onto increasingly more intense terrain.

A similar analysis is offered by Moody's groundbreaking *On New Terrain*, which conducts a finely honed analysis of capital's current global technical composition supported by extensive detailed research provided by capital itself. Noting that the composition of the working class has been transformed by the changing technical composition of capital, Moody reminds us that "The terrain on which the working class and the oppressed fight necessarily changes as the structure and contours of global and domestic capital changes." As the class composition changes, the working class is responding by developing new tactics and strategies that increase its potential for recomposing its own power. The old industrial system, Moody concludes, "has been replaced by new and mostly different geographic patterns and structures of concentration with the potential for advances in working-class organization and rebellion" (2017: 2–3).

WORKERS' INQUIRY AS STRATEGY

This book, however, takes a relatively unique path in that it focuses on an analysis of the class composition and how it can inform new tactics, strategies, objectives, and organizational forms. While not all of the contributions in this book take entirely the same approach or reach the same conclusions, what ties them together is an attempt to carry out, either in part or whole, what is called a "workers' inquiry" *from below* when conducted by workers themselves, and *from above* when conducted by academic and independent scholars, as partners engaged in co-research (Woodcock 2014: 505; Monaco 2015a, 2015b, and 2017; Curcio and Roggero 2018).

What emerges from these workers' inquiries is not only that class struggle has never ceased or gone underground during the decades of defeat, but also that workers have been experimenting with new forms of organization, strategies, and tactics that can be found inside, outside, or in conflict with unions. These struggles rarely show themselves in the form of strikes, let alone strike waves, but they are disruptive threats to the accumulation of capital nonetheless.

This observation is informed by re-reading the voluminous economic reports on rates of private investment, return on investment, "redundancies," "flexibility," automation, productivity, efficiency, and innovation from the perspective of the working class. This careful re-reading—what Cleaver (1992) calls the "inversion of class perspective"—finds class struggle to be ubiquitous throughout the global capitalist system. Mario Tronti made the case for inverting capital's perspective as follows:

> We too have worked with a concept that puts capitalist development first, and workers second. This is a mistake. And now we have to turn the problem on its head, reverse the polarity, and start again from the beginning: and the beginning is the class struggle of the working class. At the level of socially developed capital, capitalist development becomes subordinated to working-class struggles...
> (Tronti 1966)

This inversion, Tronti argues elsewhere, can demonstrate that "the pressure of labour-power is capable of forcing capital to modify its own internal composition, intervening *within* capital as [an] essential component of capitalist development" (Tronti cited in Wright 2002: 37). Panzieri made a similar point when he observed that "the sole limit to the development of capital is not capital itself, but the resistance of the working class" (1976: 11–12). Kolinko's workers' inquiry into call center workers' struggles in Germany in the 1990s and 2000s spoke to Tronti and Panzieri's point about how working-class struggle drives capitalist development:

> Our starting-points are the specific conditions in a specific sphere of exploitation, we have to try to relate them to the global class contradiction. In reference to ... the usage of class composition (the relation of workers to the organic composition of capital): Workers are confronting the "organic composition" of capital and socialisation of work in many different ways ... We have to face and analyse the problem of how these differences can be overthrown in class struggle. (Kolinko 2001: 10)[4]

In short, if we channel the insight of Galeano, a workers' inquiry into class composition provides us with confirmation that if there is no worker struggle then there is no need for capital to innovate. Or, as Cleaver observed, "The violence that capitalists required to impose their order reveals the depth of resistance" (2019: 19).

This book is an attempt to identify newly emerging strategies used by workers and the lessons that can be learned from them and circulated globally. We know a lot about capital's strategy but what do we really know about workers' strategies? The book is a response to this deficiency, lamented by John Womack in his sweeping history of the strategy of disruption:

> many Marxist academics considering questions of strategy took only capitalists or managers for strategists. In their accounts workers acted only in "resistance," on the strength of interests, indignation, or solidarity, maybe by "stratagem," but never strategically ... In many other Marxist accounts industrial workers (even "the working class" at large) appeared capable of strategy, but only away from work, in labor markets or politics or culture. (Womack 2006: 207)

From this perspective, accounts of capital's power and working-class weakness come up short. They mistake capital's current effort to impose a new technical composition for a decisive hegemonic victory. This book will argue, counter to Moody's otherwise splendid analysis of that technical composition, that the move to platform-based metric-driven production using contingent labor is capital's strategic *response* to efforts to recompose working-class power. This struggle between the potential recomposition of working-class power and capital's quest to devise tools to control, discipline, manage, and repress it is constantly in flux, pushed and pulled from one pole to another, and never entirely resolved. Marx read class struggle into capitalist innovation when he observed that machinery "is a power inimical to him [the worker]. It is the most powerful weapon for suppressing strikes, those periodic revolts of the working class against the autocracy of capital ... It would be possible to write a whole history of the inventions made since 1830 for the sole purpose of providing capital with weapons against working-class revolt" (Marx 1976 [1867]: 562–3).[5] The same could be said today: beneath capital's strategy lies class struggle.

Depending on the period we focus on, the tools we use to examine it, and on whose behalf we choose to look, the struggle between capital and labor continues to ebb and flow. Capital's continued assault on the global working class is not without cause. Class struggle has never gone away but has only adapted, evolved, improvised, and transformed to meet the challenge. Capital and workers are continually engaged in what Alquati (1967) called a "decisive spiral" of struggle that plays out over historical periods. As capital plays its hand, workers regroup, alter their strategy, play their own hand, and take a win. In response, capital withdraws, regroups, alters its strategy, and then plays a new hand, putting workers on the defensive and perhaps even defeating them.

We call this understanding of the dialectical push and pull of class struggle the theory of *class composition*. To push the ebb and flow of that struggle back in favor of workers it is critical that we carry out a global workers' inquiry to understand the strategies, tactics, organization, and objectives of capital and how workers are adapting their own strategies, tactics, and organization to achieve their objectives of responding to, defeating, and transcending capitalism. Marshall Ganz described this interplay between tactics, strategy, and objectives as "turning *what* you have into what you *need* to get what you *want*" (cited in McAlevey 2016: 5).

A NEW CLASS SCIENCE

A workers' inquiry into class composition is not an academic exercise but what Tronti called a "class science." It is clearly partisan in its attempt to identify, document, understand, and circulate the tactics, strategies, organizational forms, and objectives of the workers' struggles being examined (Tronti cited in Wright 2002: 38). As Woodcock explains, "the inquiry aims to uncover the composition of the working class at particular points or in different contexts to understand how struggle will develop" (2014: 507).

A workers' inquiry serves a critically dual role: for workers to inform themselves about their own class power in a particular struggle, and to provide a model for workers to emulate in their own struggles elsewhere. An inquiry uncovers the tactics, strategies, organizational forms, and objectives of both capital and workers with the intention of providing the necessary information about the positions of power of each in order to further the success of the workers' struggle. In this way, just as the methods of anthropology, psychology, sociology, and engineering are partisan—intended to serve the interests of dominant economic, political, and social institutions—a workers' inquiry is similarly partisan in its intention to serve the interests of workers. For this reason, workers' inquiries are sometimes referred to as "co-research," "militant co-research," or "militant inquiries" (Hoffman 2019: 3).[6] Whatever they are called, they serve to develop a proletarian methodology for documenting, analyzing, understanding, and articulating the current class composition in the interests of workers both inside and outside the waged workplace.

The partisan function of a workers' inquiry can be as varied as those who conduct the inquiries. Many inquiries are a variation on what are called "assets" and "needs" maps of both sides in the class struggle. The intention is to uncover capital's weakness, identify tactics that would create leverage to exploit these choke points, strategies that assert and shift power to workers at the point of production or reproduction, and the objective of extracting a series of concessions that makes the workforce ungovernable in order to disrupt the capital accumulation process. "Workers' *self*-inquiry" has "a tactical agenda" (Thorn 2011: 2).[7]

Workers' inquiries are not used to merely extract concessions but also have the greater objective of rupturing capital and transitioning out of and beyond capitalism. With the myriad of insurmountable and catastrophic crises facing humanity, non-human life, and the entire planetary ecosystem, there is currently no more urgent need than to find a strategy to end capitalism in the immediate future. Because we still live under what Cleaver (2017) calls the "dialectic of capital," that strategy must be rooted in the refusal of work in the spheres of production and reproduction where capital is organized. Strategically, Tronti reminded us, "When the development of capital's interest in the factory is blocked, then the functioning of society seizes up: the way is then open for overthrowing and destroying the very basis of capital's power" (1980: 28). Because capital is clearly global, the working class, too, needs a global workers' inquiry. Before it can can make the politics of revolution, a workers' inquiry into the global working class and its adversary is needed.

In contrast, establishment social sciences utilize methods to obtain findings that inform capital's strategy and its objective of maintaining or restoring control on and off the shopfloor. Such an approach freezes the subject in time and context in order to gather information about it as an *object* to be acted upon, controlled, and managed.

A workers' inquiry is also distinguished from a union survey gauging the issues, grievances, and problems that inform collective bargaining; such surveys are rarely shared with the workers and rarely used as an organizing tool. They are intended to serve the institutional prerogatives of the union by providing it with essential information about the mood of the membership as the bargaining team prepares to engage with management. Surveys are used to gauge the lower limits of what members would be willing to accept and the upper limits of what they would be willing to trade to get it, for example how much new pain they would accept to achieve some relief for chronic pain.

The workers' inquiry is also distinct from McAlevey's innovative "structure test," which is used to organize workers for collective action and to assess the level of commitment to striking. Despite being a valuable tool for analyzing workers' organized power, the structure test is presented as serving the limited purposes of collective bargaining (McAlevey 2016). McAlevey's method is for workers or union staff to carry out a study of the composition of the workers in a particular workplace and in their communities in order to organize as many as possible to engage in gradually intensifying shows of worker strength in preparation to strike.

The structure test methodology has much in common with class composition theory and the method of the workers' inquiry. However, McAlevey's objectives are short-term and focused on winning localized victories that are enshrined in the next collective bargaining agreement, rather than serving the long-term interests of expanding the struggle in order to recompose working-class power to take on capitalism. While either union staff or workers may conduct structure tests, the workers' inquiry is conducted by workers themselves, with or without co-research partners, with the intention of identifying other workers with whom they can develop their own tactics, strategies, organizational forms, and objectives to collectively struggle against work.[8] In this way, the workers' inquiry is a method for workers to understand their own power, self-organize, and act autonomously against the rationalization of work with the aim of reducing exploitation or achieving their liberation from it. While McAlevey has little to say about assessing capital's technical composition, the structure test, as we will see shortly, could be a useful tool for assessing the potential for recomposing worker power.

OBJECTIVES OF A WORKERS' INQUIRY

Despite the re-emerging interest in workers' inquiries there is still some confusion over their methods and objectives. A workers' inquiry expresses workers' daily experiences at work while connecting their unique grievances to an analysis of the larger division of labor and the capital composition (see Wright 2002: 50).[9] The new organizational forms, tactics, and strategies informed by the workers' inquiry can be deployed by the workers to win their struggle, be it in their workplace, community, sector of the economy, or as a class. It is the method for studying, understanding, and overcoming the current class composition from the workers' perspective. While the method of the workers' inquiry is in flux, its objective could be characterized by *three key objectives* for understanding capital's and workers' tactics, strategies, organizational forms, and objectives (Lefort 1952: 88–9).[10] In short, a workers' inquiry should be conducted from the perspective of the workers, assess capital's current power, and devise the means to assert the workers' power to overcome it.

First, a workers' inquiry is conducted by workers themselves or in collaboration with a co-researcher in order to understand the current class composition from the perspectives of the workers. The most commonly used model for the workers' inquiry comes from Romano Alquati's co-research at the Italian firms Fiat and Olivetti in the early 1960s, conducted with the Italian Socialist Party and union militants and published in the *Quaderni Rossi*, of which Alquati was a member. What sets a workers' inquiry apart from other forms of academic or militant research is, as Hoffman observes, its aim "to enable workers to act politically on their own knowledge of their own conditions and struggles" (2019: 6).[11] As Lefort has written, a workers' inquiry begins from the immediate daily experiences of the worker because

> This class can be known only through itself and only on the condition that whoever inquires about it acknowledges the value of proletarian experience, is rooted in its situation, and makes his own this class's social and historical horizons—on the condition, therefore, that he break with the immediately given, that is, with the conditions of the system of exploitation. (Lefort 1952: 87)

In other words, the methods are developed in the context of the struggle and "flow ... from the political orientation of the investigation and determine its realization" (Hoffman 2019: 7–8 and 15–16). The orientation of the inquiry is to create a collective body of workers that can use the knowledge acquired in their own self-study to inform their struggle, rather than merely studying them for the purpose of documentation.

The second feature of the workers' inquiry is to examine the current class composition by analyzing the organization of work or the technical composition of capital. This analysis is conducted in order to understand how each change in that organization serves capital's objective of decomposing workers' power by fragmenting their collective forms of work and struggle and reimposing work on isolated individual workers. As Kolinko insightfully observed in their workers' inquiry into call-center workers in Germany, the forms of struggle are shaped by the conditions in which workers find themselves:

> Struggles of workers arise from concrete work-conditions, from actual situations of exploitation. Workers' struggles take different forms (in the past, in different regions or sectors etc.), because the concrete labour-process and therefore the material form of exploitation differs ... specific forms of production influence the ways, contents and perspectives of struggles. (Kolinko 2001: 3)

Closely related is the third aspect of the workers' inquiry, the flipside of the study of class composition: understanding workers' potential to recompose their power for the dual purpose of disrupting and transcending the relations of capitalist production and reproduction. This requires two things. First, workers must identify and understand capital's weaknesses and choke points. Second, in order for workers to attack capital's vulnerabilities and apply leverage they must assess their own strengths and weaknesses, and what they can do to wield it.

How an inquiry is designed, conducted, and assessed must necessarily vary depending on the capacities, resources, and skills of the workers and their allies. However, these three features of the inquiry are critical for the resulting analysis to provide the richest possible intelligence about capital's power and the workers' potential to disrupt and surpass it.

CLASS COMPOSITION

A workers' inquiry is an investigation into the current organization of capital and the working class, the make up of their forces, and the struggle of each to assert its power over the other. The study of class composition examines three dynamic cycles: 1) the current organization of work and capital's power in the workplace (technical composition), 2) workers' ability to reorganize their power to respond to and disrupt capital's power (working-class recomposition), and 3) capital's power to attack and undermine workers' power and to restructure the technical composition to reimpose its own power (working-class decomposition).[12]

For Kolinko, "The notion of class composition could help us to understand the coherence between the development of the material conditions within these sectors, and the re-emergence of workers' power" (Kolinko n.d.). Class composition can thus be thought of as a dance between the current technical composition of capital, workers' capacity to recompose their power, and capital's counter-attack intended to decompose organized workers' power and impose a new technical composition. Hardly static, this dance spirals about as it increases and decreases in intensity. Cleaver portrays it in the following way:

13

While it can be said that capital seeks a "class composition," i.e., a particular distribution of inter- and intra-class power which gives it sufficient control over the working class to guarantee accumulation, it is also true that workers' struggles repeatedly undermine such control and thus rupture the efficacy (from capital's point of view) of such a class composition. Such a rupture occurs only to the degree that workers are able to *recompose* the structures and distribution of power among themselves in such a way as to achieve a change in their collective relations of power to their class enemy. Thus the struggles which achieve such changes bring about a "political recomposition" of the class relations—"recomposition" of the intra-class structures of power, and "political" because that in turn changes the inter-class relations. (Cleaver 1992: 114)[13]

Capital's technical composition

In the first instance, the existing technical composition of capital is a response to the working class's existing or potential power to disrupt production and reproduction and thereby potentially rupture what Cleaver calls capital's dialectic. Rupture of class relations promises to ultimately free the working class from imposed work and bring about their liberation as human beings, or what Cleaver calls "the power of creative affirmation, the power to constitute new practices" (1992: 129). It cannot be emphasized enough that the study of class composition is the study of the power of the self-organized working class to attack, disrupt, and transcend the bounds of capital by constructing multiple others ways of organizing life. Capital is continually pursuing new tactics, strategies, and organizational forms in order to absorb, coopt, discipline, manage or repress this force, restore production, and reimpose its domination in the form of a new technical composition. To overcome the recomposition of working-class power, Cleaver emphasizes, capital

must seek to "decompose" the workers' newly constructed relations among themselves and create some new, controllable class composition. The introduction of new technologies, of new organizations of machinery and workers, if successful, results in the undermining of workers' struggles and their reduction, once more, to the status of labor power. But whatever new "class composition" is achieved, it only becomes the basis for further conflicts because the class antagonism can only be managed; it cannot be done away with. (Cleaver 1992: 114)

Working-class recomposition

Once the new technical composition of capital is in place workers must examine it to design new tactics, strategies, organizational forms, and objectives to counter and overcome it both within and outside the workplace. Martin Glaberman (1947) described the role of a workers' inquiry as "understanding the different strata within the working class and their movement" in the class struggle. For Cleaver, the process of recomposition can be seen in capital's reorganization of production and work. As he observed,

> the concept of political recomposition theoretically articulates the central role of working class struggle at the heart of technological change and the concepts of class composition and decomposition provide vehicles for rethinking the issue of technological domination in terms of capital's efforts to cope with an autonomously active, and opposed, historical subject. (Cleaver 1992: 114)

Working-class decomposition

As capital and the working class spiral about one another in the ever growing intensity of struggle, the possibilities of a rupture of capital or a defeat of the working class are ever present. Cleaver describes this process in terms of "cycles of class struggle, wherein the upswing in such a cycle involves a period of political recomposition by workers and the downswing, however much the workers win or lose, a process of class decomposition through which capital reestablishes sufficient control to continue its overall management of society" (1992: 114).

Capital's new technical composition

The decomposition of working class power is accompanied by a new technical composition of capital. Constant technological development and innovation are the outer signs of this perpetual class struggle as capital seeks to achieve the impossible: breaking free of its dependence on human labor to produce the very profits it must generate in order to reinvest in developing a new technical composition to restore its control over the working class. Capital's simultaneous mission to escape from its dependence on workers even as it remains bound to them as the only source of surplus value is what Caffentzis calls capital's "zerowork paradox" (2013: 150–7). To adapt Eugene Debs's warning that "where there would be no resistance, ... slavery would come," a workers' inquiry into the class composition would observe that "where there were no struggle, capital would have no need to innovate".[14] In such a case, the new division of labor would put capital entirely in control to extract as much work as it demands and with no need to innovate. Only a workers' inquiry can get to the bottom of this mystery.

CONDUCTING A WORKERS' INQUIRY

Although workers' inquiries are not yet widely used there has been an upsurge in recent years. Considering the sensitivity of information obtained in an inquiry, it is likely that some inquiries will remain confidential while they are being used in an active struggle.[15] Two exceptions are the new magazine *Notes from Below*—whose editors have contributed a chapter to this book—which actively publishes workers' inquiries for ongoing struggles in many primarily European sectors, and fellow contributor Lorenza Monaco's work in Italy and India.

The one common thread among the workers' inquiries that are publicly available is that they do not merely gather information. Rather, they serve to identify current forms of cooperation and ongoing relationships among workers that can develop into powerful organizational forms to circulate the workers' struggle and confront the existing technical composition of capital.[16] The methodology for carrying out an inquiry is as important as the uses for which it is intended.

Methodology

Kolinko's workers' inquiry in ten call centers provides the most detailed discussion of the method for conducting a workers' inquiry.[17] They conducted their inquiry in three stages. First, the core group began with an inquiry from above in which they examined the existing body of research into call centers and conducted theoretical discussions among themselves about capitalism, work, and technology. They then conducted an inquiry from below by seeding themselves in jobs in call centers and investigating the organization of work using interviews and surveys. Finally, they engaged in co-research by identifying other workers already engaged in collective action and collaborating with them to produce a website and flyers inviting workers to document forms of cooperation and connect with one another. They expected the participating workers to connect the knowledge they generated with existing organizational forms, tactics, strategies, and objectives (see Woodcock 2014: 510). Their culminating inquiry was published as the book *Hotlines* to share their "political evaluation" and promote further inquiries (Kolinko 2002: 6–7).

The Kolinko group faced a difficult quandary in conducting their inquiry: absent any observed forms of struggle should they organize such struggles and then use the inquiry to inform them? Frustrated at the lack of existing worker cooperation, Kolinko ultimately decided to end their workers' inquiry and document it in *Hotlines* rather than organize the struggle themselves. Reflecting on the difficulty of inquiring into something that doesn't exist they asked, "What is the point in leaflets and other kinds of intervention at all if there is no workers' self-activity to refer to?" (Kolinko 2001: 12).[18]

Although there is no single methodology for conducting a workers' inquiry—because the dynamic and specifics of class struggle make it a constantly moving target—there are some common approaches, features, criteria, and details that can be borrowed, adapted, and applied for inquiring into the current class composition.

Capital's technical composition

While the word "technical" implies technology, the technical composition of capital includes far more than just the type and level of technology used in the workplace. In short, the technical composition of capital concerns the methods of organizing work and the strategies for imposing and intensifying it, the command structure in the workplace, and the location of the workplace in the global system of production. The objective of such a comprehensive study of the organization of capital is strategic. It should ultimately lead to identifying choke points, vulnerabilities, and weaknesses where well-organized workers can strike most effectively to disrupt the relations of production, shift power, and assert control.

There are many aspects of the technical composition throughout the entirety of the production process that can be assessed. There is no exhaustive list because as capital devises new responses to class struggle new strategies will emerge that need to be identified and understood. These include the rationalization and organization of work (the division of labor); the concentration and diffusion of functions; vertical and horizontal integration; sectoral and territorial distribution; deskilling; the separation of conception from execution; routinization; regimentation; the structure of authority in the workplace, firm, and industry; methods of control and workplace rules; tactics for intensifying and lengthening the work day; pay and benefits; colonization of non-work time; management strategies; public relations; disciplinary mechanisms; forms of state intervention such as regulation and enforcement of property law; and the roles of technology in the production process, among other features.

An inquiry into the organization of work would map the existing division of labor by outlining the hierarchical command structure of the workplace, the types of jobs with their different responsibilities, and the role of each in the production process. The workforce could also be mapped to identify the pay and benefits structure at every level, how many workers are involved in each aspect of the work, the impact of deskilling on the workforce, length of tenure and physical location, existing conflicts and tensions, horizontal and lateral mobility across positions, and the size and respective responsibilities of administrative, management, and production staff. The workplace should be situated in the global division of labor by identifying workplaces down- and upstream from it. Historical changes in the conditions, distribution, organization, and pace of work, including any recent changes, their causes, and struggles over them, are also critically informative. An important resource here is Harry Braverman's (1974) work on the deskilling process, by which the separation of conception from execution is carried out as higher level skills are fragmented into lower skilled component competencies and automated, dispersed among multiple workers or outsourced to unrelated firms. It is also critically important to assess the effectiveness of the new division of labor for the management goal of preventing interruptions to production, disruption, tensions, and other conflicts. Any failure in management strategy would point to everyday forms of resistance and refusal of work that can inform new forms of overt struggle.

Methods are just as critical as technology to capital's strategy of control. As Panzieri (1980) reminds us, "'methods', organizational techniques, etc., are incorporated into capital and confront the workers as capital: as an extraneous rationality." Methods, rules, and tactics of control and discipline for intensifying and lengthening work should also be studied. These can include the introduction of new technologies such as audiovisual equipment, operating systems, apps, surveillance devices, data gathering, and the use of metrics for assessing work. Alterations in the workplace command structure, job roles, work process or rules should also be examined. Who made these changes, when, and why should also be documented, along with their effects. What impact have they had on pay, benefits, staffing, prior conflicts and tensions, productivity, and the unwaged part of the day outside work? The impacts of capital's new methods, techniques, and strategies can bring to light possible existing grievances, and the workers engaged in them can form the basis for a new organization and cycle of struggle.

Also critical to the inquiry is the relationship of the work to a larger production system connected across multiple down- and upstream workplaces and employers, and even horizontally across firms and industries. How is the particular workplace integrated with and dependent on other workplaces within and outside the industry for workers, materials, parts, supplies, coordination, and access to markets? Inversely, if the employer is relied on by other workplaces, firms, and industries, choke points will emerge that will have ramifications beyond the single workplace affecting perhaps an entire industrial or geographic sector and potentially the country and the planet.

A workers' inquiry is an "inversion of class perspective" (Cleaver 1992) by re-reading the organization of capital to use it in struggle. Analyzing the technical composition is akin to "knowing your enemy" so as to identify points at which leverage can be applied with minimum pressure and risk to achieve maximum impact. Assessing earlier changes to the technical composition can identify previous choke points and weak links and the strategies used to seal them. If small numbers of workers successfully use choke points to extract small gains they will demonstrate the effectiveness of organizing and collective action to other workers, potentially bringing them into the struggle. The analysis of the technical composition of capital can inform new tactics and strategies to take advantage of the potential opportunities in the current composition and prepare for the expected responses based on the last cycle of struggle. However, because of the globally integrated technical composition of capital, the focus, Alquati (1967) reminds us, should not merely be on the class composition in a particular workplace but on making the linkage to the global organization of capital and working-class struggles elsewhere.

Working-class decomposition and recomposition

Class composition theory is a significant departure from leftist and labor studies of the working class because the recomposition of the working class has nothing to do with their overemphasis on consciousness or culture. It is rather focused on identifying the existing tactical repertoires, organizational forms of struggle, and assets available to workers to enable them to generalize their self-organization and maximize their strength.

The analysis of the technical composition of capital will define its current strategy of control, discipline, and organization of work. Capital's strategy will have *decomposed* the previously existing forms of organization and collective action by breaking their social connections and repressing the "unknown committees" (Ovetz 2019:

365–70; 438–54) among the workers in order to reassemble them in such a way as to restore control and discipline and reimpose work. To *recompose* their power workers must understand their own current composition, including demographic characteristics, associations, connections, resources, networks of cooperation, and past and present forms of collective organization and action, in order to form a new organization of workers, build their own tactical repertoire, and develop and deploy a new strategy. Knowing who the workers are will help explain why they have not engaged in collective action, why previous efforts failed, and what is needed to overcome the impediments to collective action. Understanding the basis for prior and future collective action is critical for understanding how workers' actions can tip the balance of power by moving around, over, and through hierarchical barriers to circulate the struggle throughout a workplace, firm, industry, country or even globally.

Even in the absence of strike-related activity workers are still engaged in various forms of resistance to capital's plan, including the refusal of work. Understanding and circulating the recomposition of worker power begins with seeking forms of existing cooperation and collective action carried out by unknown committees. Such self-organized anonymous groupings of workers will utilize a range of tactics from their repertoire depending on the balance of power and conditions of work. Watson (1971) identified how such committees engage in "counterplanning on the shopfloor" that both undermines the existing technical composition of capital and points to a new recomposition of workers' power. A workers' inquiry should identify the known and unknown committees, their tactical repertoire, and when and why they draw on it to engage in action.

On the other hand, even if collective action is occurring there may be barriers to circulating and generalizing it. The part of the workers' inquiry focused on the technical composition of capital should identify the internal divisions, hierarchies, rivalries, concentrations of decision-making power, and contractual disciplinary tools constructed by the rationalization of the production process. These barriers must be overcome in order to connect, circulate, and generalize the struggles of worker committees across departments, firms, and worker hierarchies, thereby resisting exploitation and attacking, disrupting, and transcending the relations of production.

The diversity of identities that divide workers among themselves must also be overcome. An inquiry into the composition of the workforce should focus on the ethnic, gender, sexuality, and racial characteristics of the workers and how the boss promotes and exploits them, on issues of language, cultural norms, and community associations, and on their history of internal division, prejudices, isolation, group formation, collective action, and cooperation. Hierarchical stratification of workers by job type, work responsibilities, location, date of hire, seniority, wages, benefits, accommodations, promotion, previous lay offs, and other characteristics must also be identified and transcended.

Understanding the diversity of the workers, how they are interconnected both inside and outside the workplace, and their commonalities and differences can also help uncover the ways in which they are already self-organized and the barriers to further organizing and exercising their strength. The gendered and racialized divisions in the labor force are likely to be reproduced in the composition of the workers in the shop and the firm. Detailing the demographic diversity of the workers by their gender, racial, sexuality, and ethnic characteristics will help provide the necessary information about how to identify connections among different groups, who is best situated and prepared to reach and connect with them, and the possible outcomes from doing so.

These demographic details are critical for uncovering forms of social cohesion, collective action, and non-work associations that already provide a form of cooperative organization and action. It is common for workers who share a national origin, a language, and familial or neighborhood affiliations to already have a close connection with one another. These connections form what William Foster called "list and chain systems" among workers through various family, school, club, sports, faith, or other union solidarity networks which often have a key influencer who can bring these groups together in or outside the waged workplace.[19] McAlevey calls these key influencers "organic leaders" and suggests they should be the focus of organizing rather than union "activists" who are already committed to the struggle but have little or no influence among other workers (2016: 13 and 34).

Key influencers maintain their credibility by helping others get jobs, receive promotions, pay increases or benefits, and address grievances to management, and by protecting them from cutbacks or assisting them in other ways in the community. Because they are already leaders who are listened to and trusted, some of these key influencers can organize large numbers of workers who can provide solidarity and even bring other groups of workers into collective action. Such leaders commonly play the role of problem solvers, informal grievance officers, organizers, and strategists among a core group of workers who operate as an already functioning unknown committee. However, caution is called for as other organic leaders may use their status, family, paternalism, or power as an informal labor contractor to impede the struggle.

Already existing forms of collective action carried out by organic leaders and unknown committees in the workplace must be identified, understood, and connected to one another in order to prepare a further tactical intensification of action. Key influencers are capable of translating and relating demands and other communications into the vernacular and norms of the larger group, making introductions to other key influencers, and providing other intangible resources. Bring in these organic leaders and you will bring over most or all of the workers they influence. Working together, such key influencers can provide a knowledge base of what types of organization, tactics, strategy, and objectives work in order to engage other workers and defeat management's plan. Tapping into and working with these existing unknown committees and their solidarity networks is critical to circulating the struggle across the barriers put in place by the current technical composition, to defeating capital's strategy, and to recomposing worker power. This is an effective strategy of self-organization workers use without a formal union, and once it is up and running it will become a *de facto* union.

Key influencers are also critical for connecting to larger networks beyond the workplace such as religious institutions, community centers, sports teams, charities, neighborhood organizations, and local media. For this reason, they can be a bridge between the waged workplace and the community that can circulate the struggle throughout what Panzieri and Tronti both called the "social factory."[20] Reflecting on the strategy that connected key influencers both inside and outside the school workplace ahead of the 2012 teachers' strike in Chicago, McAlevey observed that "a workplace struggle led as a community struggle can be transformational for the whole working class" (2016: 204). Similarly for Alquati (1964), such strikes can illustrate "the political unification and capacity of workers to rapidly circulate, at a general level, making use of the entire social fabric 'inside' and 'outside' the plant."

Unions commonly rely on the community to provide tangible support such as money, child care, meeting spaces, picket line volunteers, and food, and to help swing wider public opinion towards the workers during a strike. However helpful all this is, there is much more such social networks can provide. Key community influencers can organize broad public support for the workers to apply pressure on the employer to settle. They can do this by connecting to other critical groups who can provide bodies to disrupt other locations along the global supply chain in order to circulate the struggle and extract concessions.[21] While disruption of choke points along the fragile global supply chain is finally attracting renewed focus, such networks tying together the workplace and non-workplace spheres can help spread the disruption and amplify it (see Bonacich 2003: 41–8; Bonacich and Wilson 2008; and Alimahomed-Wilson and Ness 2018).[22]

Not all forms of struggle are conducted overtly or even coordinated around a network tied to a key influencer. Often unknown committees of self-organized workers may be engaging in individual or collective action such as work to rule, going slow, non-collaboration, "informal coagulations," or "sabotage" on a microscopic scale, drawn from their tactical repertoire according to the balance of power and conditions of work.[23] Common tactics include shaving time off of work by showing up late or leaving early, calling in sick, doing or approving shoddy work, staying logged in even when not working, providing inaccurate information, and altering equipment to run poorly or break down.

Such tactics can be hard to identify because those using them want to remain anonymous, which makes it more difficult, if not impossible, to extend them into overt collective action. A workers' inquiry can identify and connect these forms of refusal to the concrete relations of production and socialize otherwise anonymous, individual, or invisible forms of struggle. The objective should be to establish cooperative relations among workers to identify, escalate, and organize such tactics into explicit organizational forms of refusal that disrupt the relations of production (Woodcock 2016: 114).

However, it is not necessary that these everyday forms of refusal be "organized" overtly since they can play a complementary role to more public forms of struggle. First, they can be indicators of wider dissatisfaction with and refusal of work although they may also indicate a fear of acting publicly due to repressive forms of retaliation which can be challenging to overcome. Second, they can draw attention to widely held grievances in the workplace and provide an opening that will bring more workers into the organizing. Lastly, they also provide leverage for overt collective action because they generate costs to the employers, reduce profits, and create vulnerabilities that will make the management more likely to concede to organized workers' demands.

The forms of refusal carried out by individuals and unknown committees also provide a check on the collective bargaining agreements (CBAs) of contract unionism, which trade concessions on wages and benefits, and prohibit collective action, in exchange for addressing control issues and the ability to strike. Because CBAs leave the current technical composition of capital, and the class tensions it engenders, in place, the future role for contract unionism in managing class struggle, despite attempts to relabel it as social movement unionism or bargaining for the common good, will continue to decline. This makes it possible to recapture the meaning of the "union," directing it away from its current status as a disciplinary auxiliary of capital to a body of self-organized workers engaged in autonomous struggle.

CBAs serve to harness workers to the current technical composition policed by the union, management, and the state long enough for capital to devise a new strategy. A concession can serve as a delaying tactic to give the employer more time to identify and remove key influencers or organizers, alter the division of labor, or drive productivity back up. If workers delegate to key influencers or organizers, these individuals may also be coopted or integrated into the command hierarchy by being given promotions as low level managers or as enforcers of the contract providing the concession in cases where a union exists in the workplace.

Alquati's participation in the workers' inquiry at Fiat in the early 1960s followed the catastrophic defeat of the established unions and a wave of wildcat strikes carried out by unknown committees of workers that proved difficult to suppress. He observed "invisible organization[s]" of workers adapting their tactics and strategies to use "non-collaboration," countering the disciplinary role of the unions and management. For Alquati (1964), these wildcat strikes illustrated two critical features of self-organized workers' struggle: "it demands an 'invisible organization' that does not institutionalize itself as an autonomous organization within the capitalist production process; it actualizes itself through a continuous and *unpredictable* rotation of the tactics, methods, times, and places of the strike." To demand nothing is to refuse concessions, institutionalization, and cooptation. The difficulty with wildcat strikes and collective action by unknown committees is translating it into overt forms of action that do more than refuse but transcend without becoming a new disciplinary tool.

Self-organized workers who extract concessions while maintaining their own autonomous form of organization rely on their recomposed power, rather than a CBA, to defend and exceed their current gains. Absent a CBA there will be no union to police it or a social democratic party to harness the working class to the state. In short, no contract, no rules.

Decomposition or a new cycle of struggle?

Mapping these connections in and outside the waged workplace, and the tangible and intangible assets and resources they bring with them, is critical to understanding how and why workers are capable of devising and using new forms of self-organization and collective action that can recompose working-class power.

A workers' inquiry can uncover key influencers and unknown committees, and identify choke points that can be targeted by tactics of gradually escalating intensity (see Ovetz 2019). As the inquiry informs tactics, strategy, and organizational forms, each action reflexively further informs the inquiry. According to the banking model of organizing, with each successful action self-organized workers make a "deposit" into a bank of credibility, on which they can then draw to bring in more committed workers to take and circulate further action.[24] Each time workers coordinate and lead a successful collective action they establish more credibility, both with other workers and with the employer. The employer knows that the workers will respond in an organized fashion and will circulate the struggle beyond the local shop if the employer fails to respond to their grievance or to concede to some or all their demands. When even a small number of workers with a high level of strategic power disrupt their workplace and connect it both up- and downstream this demonstrates to their fellow workers that organized struggle can get the goods and so they will get involved.

To the degree that these self-organized groups can circulate their existing struggles to other groups in and outside their waged workplace by overcoming differences of demographics, job roles, wages, work status, and geography, workers can recompose their power in the workplace or across an entire industry, even crossing borders. When these struggles connect across employers in a variety of geographical locations or even nation states such a recomposition can trigger a new wave of global class struggle.

As each effort to organize, act, and disrupt demonstrates the effectiveness of workers in shifting the balance of power, the employer will seek to respond with a strategy to once again decompose the bonds and forms of workers' power. Precious time to prepare a new strategy of decomposition will be bought with relatively low cost concessions on layoffs, wages, and benefits. The employer's strategy will be to impose a new division of labor in order to achieve a new technical composition through which it can reimpose work and restart accumulation. As described above, capital will use automation, deskilling, dispersal, and other aspects of a new rationalization of work at the local, regional, or global level. As Kolinko observed,

Capital reacts to the "political class composition" (the generalization of class struggle) with a "technical re-composition," with the reproduction of uneven development on a higher level: regions are "de-industrialized," in others capital makes the great technological leap forward, old "core" factories are divided into different units of a production chain, the production is "globalised" etc. Capital creates new centres of development which can become new points for the generalization of future class movements. So the inner coherence of the coming class movements is anticipated. Their strategy will not grow detached in the heads of revolutionaries, but lies within the process of the material development (of division of labour, machinery, etc.) itself. (Kolinko 2001: 7)[25]

On the shopfloor, in a particular firm, or in the national polity, capital's strategy of decomposing workers into atomized individuals commonly includes the tactics of making concessions, cooptation, institutionalization, and repression. An inquiry is always evolving and should be sensitive to these changing tactics and prepare responses in advance that will defuse their power and prevent them from succeeding.

Similarly, repressive measures such as firing key workers, lock outs, or displacement by new organizational strategies ("downsizing" and "outsourcing") or technologies ("automation" and "predictive analytics") are likely to be met by unknown committees engaging in tactical escalation, targeting choke points and other already identified vulnerabilities. Support networks outside the workplace could be called into the struggle to support escalating tactics and to help circulate the struggle and raise the costs of potential repression.

To avoid cooptation, institutionalization, and repression a long-term strategy of adopting tactics with ever increasing levels of intensity along the global supply chain must be planned. The continuing intensification of tactics in dispersed locations could immediately follow successful concessions, leading to yet greater concessions before any single firm or industry can regroup. This would allow each struggle to snowball, keeping the employers off balance and shifting power more and more to the workers before capital can devise a new strategy, state power can be mobilized and deployed, and workers' organizations are either coopted, or decide to de-escalate and demobilize, or are institutionalized with a CBA used as a disciplinary and control mechanism.[26]

By spacing out workers' actions in a strategic sequence across single or multiple workplaces, industries, and countries along the global supply chain, class struggle transforms itself into a game of "whack a mole" in which capital can never know or accurately predict where the next disruptive collective action will pop up.[27] While it's busy trying to coopt, institutionalize, and repress workers in one place, other more tactically intense struggles break out simultaneously and without warning in several other places. During such moments a new cycle of global class struggle extends across demographic divides, workplaces, industries, and nation states in a revolutionary wave that threatens to rupture capital's dialectic.

Workers' inquiries should plan not only for gains and successes but also for defeat, preparing for potential cooptation, institutionalization, and repression. By cataloging and mapping all of capital's previous tactics and strategies, workers can be well prepared for the employers' inevitable responses. Even if the workers are ultimately defeated and decomposed, each preceding struggle can provide workers lessons from the road taken that will allow workers to avoid the same pitfalls, risks, and threats when the next cycle of class struggle is relaunched and further escalates.

THE ORGANIZATION OF THIS BOOK

As work has changed so have the forms of worker self-organized struggle. Each of the chapters in this book examines some or all of the elements of a workers' inquiry into the current class composition in a particular country, including capital's technical composition, the working class's composition and possibilities of recomposition, and the threat of decomposition. The objective of assembling these workers' inquiries from across the global capitalist system is to realize Emery's project of mapping out the next terrain of class struggle at the global level. This objective was captured by Alquati (1961), who reminded us that the hypothesis of general aspects of capitalism comes from the analysis of connections that the workers themselves grasp in isolation as "facts," in a process that starts from the factory. Precisely as a hypothesis concerning the general aspects of capitalism, this allows us to provide an interpretation as one step towards a class alternative, that can pay off as a political perspective in more general terms.

Each chapter of this book is an attempt to uncover the general features of capital in the struggle over work that can help us articulate new organizational forms, tactics, strategies, and objectives. After four decades of defeat, this book endeavors to continue carrying out a collective global workers' inquiry to identify if and how far workers have returned, as Alquati (1964) put it, to openly "unify, recompose, and massify the working class 'for itself'" and "to determine the methods and objectives of the struggle for themselves as a social class, increasingly dropping the 'union' aspect."

There is no doubt that attempting a collective global workers' inquiry is a monumental task that is both long overdue and critical for turning back the rampant exploitation and ecological collapse brought on by unrestrained capitalism. Because the problem stems from the relations of production the answer has to be sought there. Claims that we have somehow transcended production, reproduction, and industrial capitalism are misguided and plain wrong. The exploitation and growth of the global waged and unwaged working class in the production, reproduction, and service sectors continue virtually unabated, particularly in the global South.[28]

No "green new deal" or other new social contract is likely to happen without the application of an irresistible leverage provided by the organized working class. Even if they are realized, such policies are unlikely to bring an end to the exploitation of the waged and unwaged labor of billions of people and the relentless destruction of the ecosystems that sustain all life. As has been said to the point of being a cliché, because the problems we face are global the solutions must be as well. As long as capitalism continues to impose its global hegemonic plan, disrupting that plan depends entirely on recomposing a powerful global working class with new strategies, tactics, organizational forms, and objectives. At a moment when we have been warned that time has run out, the contributors to this book have given us reasons for optimism that this recomposition has already begun even if it still has a very long way to go.

The book is organized thematically in three parts, beginning with workers' inquiries into transport and logistics, before proceeding to inquiries into education, call centers, cleaners, platform work, and gamers and concluding with manufacturing and mining.

Transport and logistics

In "*Camioneros*: The Argentine Truckers' Union that Can Paralyze the Country," Dario Bursztyn conducts a workers' inquiry from above across the more than two-century history of post-colonial Argentina. He explores how the changing technical composition of capital shaped and was shaped by the recomposition of working-class struggle, from workers on the ranches, the railways, and in the factory, to the truckers who today belong to the powerful *Camioneros*. According to Bursztyn, the *Camioneros* have tremendous disruptive power over the Argentine economy and global trade because of their strategic position in a critical export economy. With nearly all cargo moved by truck, the recomposed power of the transport workers provides a potent power that could disrupt the global economy.

Logistics and disruptive power are also central to Alpkan Birelma's chapter, "When Class Unionism Leads to Working-Class Recomposition: The Case of TÜMTİS in Turkey." Birelma's workers' inquiry uncovers the strategies, tactics, organization model, and objectives that have led to the meteoric rise of the logistics sector union, TÜMTİS, in the midst of the continuing decline of organized labor throughout Turkey. With their strategic location in the delivery sector, the union has long pursued a careful path of deep organizing in mid-sized logistics firms to extend their credibility with workers in the large global firms. Characterized by a flat organizational structure in which workers are organizers, the union has many lessons to teach workers in countries where defeat is the order of the day.

The Italian logistics sector has received attention in recent years for the effectiveness of self-organized workers in overcoming divisions of gender, immigration status, and race. In "Resisting Sexism and Racism in Italian Logistics Worker Organizing," Anna Curcio assesses how the workers' own inquiry informed their tactics, strategies, and organizational form in their successful struggle at the Mr. Job logistics firm, strengthening its independent union ally, and posing a threat to the global supply chain.

Education, call centers, cleaners, platform work, and gamers

In "Making Threats: Credible Strike Threats in the US, 2012–2016," Robert Ovetz focuses on a new strategy of making credible strike threats, which are on the rise in the US. While the number of strike threats between 2012 and 2016 was about 30 percent greater than the number of actual strikes, more than twice the number of workers were involved in making them. How do workers organize for a strike in a way that makes the threat credible enough that the employer will concede to the workers' demands to avoid a strike? Ovetz develops a model structure test to assess the level of recomposition of disruptive power among workers making a credible strike threat. Using the 2016 strike threat by about 26,000 members of the California Faculty Association as an example, he analyzes why it lacked the features of a credible strike threat.

In recent decades in Mexico—a country in which the unions have long been almost entirely harnessed to the ruling PRI party—militant workers' unions such as the CNTE have emerged to counter the neoliberal consensus. In his chapter, "The Self-Organization of the Mexican Multitude Against Neoliberal State Terror: The CNTE Dissident Teachers' Movement Against the 2013 Education Reform," Patrick Cuninghame presents a workers' inquiry into the tactics, strategies, organizational form, and objectives of the militant breakaway teachers' union. Facing violent state and non-state repression, the CNTE has provided the foundation for a working class in the midst of recomposition.

Taking an expansive view of numerous key and emerging sectors in UK education, retail, platform capitalism, call centers, and gaming, the editorial collective of *Notes from Below* magazine have shown us the richness of the workers' inquiry approach when applied to the current technical composition of capital and the potential for working-class recomposition. Their chapter, "Notes from Below: A Brief Survey of Class Composition in the UK," is a sweeping reassessment of their first year of workers' inquiries into all of these sectors. It provides a model for how to replicate such a nationwide workers' inquiry elsewhere.

Manufacturing and mining

While the Chinese economy has been the focus of much study we still know precious little about workers' struggles there. In her chapter "Worker Organizing in China: Challenges and Opportunities," Jenny Chan contributes an expansive workers' inquiry from above of the past four decades of class struggle. Examining changes in law, labor relations policy, and economic data, Chan inverts capital's perspective to demonstrate how self-organized workers are attempting to make their voices heard through legal and extralegal struggles. The workers' efforts to innovate new tactics, strategies, and organizational forms provide a glimpse into the barriers impeding the recomposition of the Chinese working class.

Self-organized precarious mine workers in South Africa have questioned the need for a formal union in their struggles against capital, bureaucratic unions, and the corporatist ANC government. In their chapter, "Self-Organizing is Breathing Life into Workers' Struggles in South Africa," Shawn Hattingh and Dr. Dale T. McKinley provide a workers' inquiry from both above and below. To understand the self-organized wildcat strikes in the mining sector that captured global attention it is critical to understand the trajectory of black workers unions from militancy to collaboration in the post-apartheid era. Ultimately, state and union repression forced some workers back into the unions. However, many others took their self-organizing experience further by innovating new workers' advice centers and forums from which a new cycle of struggle has erupted.

The wave of worker self-organizing and strikes in the Indian auto sector underpins Lorenza Monaco's case for extending the workers' inquiry to the global level. In her chapter, "Towards a Global Workers' Inquiry: A Study of Indian Precarious Auto Workers," Monaco reflects on her experiences of conducting militant co-research in the

UK and South Africa and how it informed her workers' inquiry into the struggles of Indian autoworkers in the National Capital Region during and following the 2011–12 Maruti-Suzuki strikes. Amplifying Emery's 1995 call "no politics without inquiry" by carrying out workers' inquiries at the global level, Monaco illustrates both the promise and opportunities of doing so.

NOTES

1. See, for example, the debate in the pages of *Jacobin* on whether or not there is a strike wave occurring in the US in the midst of a series of teacher strikes.
2. Among these works in recent years are Ness 2014; Atzeni and Ness 2018; Azzelini and Kraft 2018; McAlevey 2016; Dutta, Nowak, and Birke 2018; Sinwell and Mbatha 2016; and Woodcock 2016, as well as the magazines *Labor Notes*, *Notes From Below*, and *Viewpoint*.
3. Alquati (1964) addressed the collaborationist role of social democratic parties and unions, and Glaberman (1947, 1965) demonstrated the role of contract unionism in disciplining the working class.
4. Kolinko's use of "organic composition" of capital is here referred to as the "technical composition."
5. See also Tronti 1980: 30; Lefort 1952: 82; and Panzieri 1980.
6. Hoffman describes a "militant investigation" as "fluid and adaptable" but focused on "the production of forms of collective political subjectivity rather than the extraction, accumulation, and publication of purely informational contents" (2019: 3).
7. See also Woodcock 2016: 30.
8. McAlevey considers this the process of identifying natural leaders who can bring with them a group of workers in which they are influential (2016: 4–6).
9. Among the other early workers' inquiries are Alquati 1961, 1964, and 1967; and Romano and Stone 1972.
10. Lefort identified four features: 1) workers' relation to work, 2) workers' relations with one another, 3) life outside the factory, and 4) links to the history of workers' struggles (1952: 88–9). However, I depart from this composition as it lacks any emphasis on tactics, strategies, and objectives.
11. See also Woodcock 2014: 493 and Alquati 1961.
12. While *Notes From Below* has introduced the term "social composition" to refer to the working class's current composition of power, Cleaver and others retain "political composition" to reflect the level of the recomposition of working-class power. However, I avoid using the modifying terms "political" and "social" for several reasons. First, "political" and "social" imply the current hegemonic institutions of capitalist society. Second, they are static terms lacking the valuable reference to the dynamism of the struggle over the class composition. Third,

they imply that they are distinct spheres in which politics occurs apart from the social and the economic. Lastly, referring to both as composition muddles the distinction between the working class in a state of subordination to capital's plan (social composition) and the working class's self-organizing to refuse it (political composition). Instead, I prefer to distinguish between capital's "technical" composition and the varying states of the working class's composition, "recomposition," and "decomposition."

13. On class composition theory, see also Alquati 1967 and Woodcock 2016: 31.

14. Debs's complete testimony at his trial on charges of contempt for violating a court injunction stemming from the 1894 Pullman railroad strike is worth reading in full. He warned that "It seems to me that if it were not for resistance to degrading conditions, the tendency of our whole civilization would be downward; after a while we would reach the point where there would be no resistance, and slavery would come" (quoted in Zinn 2015: 281; see also Part 2 in Ovetz 2019).

15. See Alquati 1961 and 1964. More recent workers' inquiries have been conducted by the German group Kolinko into call centers and the Swedish group Kämpa Tillsammans.

16. Ironically, the conflict over the use of sociological research methods and the role of the leftist parties and unions in the Fiat and Olivetti workers' inquiries led to the split in *Quaderni Rossi* and the founding of *Classe Operaia*. See Haider and Mohandesi 2013; Monaco 2015a and 2015b; and especially chapter 3 in Hoffman 2019.

17. Woodcock has written a similarly detailed account of his own workers' inquiry into a call center in the UK. Like Kolinko, Woodcock shies away from drawing lessons from the lack of existing everyday and overt forms of struggle (see chapters 5–6 in Woodcock 2016).

18. Woodcock (2016) similarly found little worker cooperation although he went further to try to organize workers. Ultimately, he ended his study with rich examples of cooperation but little observation of struggle.

19. Cited in McAlevey 2016: 33. For a useful illustration charting workers' social networks see p. 69.

20. Alquati (1961) denounced the question of inside or outside the factory as "a false problem: today the factory does not exist as a moment that can be separated." However true theoretically, the day to day barriers between inside and outside the waged workplace necessitate specific tactics and strategy to overcome them.

21. Writing about the 1919 steel general strike, William Z. Foster called this the "link and chain" system by which workers organized networks both inside and outside the waged workplace that could be called into action when needed (cited in McAlevey 2016: 33).

22. Alquati (1964) described how the unified movement of open struggle connecting these "nodes" would become a wave of struggle.

23. For the term "informal coagulations" see Womack 2006: 83. See also Ovetz 2019: 438–54, and chapter 4 in Woodcock 2016.
24. I am indebted to Joe Berry for sharing this analogy with me.
25. On capital's strategy of decomposition see also Alquati 1961 and 1964.
26. See my explanation of the use of "trajectory theory" in Ovetz 2019: 2–4.
27. Wright refers to these as "checkerboard strikes" (2002: 34).
28. This is extremely well documented by Silver 2003 and Ness 2015.

REFERENCES

Alimahomed-Wilson, J. and Ness, I. (eds.) (2018). *Choke Points: Logistics Workers Disrupting the Global Supply Chain.* London: Pluto.

Alquati, R. (1961). Organic Composition of Capital and Labor-Power at Olivetti. At www.viewpointmag.com/2013/09/27/organic-composition-of-capital-and-labor-power-at-olivetti-1961.

Alquati, R. (1964). Struggle at FIAT. *Classe Operaia* 1 (January). At www.viewpoint-mag.com/2013/09/26/struggle-at-fiat-1964.

Alquati, R. (1967). Outline of a Pamphlet on FIAT. *Classe Operaia* 3(3) (March). At www.viewpointmag.com/2013/09/26/outline-of-a-pamphlet-on-fiat-1967.

Atzeni, M. and Ness, I. (eds.) (2018). *Global Perspectives on Workers' and Labour Organizations.* Singapore: Springer.

Azzellini, D. and Kraft, M.G. (eds.) (2018). *The Class Strikes Back: Self-Organised Workers' Struggles in the Twenty-First Century.* Leiden: Brill.

Bonacich, E. (2003). Pulling the Plug: Labor and the Global Supply Chain. *New Labor Forum* 12(2) (Summer), 41–8.

Bonacich, E. and Wilson, J. (2008). *Getting the Goods: Ports, Labor, and the Logistics Revolution.* Ithaca, NY: Cornell University Press.

Braverman, H. (1974). *Labor and Monopoly Capital.* New York: Monthly Review Press.

Caffentzis, G. (2013). *In Letters of Blood and Fire: Work, Machines, and the Crisis of Capitalism.* Oakland, CA: PM Press.

Cleaver, H. (1992). The Inversion of Class Perspective in Marxian Theory: From Valorisation to Self-Valorisation. In Bonefield, W., Gunn, R. and Psychopedis, K. (eds.), *Open Marxism, Vol. II.* London: Pluto, pp. 106–44.

Cleaver, H. (2017). *Rupturing the Dialectic: The Struggle Against Work, Money, and Financialization.* Chico, CA: AK Press.

Cleaver, H. (2019). *33 Lessons on Capital: Reading Marx Politically.* London: Pluto Press.

Curcio, A. and Roggero, G. (2018). Logistics is the Logic of Capital. *Viewpoint Magazine* (October 25). At https://www.viewpointmag.com/2018/10/25/logistics-is-the-logic-of-capital.

Dutta, M., Nowak, J., and Birke, P. (eds.) (2018). *Workers' Movements and Strikes in the Twenty-First Century: A Global Perspective*. London: Rowman & Littlefield International.

Emery, E. (1995). No Politics Without Inquiry: A Proposal for a Class Composition Inquiry Project 1996–7. *Common Sense* 18 (December), 1–11. At https://notes-frombelow.org/article/no-politics-without-inquiry.

Galeano, E. (1997). *Open Veins of Latin America: Five Centuries of the Pillage of a Continent*. New York: Monthly Review Press.

Glaberman, M. (1947). Strata in the Working Class. *Internal Bulletin of the Johnson-Forest Tendency* (August). (Originally published under the name Martin Harvey.) At www.marxists.org/archive/glaberman/1947/08/strata.htm.

Glaberman, M. (1965). Be His Payment High or Low: The American Working Class in the Sixties. *International Socialism* 21 (Summer), 18–23. At www.marxists.org/archive/glaberman/1965/xx/uswc.htm.

Haider, A. and Mohandesi, S. (2013). Workers' Inquiry: A Genealogy. *Viewpoint* (September 27). At www.viewpointmag.com/2013/09/27/workers-inquiry-a-genealogy.

Hoffman, M. (2019). *Militant Acts: The Role of Investigations in Radical Political Struggles*. New York: SUNY Press.

Kämpa Tillsammans (n.d.). (no title) At https://libcom.org/tags/k-mpa-tillsammans.

Kolinko (n.d.). Discussion Paper on Class Composition. At https://libcom.org/library/discussion-paper-class-composition.

Kolinko (2001). Class Composition. At www.nadir.org/nadir/initiativ/kolinko/engl/e_klazu.htm.

Kolinko (2002). *Hotlines*. At www.nadir.org/nadir/initiativ/kolinko/lebuk/e_lebuk.htm.

Lefort, C. (1952). Proletarian Experience. *Socialisme ou Barbarie* 11 (November–December). At www.viewpointmag.com/2013/09/26/proletarian-experience. Reprinted in Curtis, D.A. (ed.), *A Socialisme ou Barbarie Anthology: Autonomy, Critique, and Revolution in the Age of Bureaucratic Capitalism*. La Bussière, Acratie, 2007.

McAlevey, J. (2016). *No Shortcuts: Organizing for Power in the New Gilded Age*. Oxford: Oxford University Press.

Marx, K. (1880). Workers' Questionnaire. In *Marx-Engels Collected Works, Vol. 24*. New York: International Publishers. At www.marxists.org/history/etol/newspape/ni/vol04/no12/marx.htm.

Marx, K. (1976 [1867]). *Capital: A Critique of Political Economy, Vol. 1*. London: Penguin.

Monaco, L. (2015a). Nuova Panda schiavi in mano: Workers' Inquiry as a Tool to Unveil Fiat's Strategy of Labour Control. *Historical Materialism* 23(1), 221–42.

Monaco, L. (2015b). *Bringing Operaismo to Gurgaon: A Study of Labour Composition and Resistance Practices in the Indian Auto Industry*. Doctoral thesis, SOAS, University of London.

Monaco, L. (2017). Where Lean May Shake: Challenges to Casualisation in the Indian Auto Industry. *Global Labour Journal* 8(2). At https://mulpress.mcmaster.ca/globallabour/article/view/3040.

Moody, K. (2017). *On New Terrain: How Capital is Reshaping the Battleground of Class War*. Chicago: Haymarket.

Ness, I. and Azzellini, D. (2011). *Ours to Master and to Own: Workers' Control from the Commune to the Present*. Chicago: Haymarket.

Ness, I. (2014). *New Forms of Worker Organization: The Syndicalist and Autonomist Restoration of Class Struggle Unionism*. Oakland, CA: PM.

Ness, I. (2015). *Southern Insurgency: The Coming of the Global Working Class*. London: Pluto.

Ngwane, T., Sinwell, L. and Ness, I. (2017). *Urban Revolt: State Power and the Rise of People's Movements in the Global South*. Chicago: Haymarket.

Ovetz, R. (2019). *When Workers Shot Back: Class Conflict from 1877 to 1921*. Chicago: Haymarket.

Panzieri, R. (1976). Surplus Value and Planning: Notes on the Reading of *Capital*. In *The Labour Process and Class Strategies*, CSE Pamphlet No. 1, pp. 4–25.

Panzieri, R. (1980). The Capitalist Use of Machinery: Marx versus the Objectivists. In Slater, P. (ed.), *Outlines of a Critique of Technology*. New Jersey: Humanities Press. At https://libcom.org/library/capalist-use-machinery-raniero-panzieri.

Rawick, G. (1969). Working Class Self-Activity. *Radical America* 3(2), 23–31.

Romano, P. and Stone, R. (1972 [1947]). *The American Worker*. Detroit: Bewick.

Silver, B. (2003). *Forces of Labor: Workers' Movements and Globalization Since 1870*. Cambridge: Cambridge University Press.

Sinwell, L. and Mbatha, S. (2016). *The Spirit of Marikana: The Rise of Insurgent Trade Unionism in South Africa*. London: Pluto.

Thorn, J. (2011). The Workers' Inquiry: What's the Point? *The Commune* (May 16). At https://libcom.org/library/workers%E2%80%99-inquiry-what%E2%80%99s-point.

Tronti, M. (1962). Factory and Society. In *Quaderni Rossi*, 2, 1–31. English translation at https://operaismoinenglish.wordpress.com/2013/06/13/factory-and-society.

Tronti, M. (1966). Lenin in England. In *Operai e Capitale*. Turin: Einaudi. At https://libcom.org/library/lenin-england. English translation at https://operaismoinenglish.wordpress.com/2010/09/30/lenin-in-england.

Tronti, M. (1980 [1965]). The Strategy of Refusal. In *Italy: Autonomia, Post-Political Politics*. New York: semiotext(e), pp. 28–35.

Watson, J. (1971). Counter-Planning on the Shop Floor. *Radical America* 5(3), 77–85.

Womack, J. (2006). Working Power Over Production: Labor History, Industrial Work, Economics, Sociology, and Strategic Position. XIV International Economic History Congress, Helsinki 2006, Panel 56: The Economics of Latin American Labor. At www.helsinki.fi/iehc2006/papers2/Womack.pdf.

Woodcock, J. (2014). The Workers' Inquiry from Trotskyism to Operaismo: A Political Methodology for Investigating the Workplace. *ephemera: theory & politics in organization* 14(3), 493–513. At www.ephemerajournal.org/sites/default/files/pdfs/contribution/14-3woodcock.pdf.

Woodcock, J. (2016). *Working the Phones: Control and Resistance in Call Centers*. London: Pluto.

Wright, S. (2002). *Storming Heaven: Class Composition and Struggle in Italian Autonomist Marxism*, London: Pluto.

Zinn, H. (2015). *A People's History of the United States*, New York: HarperCollins.

Part I

Transport and Logistics

1

Camioneros: The Argentine Truckers' Union that Can Paralyze the Country

Dario Bursztyn

The integration of the Argentinian economy into world capitalism as a supplier of raw materials to the world's largest economies— Great Britain in the nineteenth century, the US in the twentieth, and China and Brazil in the twenty-first—is critical for understanding the emergence of the *Camioneros'* struggle for social justice. To do so we must trace the history of Argentina's insertion into the global model of accumulation as well as the changing technical composition of capital. We will see that the agro-livestock exporting *latifundio*, the railroads system, the dependence on British capital, and the transport of cargo by truck are stages along a continuum in time to the present. Over the past several decades, and particularly the last one, partial or total strikes by the *Camioneros* have left the country paralyzed. The central role of trucking in moving cargo to global markets has provided the Argentinian working class with strategic leverage. This chapter offers an historical analysis of how the changing technical composition of Argentinian capital has affected the composition of the working class and the consequences for class struggle.

HISTORY OF A LONG DEPENDENCE

The Argentine Republic was initially inserted into the world capitalist economy as a satellite of the British Empire. This relationship dates back to the period prior to the development of capitalism in its mature stage. Already at the beginning of the eighteenth century the privileged commercial sectors of the Viceroyalty (*Virreinato*) of the Río de la Plata were trading fluidly with London. They dodged the regulations set by the Spanish Crown—the owner of those territories—that demanded exclusivity of trade with Cadiz and Seville from the Customs of Buenos Aires. Through smuggling they provided the English with salted dried meat—food for the slaves of the colonies in the Caribbean—and tallow and cowhides, in exchange for yarn, slaves, and other goods entering South America (Villalobos 1977: 82–5). It was this *genetic* and pivotal point in the history of the region that kept the economy of the philo-Europeanizing Río de la Plata tied to London. This relationship did not diminish with time but increased to constitute Argentina as a semi-colony. The history of colonialism and dependency helps us understand the changing composition of capital and the resulting class struggles.

In the early nineteenth century, two English military invasions of Buenos Aires were attempted, to turn the lands of the Spanish Viceroyalty into a British colony. However, both were resisted and the British were expelled by a local population that already had an elementary awareness of the French Revolution, the events in Spain, the Enlightenment, and the expansion in South America of libertarian and republican lodges modelled on those in Europe. On May 25, 1810, a revolutionary movement that united some Spaniards with native creoles and some other popular sectors became the only independence (and later republican) movement to triumph and be sustained throughout Latin America.

Following the revolution, the links between the privileged sectors of Buenos Aires and the British—owners of the seas and commerce—expanded. London banks funded abusive British investments in lands and undertakings such as the extraction of wood, *tañino*, and minerals for the war, and the setting up of settlements to breed ovine herds to obtain wool, which were a constant feature during the nineteenth century. It is in this context that we can understand the 1833 British invasion and possession of the Malvinas Islands, in the extreme South Atlantic, a territory that continues to be under British colonial rule.

This brief introduction provides a glimpse into the role of the Río de la Plata economy as a supplier of raw materials to the heart of world capitalism for more than a century and a half. In fact, Argentina was constituted as the result of a bifrontal struggle, one that was not resolved even after the formal declaration of independence in 1816. On one front, it was a struggle against foreign invaders (i.e. Spaniards), but on the other it was also a struggle against the pro-British landowners and commercial powers of Buenos Aires, who under no circumstances wanted to lose the innumerable privileges they held. Thus, the Customs Port of Buenos Aires was the entry and exit point for everything. The city, which at the turn of the nineteenth century had been no more than a village far from the heart of Spain's interests (centered on Lima, Upper Peru, and Mexico), became a center of power from east to west, from the sea to the Andes mountain range. But the growth of Buenos Aires was due not to the connection with the old metropolis, Spain, but to its link with British imperialism.

In the provinces, the *caudillos* ruled (except in Patagonia, which was in the hands of the native peoples, and whose incorporation into the agro-livestock production system was achieved decades later by blood and fire from Buenos Aires with British collaboration). *Caudillos* were figures with territorial and military power, landlords owning small or large portions of land, at a time before it was divided into plots, or *latifundios*. The *caudillos*, men and some women, built the respect of the local population with their personal charisma, but they were targeted for elimination by the great merchants, exporters and landowners of Buenos Aires in order to implement the bourgeois nation state with all its legal and administrative apparatus. In that process, a crack between "the interior" and Buenos Aires emerged that was to be permanent. Buenos Aires was perceived as the internal invader, and as the partner of "Europe." In the center-west, north-west and north-east interior all kinds of small artisans and local production processes were gradually destroyed or reduced to a barely residual value, making way for the country's growing dependence on goods imported from England.

However, we cannot say that the *caudillos* were a group homogeneous in their ideals and attitudes, let alone a class. The reason for this is that they had followers in the provinces among both the land-owning elites—some of them heirs of wealthy families—and the poor and the *gauchos*. The *caudillos* represented another type of territorial power, independent of the aristocracy of the port (e.g. Buenos Aires), hence earning the latter the nickname of *porteños*. At the time, what is now Uruguay was part of the United Provinces of the Río de la Plata; its main leader was José Artigas, who as early as 1815 carried out the first known agrarian reform, which earned him intense and persistent persecution (Bruschera 1969).

These elements of the history of Argentina are relevant to the analysis of social and labor struggles because they are constitutive: although on the periphery, Argentina always formed part of the development of capitalism and imperialism. The productive forces that developed in their bosom moved rhythmically and in parallel. Since then, *"caudillismo"* has maintained a permanent place in Argentine politics, expressed and crystallized in the leaders of the great mass political movements, the strong presidential and non-parliamentary model, and in the traits of union leaders. At the same time, and still resonating even in the current social and political situation in Argentina, the notion of the "invader" has been an element perceived among the most humble, applied not only to the Spanish or British foreigners, but also to the rich *porteños* who were always their partners. The mixtures of ethnicities during colonization, mainly of Spanish and later Italian immigrants with indigenous and former black slaves, produced a *"mestizo"* population. The majority were workers in the plantation fields, in local industries in the provinces, and housekeepers—the so-called "darkies." When, many years later, the "darkies" of the provinces came together in the port cities to join the industrial proletariat, the privileged sectors described them as "blacks" or "indians" or "little black heads" that had invaded *civilization*. It was Eva Peron, Evita, who said *"mis queridos cabecitas negras"* ("my beloved black haired"), in an attempt to give these masses of workers a positive identity.

Understanding the germinal struggles of the masses in Argentina during the twentieth and twenty-first centuries means going back to the men and women who were dedicated to various rural labor tasks, the artisans, and the railway workers. Their struggles bring us back to the issue of the expansion of the nascent bourgeoisie and the local oligarchy in partnership with foreign capital. While productive enclaves in other territories of the Southern Hemisphere were French, Dutch, or German, in Argentina they were British. American capital only appeared in the industrial sector in the first thirty years of the twentieth century. British capital invested in the creation and expansion of the railroad, which was constructed radially on the basis of where the areas to be exploited were located. The rails naturally converged (and still do) towards Buenos Aires and the grain export ports (Rosario, Bahía Blanca, and Quequén). They also extended to the *quebrachales* (north of the province of Santa Fe), the cotton plantations (Chaco), and then to the sugar plantations or the sheep production *estancias* in Patagonia. The subject of the railroad and its vast network is one to which we will later return.

The historiography of capital in Argentina provides an abundance of material relating to the expansion of the railroad, foreign bank loans, the arrival of immigrants, the distribution of land, and the struggles of workers. One chronicler to these developments, Germán Avé Lallemant, served a double mission. He was born in Lübeck, Germany, and in 1868 settled in Argentina to develop his work as a geographer, geologist, and surveyor. He also occupied the rectorate of the National College in San Luis, a province in the center-west that was at the time a "territory" without its own legal demarcation. What interests us about Lallemant, beyond his scientific work, is that, in addition to founding the Argentine press organization Federación Obrera (Workers' Federation), he was a correspondent for *Die Neue Zeit*, the newspaper of the international labor movement, edited by the German socialist Karl Kautsky from 1894 and 1909. Unfortunately, Avé Lallemant's contributions to the *Die Neue Zeit* were not translated until the 1970s.

Lallemant warned that "without political conquests, without ships or cannons, English capitalism extracts from Argentina 17 times in relative value what it extracts from its subjects in India … and worse, five or six London bankers—the Rothschilds, Baring, Morgan and Greenwood—give orders to the Argentine ambassador and the government of Buenos Aires" (Paso 1974: 37). It is clear that Argentina's situation was that of a permanent semi-colony.

Incipient organizations of workers began to operate in the nineteenth century, and were greatly enhanced by the arrival of workers from Europe in successive waves subsequent to the revolutionary attempts of 1848, 1871, and others. Tens of thousands of Italian and Spanish peasants arrived during the time of agricultural harvests, meeting the need for an agricultural labor force in a country that was first and foremost dominated by ranching. Many returned home, but many others stayed. Hence, the early entry of the internationalist ideas of anarchists, socialists, and communists in Argentina, embodied in the struggles that were already taking place. Among these were struggles for the land, or against the abusive taxes set by Buenos Aires, against internal customs duties, and against the massive conscription of the "*gauchos*" to the armies fighting against the Indians. The historian Leonardo Paso points out that

> The new social ideas of that time looked like anticipations of those that would last, a fact that is not causal if the conditions of the socio-economic development of Argentina are taken into account. Augusto Kühn, one of the founders of the German club *Vorwärts* in 1882 (he would later also be a founder of the Communist Party), confirms that that was the starting point of the socialist work in the country, never interrupted afterwards. From that point to the constitution of the organizing Committee of May 1, 1890 ... and the appearance on December 12, 1890 of the newspaper *El Obrero*, a period elapsed whose brevity interweaves with the rapidity of the events ... [together with] the constitution of the Workers' Federation, [these] are three manifestations of the organized presence of the Marxist current in Argentina ... that in the meeting of Paris of 1889 was represented by order of the club *Vorwärts* of Buenos Aires by Wilhelm Liebknecht ... All authors agree that in Argentina and Chile the reception of Marxism preceded the rest of the countries of Latin America. And this is linked to the characteristics of its development, not to the circumstantial presence of any man. (Paso 1974: 8–14)

The enormous expansion of land for livestock and agriculture during the so-called "Conquest of the Desert" in the 1870s—that is, the genocide of the indigenous peoples who lived in the regions south of the province of Buenos Aires to the extreme of Patagonia in Tierra del

Fuego—put the local and foreign landowner oligarchy in a position of incomparable advantage that seemed to have no end. That "golden" period sealed the conflict in the hegemonic bloc over what kind of insertion Argentina should have in the world market. The question was whether agriculture and ranching would supply raw materials or if progress was to be made through an expanded industrialization. In the 1910s, 1930s, 1980s, and from 2015 to the present, it has been insisted that Argentina's role is to be a "granary" or "supermarket of the world." To some extent, the brief years before Peronism and the period of Peronist government were the watershed, giving rise to an effective and powerful policy of industrialization and import substitution. We'll return to this point later.

In 1898, Lallemant, wrote in *Die Neue Zeit*:

> the industry has been forced to consume only imported coal of English origin, and it is for this reason that the large industry has developed almost entirely in the city-port of Buenos Aires, at least 95% of the industry ... The landowners are 40,362 according to the census of 1895, who take great profits and dominate the country at will, thus forming an all-powerful oligarchy despite the fact that by number the oligarchy is worth only 1.02 per cent of the total population ... there are 261,453 farmers, settlers, tenants and stable laborers and 342,493 day laborers without fixed occupation (the so-called *peón golondrina* or "swallow workers") ... the number of people employed in the industry and trades amounted to 366,087, 23.24 percent of all wage earners over 14 years. According to the data provided by the manufacturers in December 1898, the industry in the capital of the country in the last 10 years went from 6,500 factories and workshops with 42,000 workers to 24,000 factories and workshops with 215,000 workers, and of that total 180,730 are women and children. (Paso 1974: 182–8)

From this precise picture at the end of the nineteenth century emerges the character of the productive matrix of Argentina. But it was not only the big landowners who pushed in this direction, the model also provided huge dividends to British imperialism. In one of his last articles, from 1909, Lallemant (as Raul Scalabrini Ortiz and the members of FORJA would carefully observe later) gave an account of how the British secured power through the railways: "In 1904 the extension of the railways was 16,703 kilometers and in 1908 it was 24,763 kilometers; there are 6,500 kilometers under construction and concessions have been awarded to build another 10,000 kilometers. English rail capital has a dividend of 8%. The big railway companies are really the true owners of the country" (Paso 1974: 207). During strikes in 1879,

> bakers, masons and cigar workers entered the struggle, among the latter there [were] many anarchists. In 1881 the Society of Dependents of Commerce demanded Sunday rest and reduction of the working day; hotel employees, milkmaids, domestic laborers and servants [protested] against the *labor document* that the authorities tried to impose ... In 1882 the plasterers went on strike and got a wage increase ... in 1883 there is a strike among workers on the construction of La Plata, the new capital of the province of Buenos Aires. (Zaragoza Rovira 2015: 84)

As early as the late 1880s, the Brotherhood of Machinists and Boilermakers was born. In no way was the origin of the labor movement in Argentina a "product" of the later Bolshevik Revolution, and even less of Peronism in the 1940s. The Russian Revolution of 1917, and the granting and extension of labor rights by Juan Perón, only crystallized the various struggles that had already existed for several decades and gave a particular character to the Argentine labor movement. Undoubtedly, the majority of workers have since identified with Peronism, and in a much smaller proportion with leftist ideas, once the state had granted or promoted the institutionalization of historical labor demands. Needless to say, what is left of the Peronism of 1944/1955 is the subject of another debate.

BRITAIN FALLS, THE UNITED STATES RISES: WHAT ABOUT ARGENTINA?

Before World War II, the axis of world economic power was already beginning to turn towards the United States, generating a dispute over "zones of influence." Argentina had belonged to the "British sphere," but in the 1920s the installation of factories relying on inputs from the US began to change that dependency. This was reflected in the 1929 D'Abernon Report of the British Economic Mission to South America. The British wondered how they could sustain their influence in the face of American investments in industry (Normano 1932), which, by the end of that decade, had led to a decline in imports of British goods and their replacement by US raw materials and equipment. This definitive substitution of imports was the result of a change in the composition of the industrial product, and in particular an increase in the importation of machinery that would bear fruit shortly afterwards (Villanueva 1972).

We have seen how the landlords and oligarchs relied on exports of raw materials and the close relationship with the British economy, but there was already a growing industrialization. As noted by Adolfo Dorfman, who also emphasized the fact that there were workers' organizations and early struggles for improvements in living conditions, "already in 1914 the national industry supplied 71.3 percent of the consumption of industrial goods" (1986: 317). Of course, given the upheavals in the centralized core economies with World War I and later with the Great Depression, investments and local economic development were going to be dramatically affected.

As in many other cases, the abrupt decline in the prices of raw materials severely impacted the Argentine economy, particularly in rural areas. This triggered a migration to the cities, where the newcomers could find no work since industry itself had been knocked back by the lack of consumers and the lack of dollars to import parts from the US for production. The democratically elected president Hipólito Yrigoyen was deposed by a military coup in 1930, which reduced salaries. Inflation and unemployment characterized the decade. The music of the tango dance incorporated lyrics reflecting the drama of poverty. In fact, the 1930s are remembered as a decade of huge struggles for better working conditions, better salaries, and against the repression of unions and leftist activists. The only "way out" for the oligarchy seemed to be a deeper dependency on Britain, and in 1933 Argentina signed the Roca-Runciman agreement which gave full benefits to the British by protecting their investments in the country. In exchange, the local establishment could go on exporting raw materials and refrigerated meat, etc. This pact would serve only as an anchor rather than a progressive initiative.

After World War II changed the map of the world and turned the axis of power towards the US, this complementary economic relationship between Argentina and Great Britain was broken. During the last years of the 1930s until 1955, import substitutions and the growth of workshops and industries increased the mass of industrial workers. In terms of GDP, the industrial sector in the 1900 to 1946 cycle never represented more than 20 percent of the total economy (Villanueva 1972). But that does not imply that there was no struggle to define the model of capitalist accumulation in Argentina. Whether it continued to be centered on agro-livestock exports or took a more powerful industrial path, the old system of agreements with Great Britain had to break.

This transformation in the technical composition of capital was one of the ingredients that determined the birth and consolidation not only of many trade unions and workers' organizations, but also of political parties and mass movements, inaugurating a recomposition of working-class power. Hence the creation of the Radical Civic Union (UCR), the Socialist Party, the Communist Party, and later the (Peronist) Justicialist Party. These organizational forms have been common throughout the twentieth century and the early twenty-first century—with variations, multiple splits, reconfigurations, quasi-disappearances, mergers, re-namings, and diverse alliances among political representatives. The "other" power, in Gramscian terms, has been the *blocco storico*, the actual power that, with or without a party, and in alliance with the military-police-media apparatus, has governed alone or sometimes in partnership with some of these political groups, almost always at the expense of workers' rights.

Those who know the recent history of Argentina know that the so-called *Argentinazo* of December 19–20, 2001 marked a dystopia for the traditional left, Peronism, and any union because the engine of working-class mobilization was the unemployed, the *piqueteros*, the territorial-neighborhood movements, and not the trade unions or established leftist political parties. The *Argentinazo* with its cry "*que se vayan todos*" ("to leave all") introduced other actors that were not salaried, not unionized, and not militants of known political parties. They somehow recovered the grassroots assemblies deployed during the rebellious and revolutionary labor movement of the 1960s and 1970s in Argentina, assemblies that were undoubtedly mechanisms of non-hierarchical debate, and represented a way of pursuing the struggle whose place was (and still is) the occupation and blockade of the streets, public roads, and bridges. The traditional meetings, mobs, and marches with a stage and one or several speakers, were buried by the assemblies.

After Peronism was removed from power by a bloody military coup in 1955, the developmentalism of the late 1950s and 1960s opened up the economy to US and other foreign capital in key sectors such as the automotive industry and oil. The growth of those sectors, and branches of the iron and metallurgy industries, led in turn to an expansion of small and medium-sized enterprises (SMEs). In the same movement, tens of thousands of new workers arrived in the cities in direct response to the mechanization of agriculture and the industrialization of elements of livestock management. The technical composition of capital was changing yet again in response to the class struggle in industry.

An illustrative case of that change is the automotive industry, whose expansion implied a political decision to the detriment of the railroad and led to unexpected results in the 1990s. Instituto de Estudios Económicos sobre la Realidad Argentina y Latinoamericana (IERAL) researchers Juan Manuel Garzón and Inés Berniell (2006) point out that

> at the end of the 1960s, Argentina was among the 15 leading automotive producers in the world, with a market share of 0.7 percent ... [but the] automotive industry "promised" in the decade of the '60s ... over the years failed to achieve large-scale manufacturing. The opposite happened in other Latin American countries such as Brazil and Mexico ... which did manage to sustain high rates of growth in their industries.

They add that: "employment in the sector, which was less than 10 thousand in 1959, reached a ceiling of 57.4 thousand in 1974. From that moment, the industry began to dispense with labor, touching a floor of 12.1 thousand in 2002."

These figures demonstrate two simultaneous developments. First, they underline the role played by non-British foreign capital in the revitalization of the automotive industry, during which two generations of skilled labor with powerful workers' organizations engaged in a sustained battle over the model of accumulation in the hegemonic bloc. Second, they demonstrate that Argentina was reorganizing its productive structure as capital settled heavily in Brazil and Mexico. This signaled the end of the cycle of import substitution by the mid-1970s, especially from the dictatorial coup of 1976 onwards.

Meanwhile, another phenomenon was unfolding that was going to have consequences even up to the present. The oligarchy and the agro-exporter *latifundio* increasingly relied on the growing transport of cargo by trucks, thereby destroying the Argentine railways (nationalized by the first Peronist government in 1947). In other words, although auto production had periods of growth and shrinkage, the cargo sector was increasing, until it had mostly shifted from trains to trucks by the 1990s. The Inter-American Development Bank (2012), in its latest updated directory of the cargo sector, estimates that in Argentina there were a total of 593,476 freight vehicles. The Rosario Cereal Exchange, the main reference in the agribusiness market, reported that as of December 2018 these vehicles transported "a total of 537.4 million tons of merchandise ... The automobile maintains its leadership as the main mode for the transport of cargo, accounting for 92.7% of the total loads, and the tonnage transported by rail reached 18.8 million tons, 3.5%" (Calzada and Rozadilla 2020).

It is clear that at least three variables are at work here:

1) Argentina had been complementary to the British economy but not to the US economy. However, after the defeat of Peron in 1955, and due to its highly skilled workers and the liberalization of oil exploitation and chemical factories, Argentina became central for US, German, French, and Italian investments. This soon changed in the 1960s, as it became clear that the combativity of the organized working class was an issue that could not be overcome. US capital found much higher rates of surplus value in Brazil and Mexico, where they focused their investments. This was particularly because these

two countries have robust domestic markets, weaker labor laws, and much less combative union organizations.

2) The role assigned to peripheral economies arises from the Washington Consensus, and according to that scheme Argentina should be a producer of food and/or commodities, not of industrial goods, and even less of heavy industry.

3) As the neoliberal Argentine state of the 1990s withdrew from all strategic areas (energy, transport, oil, and mining), far from defending and sustaining rail transport, it privatized its profitable branches and services.

These local and international political decisions ended up sealing the fate of the powerful railroad, metallurgical, and mechanic unions, while putting in their place service sector guilds such as those of truck drivers, bankers, and insurance companies, among others. Certainly an economy based primarily on exportable goods must rely heavily on transport—in the past on trains, and today on trucks. The changing composition of capital thus opened the way for the recomposition of working-class power in the logistics sector. That is why we will analyze here the "fire power" of the truckers' union, the *Camioneros*, which since the mid-1990s has had the real capacity to paralyze the country.

TRADE UNIONS IN ARGENTINA IN THE TWENTY-FIRST CENTURY

The unions with the largest number of affiliates in Argentina are those representing commercial employees, construction workers, state employees, food service workers and hoteliers, metallurgists, and workers in the health sector. Explaining the dynamics of each one, their mechanisms of affiliation, the bureaucratization of their leadership, and their increasing distance from their membership bases would take a very long time, and is not the main goal of this chapter. We are going to say, for the time being, that these unions have not confronted the neoliberal policies used against workers during the last 30 years. But we will focus on understanding the centrally strategic role of the *Camioneros*.

The National Federation of Truck Workers (FEDCAM), known as *Camioneros*, has between 160,000 and 210,000 affiliated members, although the exact number is not available (membership numbers are not usually published by large unions). Its leader, Hugo Moyano, a *caudillo*, has been baptized as *San Moyano* or "Hugo". He has headed the guild since 1987, from a very young age, and was the leader of the General Confederation of Labor (CGT) for 13 years at the same time. He has real power. The Truckers' union has a high rate of affiliation of over 70 percent of the 300,000 total workers in the industry, and a high level of participation in the street demonstrations it calls. But the reason for the high rate of affiliation is the union's constant defense of its members' collective bargaining agreements (CBAs) and high salaries. Moyano recently captured an additional 22,800 workers who were in other unions, such as those representing post office and commercial employees, with whose leaders he was in conflict.

The *Camioneros*' federation, FEDCAM, the federation to which the *Camioneros* belong, is made up of 24 unions spread across the country, with a total of 300,000 workers in this sector. It is composed of 17 branches, though the union does not provide the exact number of affiliates per branch:

1) Freight Transportation in General (short and long distance)
2) Heavy Transport and Mobile Cranes
3) Armored Transportation
4) Transportation of Clearing and Postal Freight
5) Collection and/or Compaction of Waste and/or Sweeping and Cleaning of Streets, Public Roads and/or Sewers and/or Related Tasks
6) Transportation and Distribution of Journals and Magazines (and any other type of publication)
7) Transportation of Liquid Fuels (solid, liquid, or gaseous, in bulk and/or fractionated)
8) Transportation of Hazardous Materials
9) Transport and/or Logistics for Oil Activity
10) Long Distance, Removals, and Parcels, and/or Instant Freight
11) Transportation and Distribution of Water, Soft Drinks, and Beers
12) Logistics Operations, Storage and Distribution

13) Transportation of Construction Materials, Pre-made Concrete, Rubble by Means of Containers and/or Tippers, Movements and Assembly of Heavy Elements Intended for Civil Engineering Works
14) Cold and Frozen Transport
15) Transport of Sausages
16) Transport of Cereals, Oilseeds, and Livestock
17) Transport of Dairy Products

As is clear from this list, there is no sector of the economy that is not served by the transport of loads. Up to six of the branches are in direct connection with exports and imports, some for both the international and the domestic economy, and the rest for the everyday domestic economy. Consequently, when the *Camioneros* propose a partial or total strike, everything is paralyzed (Pontoni 2013).

The strategic role the *Camioneros* have gained, replacing the production unions' role as the vanguard of the working class, is the result of one deep and evident change in the Argentine economy. As noted above, the economy has undergone a reorganization linked to agriculture, including the export of oils and biodiesel, commodities linked to agro-industry, and extracted minerals. No less than 46 percent of its total exports have come from these items in the last decade. For example, the total harvest of the 2018–19 season was around 145 million tons: 57 million of corn, 55.6 million of soy, 19.4 million of wheat, 5.06 million of barley, 5 million of "other" crops, and 3.8 million of sunflower seeds (Agrofy News 2019).

How are these huge volumes transported? By trucks.

By comparison, during the January to May 2019 cycle, the six freight railway lines (three operated by private companies and three by the state) transported only 3.6 million tons of grain, 1.3 million tons of agricultural by-products, almost 2 million tons of minerals and construction materials, and other items totaling 8.4 million tons. The annual projection maintains the trend, with only a slight variation. In other words, the use of trains and waterways for the transportation of goods does not reach 8 percent of the total load.

In response to their disruptive power, owners of the truck fleets and different levels of the state administration are attempting to devise a strategy to "deflate" the power of *Camioneros*. Ironically, that power is in a sector that the owners and the state themselves created to maximize profits and tax revenues. The transport entre-preneurs, consortiums dedicated to agro-industry (including the two Chinese companies that operate in the market and export directly to China), and the state do not want to change the status quo of the wealth accumulation model nor promote the trains as a strategic tool. Trains would be a strategic alternative to the *Camioneros* because of the mixture of loads and passengers that today travel by bus. Shifting to trains would also lead to an expansion in railway construction, maintenance depots, and related jobs.

What do they want instead? To lower the wages and other benefits paid to truck drivers. If the *Camioneros* have the capacity to paralyze entire branches of the economy, *breaking their power would discipline the whole labor movement*. But the problem for capital is that each of the branches and sub-branches of the truckers' union have almost the same interests and strategic power, so weakening one is insufficient for disciplining the rest. Consequently, the establishment has tried to reform the labor laws, a policy dreamt of by the military dictatorship government in the 1970s, and more recently by the neoliberal gov-ernments of the 1990s. And now they are coming at it again, using the National Congress to eliminate the benefits obtained during more than 130 years of struggle, and in this way weaken the unions and decompose the working class's power. This is the historical and polit-ical moment that Argentina is going through, and although at the end of 2017 the state tried to push through labor law reform projects, popular mobilizations stopped them.

The pertinent question is what has remained of the long history of the workers' struggle and their resulting gains in the past three decades of the post-Fordist period? After all, this is a period charac-terized by fragmented production, with 30 percent of the population engaged in precarious non-formal work outside of CBAs, 7 to 11 percent in intermittent unemployment, and the steady growth of the tertiary service sector. How successful has capital's strategy been in decomposing working-class power?

The strategic position of the *Camioneros* was not the same in the years 1991 to 2001 as it has been ever since that year. During the 1990s, and culminating in the *Argentinazo*, the state decided to promote flexibilization, precarization, and deregulation. They aimed at the heart of the welfare state created in the 1940s and 1950s. The working masses were disciplined by mass layoffs, fixed-term labor contracts without social rights, benefits, or compensation, the extension of the working day without payment of overtime, and the elimination of sector-wide collective bargaining and its replacement with negotiations at the firm level.

If the *Camioneros* have become as powerful as they are, this is not only because their workers are in every corner of the production and distribution system, but also because their way of bargaining impacts on other unions' fights. Their bargaining for "benefits by sector" secures gains for the whole pack. The loyalty of members is built up as each sector is considered in terms of its particular demands.

During the cycle of "defeat," the *Camioneros* managed to sign only 11 CBAs. After the social and economic crisis of 2001 left more than 57 percent of the population in poverty, the state promoted the

> updating and reinstitutionalization of the *Salario Mínimo, Vital y Móvil Minimum* [guaranteed minimum income], which was a fundamental instrument to set a salary floor, especially for the lowest income workers, and, in turn, encourage a fairer distribution; the enactment of the Law on Labor Regulation [LLR] No. 25,877, which was presented as a normalizing ... labor relations, ... allowed the reversal of some of the regulations that had made work more flexible, returning unions to their capacity of negotiating on behalf of workers, promoting the generation of employment in small and medium-sized enterprises [and] the intervention of the Ministry of Labor to control and guarantee the effective exercise of labor standards with respect to the conditions, safety, and hygiene of work. (Pontoni 2013: 88)

In contrast to the previous decade, since 2003 the strategic options deployed by the truckers' union have changed significantly. Between 2003 to 2011, the *Camioneros* signed 145 agreements which together make up the CBAs (Pontoni 2013: 144). The union's strategy was not limited only to increasing wages for transport workers as a whole, but sought to carefully differentiate the sub-activities of different groups of workers to secure benefits or protections for each one. For example, they managed to get overtime payments on kilometers traveled, travel expenses for long-distance drivers, and controls on discharge payments.

After the ultra-liberal decade of the 1990s when CBAs were almost entirely suppressed and a new Labor Contract Law came into force, Moyano's strategy of organizing strikes, mobs, press conferences, and street adverts, and entering step by step into an alliance with the government to ensure full enforcement of the CBAs, paid off. The novelty of the *Camioneros'* strategy, in contrast to that of other unions, can be summarized in terms of the following elements:

1) Expanding the base of workers by incorporating union branches and sub-branches in transport, distribution, and logistics. In a concentrated export economy focused on services this makes it possible to paralyze the economy.

2) Wage bargaining with workers in the streets—a tradition that comes from the very roots of the Argentine labor movement but gained a more intense vigor from the irruption of the *piqueteros* social movements.

3) A basic salary negotiation for transport workers as a whole, but in parallel with negotiations made branch by branch to obtain specific labor rights that will empower workers in each sector.

4) Indirectly conditioning the national foreign exchange balance and the chain of payments via exports. Argentina has historically lacked dollars for development, which was one of the reasons why the Great Depression had such a strong impact on the country. Perhaps the only exceptions were the World War II period and Peronism. So, since the economy is based on exporting commodities, with trucks transporting more than 93 percent of total cargo to the ports, the pressure of the *Camioneros* is on the export consortiums and the state, which gets part of its revenues prepaid before exports.

5) Linking the whole trade union organization with the leader, Hugo Moyano. Earlier we highlighted the role of the charismatic *caudillo* in Argentine politics. Moyano is no exception and Peronism reinforces

the point. The masses act and struggle but they search for a charismatic leader. The *caudillo* is central to Argentine culture whether in relation to politics, the unions, or soccer. But it is not just a matter of an individual leader or a little emperor; it is a question of him (or her, in the case of former president Cristina Fernández de Kirchner) leading and the masses pressuring ... which is exactly what made Peron so successful.

6) The implicit or explicit support of other union leaders and unions that use the truckers' salary guidelines to put pressure on other areas where capital has ample value, for example banking and finance.

7) The highly effective operation of the medical services provided by the union. For decades, the unions have provided their own medical services (with their own hospitals) alongside the vast free public health service and costly private health services. Necessarily, the money for these union-run medical services comes from affiliates and employers through paycheck deductions, plus a contribution by the state. Among all the unions the *Camioneros* have built a very high quality health service. The union has inspectors who visit each company to check that they have made payments on time, otherwise they immediately report them to the government. People call this "*obra social*" (the social health service), which has nothing in common with the US Medicare system.

CONCLUSIONS

The *Camioneros* truckers' union is not a new type of union. It is not modeled after the popular assemblies and it does not have organized internal opposition. It works like a mass union or a movement union. It occupies the central place in this moment of the development of capitalism in Argentina. It exists within the framework of a state whose policies do not aim to modify the status quo based on agriculture and agro-industry on the one hand, and the financial apparatus on the other. The old intertwining of industrial consortiums and finance associated with the imperialist period is now an immodest marriage between agro-industry consortiums and finance. Some firms generate commodities while others are investment funds which manage the price of those commodities.

Are the *Camioneros* to be blamed for having the power and organization that they do, for securing good salaries for their members, and having achieved fully enforced CBAs during the virtual disappearance of the railway cargo system? No. Investment in a multimodal system where the railway is deployed in an effective network that generates other sources of work, and where the different systems of road transport and navigable waterways are complementary, is a necessity for the country. It would be a "greener" plan, and would result in a higher rate of capital accumulation due to the reduction of time/cost per load. This would not hurt either the truckers or the union. But the primary actors capable of realizing this gigantic investment in a territory of more than 2.7 million square kilometers are not willing to carry it forward. By primary actors we mean the national government, the truck factories, the landlords, the export consortiums, the international agrochemical manufacturers—all of them beneficiaries of the lack of investment in the railroads and the necessary multimodal transport infrastructure. Investing in such fixed capital is not worth it for capitalism. Generally, in Argentina, it was the state that made such investments for the benefit and/or development of capital. After the Washington Consensus, that was no longer the case. And since there has been no investment in the railroads, the power of the *Camioneros* has grown immensely.

Argentina has had long periods of military government and short periods of democracy. But there is no dictatorial specter at the end of the tunnel at the present time. As the country moves through the channels of democracy where laws are debated and passed by parliament, only a dictatorship deploying armed security forces in the street could prevent the application of current labor laws and repress the activities of the *Camioneros*. The power of interpellation into the establishment that the truckers' union has achieved does not seem to be under threat.

REFERENCES

Agrofy News (2019). Con más de 145 millones de toneladas la cosecha 2018/19 consolida su record. (July 3). At https://news.agrofy.com.ar/noticia/181749/mas-145-millones-toneladas-cosecha-201819-consolida-su-record.

Bruschera, O. (1969). *Artigas, 1*. Montevideo: Biblioteca de Marcha-Colección Los nuestros.

Calzada, J. and Rozadilla, B. (2020) ¿A cuánto asciende anualmente el Transporte decargas en Argentina? *Bolsa de Comercio de Rosario*. At https://www.bcr.com.ar/es/mercados/investigacion-y-desarrollo/informativo-semanal/noticias-informativo-semanal/cuanto-1.

Dorfmann, A. (1986). *Historia de la Industria Argentina: Evolución industrial Argentina 1870–1940*. Buenos Aires: Hyspamérica.

Garzón, J.M. and Berniell, I. (2006). *Los últimos 40 años de la producción automotriz ¿Radiografía de una industria argentina?* Serie Documentos de trabajo, July 8. At www.ieral.org/images_db/noticias_archivos/3597-238067361.pdf.

Inter-American Development Bank (n.d.). Los perfiles de país en transporte de carga. At http://logisticsportal.iadb.org/countryprofiles/index_es.html#cat=view69&ctr=AR.

Normano, J. (1932). The British Offensive in South America. *The Hispanic American Historical Review* 12(1), 93–9.

Paso, L. (1974). *La clase obrera y el nacimiento del marxismo en la Argentina*. Buenos Aires: ANTEO, Colección Testimonio.

Pontoni, G. (2013). *Relaciones laborales en Argentina. El caso Camioneros entre 1991–2011*. Doctoral thesis in Social Sciences-Facultad de Ciencias Sociales, Universidad de Buenos Aires, Argentina.

Villalobos, S. (1977). *Comercio y contrabando en el Río de la Plata y Chile*. Buenos Aires: Eudeba, Libros del tiempo nuevo.

Villanueva, J. (1972). *El origen de la industrialización argentina*. Buenos Aires: IDES.

Zaragoza Rovira, G. (2015). *Anarquismo argentino, 1876–1902*. Madrid: Ediciones de la Torre.

2

When Class Unionism Leads to Working-Class Recomposition: The Case of TÜMTİS in Turkey[1]

Alpkan Birelma

This chapter concerns a case of class composition led by a Turkish trade union representing road transport workers called Tüm Taşıma İşçileri Sendikası (TÜMTİS). In the mid-2000s, TÜMTİS was mainly organized in traditional, small delivery companies which were under pressure from the structural shift in the freight transportation industry towards large corporations. At that time, the union had around 1,500 members with collective bargaining agreements (CBAs). The union's revitalization began after a change in leadership in 2007. The strategic choice to concentrate on a large international firm with the support of the International Transportation Workers' Federation (ITF) and the UNI Global Union was the turning point. The ensuing United Parcel Service (UPS) campaign ended with a CBA for nearly 2,700 new members in 2011. TÜMTİS won its second large-scale organizing victory at DHL, ending with a CBA for 2,260 new members in 2014. The third victory came after an organizing drive and judicial process which took four and a half years. The union finally signed a CBA in March 2019 with Aras Delivery for nearly 4,500 new members.

How could such a small union win such consistent victories against global corporations and turn into a respected and inspirational member of the international labor movement? How can this success be explained and what are the lessons to be learned about class composition from this quite astonishing revitalization?

To scrutinize this case of class composition, I use the power resources approach in a critical way. This approach investigates the objective factors behind union agency. While it assumes a particular subjectivity, union subjectivities are in reality varied and complicated. I argue that TÜMTİS's revitalization can be only explained by taking both objective and subjective factors into consideration. The socialist orientation and class unionism of the TÜMTİS leaders explain the subjective side of the revitalization, whereas associational power from below on the workplace level plays the key role on the objective side. The new leadership refreshed the class unionism of TÜMTİS and mobilized associational power on the workplace level. To overcome the formidable local obstacles to organizing, they made the strategic choice to cooperate with the global union federations (GUFs), which soon recognized the potential of TÜMTİS and offered further support. Thereby, the union increased its associational power with additional resources from the international level, enabling its leaders to take another strategic decision to dare to organize a big player in the sector. Local union leaders adhering to class unionism managed to connect associational power at the workplace level with associational power on the transnational level. This rare conjunction brought about the union's astonishing organizing victories.

The chapter is based on field research mainly conducted in the spring and summer of 2016. I interviewed seven of the union's elected leaders and officers both individually and in groups. I met most of them more than once. I also interviewed two American unionists, one of whom interacted with TÜMTİS as an ITF officer at the time. I spent four days with a union organizing officer visiting already organized workplaces, meeting with workers who are part of an ongoing organizing campaign, and with potential members. I also participated in two crowded meetings where the union leaders and UPS workers discussed what to demand and how to prepare for the upcoming collective bargaining. I had the chance to engage in short conversations with members and potential members during these visits and meetings. For seven union members fired by DHL Express (another DHL company much smaller than the main one), the union sustained a picket line between July 2017 and January 2019. I visited this picket line seven times, which gave me the opportunity to observe the unionists and workers in action. Last but not least, I occasionally continue visiting the union or meeting with TÜMTİS unionists.

In what follows, I first review the power resources approach, and explain how and why I reinforce it with an examination of the subjectivities of the union leaders. The second section provides a short history of TÜMTİS's remarkable revitalization. In the last section, I analyze the process by tapping into the power resources approach, reinforced with a discussion on subjectivity.

THE POWER RESOURCES APPROACH
AND THE ISSUE OF SUBJECTIVITY

This chapter concerns a case of class composition led by a Turkish union. By class composition I refer to the composition of workers as a force against capital (Wright 2002: 57). Class composition has a similar meaning to more familiar terms such as the "making" (Thompson 1963) or "formation" (Katznelson and Zolberg 1986) of the working class. While making or formation often imply developments on the national or regional levels, class composition is a more elastic term useful for processes on the micro level, such as in a single workplace. In the case I examine in this chapter, the "political leap" necessary for working class recomposition (Woodcock 2014: 507) is led by a union. Therefore, I will build the discussion on the literature on trade unions, especially on trade union revitalization.

In the expanding literature on this subject, the power resources approach is prominent, especially among European scholars. Although it might have several weaknesses in its attempt to comprehend the total complexity of social reality, just like all other models (Tilly 1995: 1596), it provides an effective framework to scrutinize unions' revitalization practices comparatively and analytically (Frege and Kelly 2004: 33–5; Hyman and Gumbrell-McCormick 2013: 30–1; Schmalz and Dörre 2016; Schmalz and Thiel 2017; Schmalz, Ludwig, and Webster 2018).

The power resources model assumes that the working class in general and trade unions in particular have certain resources from which they derive their social and political power. How to discover and access these resources, and how far and how effectively they are being used, depends on the will and capabilities of the workers and their unions. The model rests on the conceptualization offered by Wright (2000: 962) and further developed by Silver (2003: 13). Accordingly, the working class has two primary power resources: structural power and associational power. While the former derives from the location of the workers within the economic structure, the latter derives from workers' collective organization in the workplace and industry in which they are located.

Scholars who have applied this conceptualization in their research have defined other power resources, which has led to an ongoing debate about what these resources are and how to classify them. I will use a quadruple model, which includes structural, associational, institutional, and societal power resources. Institutional power refers to the several support mechanisms unions may tap into, such as legislative supports, mechanisms for extending CBAs, and participation in tripartite consultation processes (Hyman and Gumbrell-McCormick 2013: 31; Schmalz and Dörre 2016: 227–30). Societal power indicates the support of different social groups for unions due to the prestige they have and/or popular demands for justice with which they can resonate (Frege and Kelly, 2004: 35; Hyman and Gumbrell-McCormick 2013: 31; Schmalz and Dörre 2016: 230–33).

The power resources approach offers a way to explain the agency of workers and unions. It elaborates the objective factors behind this agency, but subjectivities are given much less attention within the model. More recently, some scholars have added the concept of capabilities to the model in order to scrutinize the actors' subjectivities more closely. For instance, Lévesque and Murray (2010) identify four capabilities—intermediating, framing, articulating, and learning. They argue that how far unions can access power resources and how efficiently they can employ them depends on union leaders' capabilities. But what about the question of will and intention?

This question merits attention. Burawoy identifies the power resources approach with "unstated optimism," because it "assumes that labor is always interested in resisting exploitation and its success depends on its capacity, that is the mobilization of two types of resources—structural and associational power" (2010: 303). Burawoy

(2011: 73) also points to the impact of hegemony and ideology, which set limits on the workers' agency. Moreover, as Thompson shows, for the workers there are always many other and quite rational alternatives to class struggle such as "individualistic and familial strategies of survival" (1991: 266). In my field research, I observed such strategies of survival and enrichment as alternatives to acting collectively against exploitation (Birelma 2016: 208–10). Similarly, just like workers, union leaders can also have a wide range of different intentions and motivations other than organizing and class struggle (Dinler 2014; Erem 2001; Hyman 2001; Jacobs 2006). Obviously, corrupt union leaders will not care to use whatever power resources they have access to for organizing and struggle. And, more importantly, the subjectivities of union leaders are much more varied than the binary opposition between corrupt and incorrupt would suggest.

The power resources approach assumes a more or less particular subjectivity, even though subjectivities are varied and complicated (Bourdieu 2000: 164–205; Ortner 2006: 107–55). As such, I contend that the approach cannot fully explain labor's agency. In order to balance the attention given to objective factors, i.e. power resources, it needs to be complemented with an analysis of subjectivities. While the approach offers an elaborate model of the objective factors which influence the labor movement's agency, we do not yet have a model of its subjectivities as recognized. To analyze the impact of union leaders' subjectivities on the revitalization of the labor movement, I build on Hyman's (2001) ideal types of unionism, the importance Ganz (2000) attributes to leaders' motivations, research on the importance of union ideology (Benassi and Vlandas 2016; Darlington 2009), and Lévesque and Murray's (2010) work on capabilities.

More concretely, I argue that TÜMTİS's revitalization cannot be explained without taking both the objective and subjective aspects of the process into account. Without recognizing the TÜMTİS leaders' class unionism (Hyman 2001: 36), socialist ideology (Darlington 2009: 8), and ensuing intrinsic motivations (Ganz 2000: 1014), it is impossible to explain their success. But by the same token, these factors alone cannot explain the success either, because specific structural and associational power resources paved the way for the victories. On the question of which power resource was more prominent, I will contend that associational power at the workplace level has been key to TÜMTİS's revitalization, as the basis on which everything else was built.

A SHORT HISTORY OF TÜMTİS'S REVITALIZATION

The Turkish labor movement has been one of those hit hardest by neoliberal restructuring. The credible data on collective bargaining agreements is a viable measure by which to assess union power. I calculate collective bargaining coverage in terms of the proportion of the total number of employees, including civil servants and informal workers, covered by a CBA. While nearly one in four Turkish employees was covered by a CBA in the mid-1980s, a continuous fall led to a rate of 5 percent in 2013. Accordingly, wage shares have followed the plummeting strike rates, reaching new lows since the mid-1990s, as Figure 2.1 demonstrates.

The Turkish industrial relations regulatory regime does not provide any supportive mechanism for collective bargaining. Turkish unions must organize workplace by workplace to extend collective bargaining coverage. To be covered by a CBA, a worker must be a

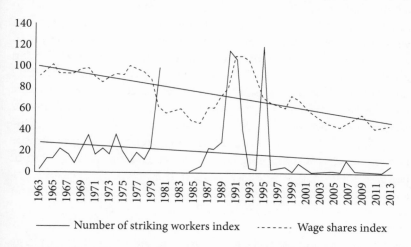

Figure 2.1 Wage Shares and the Number of Striking Workers (Index)

Source: Birelma 2017. See also Birelma 2018.

union member, and the union must exceed two thresholds. Firstly, it must organize more than half of the workers in the workplace. Since 2012, the workplace threshold for companies with more than one workplace is 40 percent of total workers in the company. The second threshold is industry wide. As of 2012, a union has had to represent at least 1 percent of the total number of registered workers in the relevant industry to be authorized for collective bargaining. The industries are defined by the law and these definitions can be changed, sometimes in an arbitrary way.

After the 2001 economic crisis the unemployment rate was never lower than 9 percent, while after the 2008 crisis it rose above 10 percent. Subcontracted employment is the most common version of flexible employment, and the ratio of subcontract workers to the total number of employees grew from 4 to 11 percent between 2002 and 2011 (Birelma 2017).

Since 2002, the one-party government of the pro-Islamic Justice and Development Party (AKP) has followed a twofold strategy concerning unions. On the one hand, the AKP has limited the activities of left-wing, militant unions. On the other, it has colonized trade unions by embracing "symbiotic syndicalism" (Çelik 2015) and fully supporting pro-Islamic and pro-AKP unions to the detriment of others (Doğan 2013; Gürcan and Mete 2017: 111). Since 2017, the government has banned seven strikes by nearly 150,000 workers in total. Due to the rising number of strike bans and arrests of union leaders, the International Trade Union Confederation (ITUC) declared that Turkey was among the ten worst countries for workers in 2018 (Birelma 2018). This formidable context, where the power resources of trade unions not aligned with the AKP have been dwindling, makes TÜMTİS's revitalization even more fascinating. As can be seen in Graph 1, the number of strikes and the share of output going to wages has declined since the mid-1990s.

TÜMTİS before revitalization

Municipal bus and tram drivers in Istanbul established TÜMTİS in 1949. It was among the founding unions of the oldest and largest trade union confederation in Turkey, Türk-İş, established in 1952. TÜMTİS was led by a politically right-wing leadership with its stronghold in Istanbul. Reporting its largest number of members in 1970 as 21,000, the union has never been a large one. Turkish unions' declarations about their membership numbers have been greatly exaggerated. The Ministry of Labor put a digital system in place and has declared membership numbers in a relatively reliable way only since 2013.

The union has suffered two setbacks in its history. The first was in 1974, when the government enacted a new regulation redefining some industries. According to this regulation, municipal bus services were excluded from the land transport sector. This caused TÜMTİS to lose almost half its membership. The second setback, the anti-labor coup of 1980, resulted in a further decrease of the membership. Nevertheless, the union leadership praised the coup due to its right-wing stance (Baydar 1998; Pala 1969; TÜMTİS 1998).

To survive, in the mid-1980s TÜMTİS engaged in organizing the workers of the traditional, small-scale freight companies in Istanbul. These companies used to be scattered throughout the city, but the municipality had forced them to operate from the same building complex since 1977. They usually employed fewer than fifty workers, a considerable proportion of which were informally employed without any formal registration or social security. Thanks to this recruitment drive, the union grew, but at a slow pace (Öztürk 2010: 99–102). Because the union's financial resources were extremely depleted, its professional leaders were paid no more than its members, which became a custom of the union.

Towards the end of the 1980s, Turkish labor made a comeback for a limited period, especially in terms of strikes. TÜMTİS was one of the forerunners of this wave by organizing a series of strikes in 1987 (Doğan 2015: 396; Öztürk 2010: 102–13), and this activism led to a significant change in the leadership. A group of left-leaning workers won the executive election in 1989. With their energy and militancy, TÜMTİS revived itself as a small but solid union of small-scale freight company workers, who were almost exclusively men (Selçuk 2002: 229). Moreover, in the second half of the 1990s, the new leadership built close ties with a small socialist party. After the 1987 strikes, the small freight companies began losing their share of the market to the growing large-scale companies. TÜMTİS tried to organize workers in one such large company at the beginning of the 1990s, but the campaign failed (Öztürk 2010: 117).

In the first few years of the 2000s the union experienced a period of lethargy, internal debate, and ensuing regression. In 2002, nearly a thousand union members working in the small delivery companies in Istanbul left TÜMTİS and joined another union. The most significant success in this period was the organizing of 200 bus drivers working in a subcontracted company serving a municipality in south-east Turkey. Due to the various deadlocks and disagreements, in 2004 a group of leaders and members began to oppose the union leadership. After a period of harsh internal debate, the opposing group, led by the leader of the successful campaign in the municipality subcontractor, won the executive election in 2007. The new leadership broke from the socialist party, which they blamed for backing the ex-leadership. This change of leadership marked a milestone in the union's history.

First step: The search for revitalization (2007–2009)

In 2008, the union began to organize in two subcontractor companies working for Unilever, which triggered the firms to dismiss 87 union members. This was the first time the union had tried to organize in an international firm, and it had received close support from the International Transport Workers' Federation (ITF). After a seven-month struggle, the union secured the rehiring of most of the workers. Nevertheless, it was prevented from signing a CBA in the following months because of a court decision which determined that the subcontractor firm was not a road transportation firm.

In the summer of 2008 the union successfully organized nearly 300 workers in a subcontracted firm at a dock in southern Turkey owned by PSA International. The employer gradually dismissed 197 members, who maintained a picket line for six months. The ITF supported the workers by visiting the picket line and pressuring the parent company in Singapore via its members in the Singapore dockers' union (Anderson 2015: 54). TÜMTİS achieved the reinstatement of all the dismissed workers and signed a CBA at the beginning of 2010. However, the managers of the dock were anxious about the combative stance of TÜMTİS, so in 2012 they transferred all the union workers employed by the subcontracting firm to the main firm. As a result, workers could not hold TÜMTİS membership, because according to Turkish labor law, dockworkers and shipbuilding workers do not belong to the transportation industry. It was because the subcontracting firm was registered as a transportation firm that TÜMTİS could originally organize its workers.

Second step: A strategic choice to organize a big player (2009–2011)

The real breakthrough came with the United Parcel Service campaign that began at the end of 2009. TÜMTİS and other unions had tried to organize large-scale freight transport companies in the past, but these attempts had failed (TÜMTİS 1998: 311). TÜMTİS targeted UPS because it was an international company with no history of failed union organizing drives. The new leadership saw an opportunity to build a campaign with support from the ITF. UPS Turkey had nearly 2,500 directly employed workers and an estimated 2,000 subcontracted and franchise workers at that time.

The union reached out to UPS workers in Istanbul and Izmir, and the UPS management began firing union members in April 2010. TÜMTİS responded by forming picket lines of sacked workers in front of three UPS transfer centers in the two cities. At that time, the union had less than 400 members among direct and subcontracted UPS workers. In the company's union-busting process, 162 TÜMTİS members were fired and most of them joined the picket line.

The picket lines and ITF-led international campaign lasted for nine months. Thanks to their combined pressure, UPS and TÜMTİS came to an agreement in February 2011. All but twelve of the sacked workers were reinstated and UPS management declared that it would respect the unionization (see Dinler and McGrath 2011). In July, the number of union members exceeded the company threshold of 40 percent and TÜMTİS received recognition from the Ministry of Labor. The ensuing collective bargaining led to the agreement signed in December 2011. During the negotiations, many non-member workers became union members, and a number of subcontracted workers became directly employed. When the agreement was signed, TÜMTİS had nearly 2,700 members among UPS workers.

Third step: Letting success breed success (2012–2014)

In close coordination with the ITF, TÜMTİS leaders chose the German Deutsche Post's DHL as the second target. This time the UNI Global Union was a more integral part of the process, because ver.di, the recognized union at DHL in Germany, is a UNI affiliate. In spring 2012, TÜMTİS began to get in touch with DHL workers. In June, DHL found out about the drive and fired 37 union members. TÜMTİS responded with two picket lines in Istanbul and Kocaeli. DHL was even more obstinate than UPS about opposing unionization, which led to a 15-month picket line campaign. UNI and ITF targeted shareholders and customers of DHL and organized many protests, although there were no on the job actions. Among other things, they filed a complaint against DHL with the German government, alleging a breach of the OECD Guidelines for Multinational Enterprises in Turkey and other countries (Conrow 2015: 109–16). The complaint led to a joint statement by the German National Contact Point for the OECD guidelines for multinational enterprises, UNI, ITF, and DHL at the beginning of 2014 (OECD 2014).

This multi-dimensional pressure overcame DHL's resistance in autumn 2013. After the recognition and collective bargaining processes, TÜMTİS finally signed a CBA with DHL in April 2014 for its 2,260 members. All but seven of the sacked workers were reinstated, wages were increased by around 40 percent, and 730 subcontracted workers were transferred to permanent positions. DHL's union-busting campaign had been so uncompromising that it provoked both leaders and members of TÜMTİS to be as stubborn as possible during collective bargaining, which resulted in a stronger first agreement compared to UPS.

Fourth step: Expanding the campaign to sustain success (2014–2019)

TÜMTİS's third target, also with the support of ITF, was the second-largest firm in the Turkish freight transport industry, Aras Delivery. By 2014, Aras was owned by a Turkish family, with the Austrian Post holding a 25 percent minority share, and employed nearly 5,000 workers. In almost a year and a half, by the end of

2015, TÜMTİS had organized nearly 2,000 Aras workers, which was enough for recognition by the Ministry.

This time TÜMTİS had followed a less contentious strategy because the Aras management had been less aggressive compared to earlier cases. Nevertheless, the company refused to respect TÜMTİS's recognition and brought the case to court. The union law grants this right to employers, who, like Aras, mostly use it to prolong the process of recognition. Including the process of appeal, these cases last usually around one and a half years, and sometimes even longer. The Aras court case lasted even longer than usual because of the failed coup attempt in 2016 which shook Turkey and brought turmoil to the political and judicial system. In September 2018, the court of appeals made the final decision approving union recognition. After the collective bargaining process, the union finally signed a CBA with Aras in March 2019, covering nearly 4,500 members. The number of members has increased over the years, especially following local court approval. Among the reasons for the increase is the organizing of smaller numbers of workers such as at DHL Express, a subgroup company specializing in international delivery, with nearly 400 employees. Once again, DHL fired seven union members in July 2017 and TÜMTİS responded by forming a picket line in front of the company headquarters which lasted for nearly 20 months. In the end, TÜMTİS became the recognized union in DHL Express and signed a CBA in January 2019.

In twelve years, TÜMTİS increased the number of its due-paying members working under a CBA from around 1,500 in 2007 to nearly 10,000 in 2019. The number of workers under CBAs in Turkey increased by approximately 40 percent in the same period, mostly due to unionization in the public subcontractor companies, mainly by unions which have close ties with the AKP (Birelma 2017). By contrast, the rate for TÜMTİS is more than 550 per cent. As noted above, since January 2013, the Ministry of Labor has begun to publish reliable statistics on union membership in Turkey. Between January 2013, when the DHL picket line was going on, and July 2019, TÜMTİS increased its total membership, including members not yet covered by a CBA, from 6,775 to 11,567.

TÜMTİS had to deal with a court decision which reveals the extreme difficulties of class unionism in the Turkish context. In March 2017, the Turkish court of appeals issued a decision involving 14 TÜMTİS leaders and members of the Ankara local. In 2012, the local court had sentenced them to prison terms ranging from one and a half to six years due to a complaint by a freight company which TÜMTİS had tried to organize in 2007. The sentence was for the "crimes" of "increasing the number of members and thus obtaining more dues" and "obstructing the freedom of work" (Çelik 2017). After the court of appeals upheld the lower court's finding, which was shocking even in terms of the declining Turkish legal standards (Çalışkan 2018), the 14 unionists were imprisoned.

ANALYSIS OF TÜMTİS'S EVOLUTION AND SUCCESS

Subjectivities: Ideology and motivations

TÜMTİS had a socialist leadership affiliated with a political party from the mid-1990s to 2007, which gave the union a militant, activist, and mobilizing stance and brought it external allies. However, such a leadership might also cause serious problems if partisan politics take precedence over unionism. This seems to be what the union experienced in the early 2000s, at a time when socialist parties and factions in Turkey were becoming marginalized after losing even the moderate social base they had. Another factor seems to have been the loss of enthusiasm and dynamism on the part of the union's leader, who had held the position for 18 years.[2] The new leadership that took over in 2007 ended their allegiance to the socialist party while maintaining their socialist ideology.[3]

As Darlington notes, "the relative neglect of the whole topic of left-wing union leadership and its significance for collective mobilization" is "a common feature of much industrial relations literature generally" (2009: 5). Similarly, Benassi and Vlandas (2016: 19) argue that ideological factors are as important as institutional ones in explaining unions' bargaining strategies. The two-centuries-long history of European labor movements reveals that for unions in general, socialism tends to be elusive, becoming at best a form of rhetoric in the long run (Hyman 2001: 17–37). Nevertheless, as

Darlington reminds us, there are exceptions, and a left-wing union leadership can have an advantage in obtaining material improvements because of its "combative stance, often involving the collective mobilization of members and the threat and use of strike action" (2009: 27).

"Class unionism," on the other hand, is one of Hyman's (2001: 1–65) three ideal types of unionism. In the first, namely business unionism, unions are interest groups with mainly labor market functions. In the second, they are members of civil society and vehicles for raising workers' status in society. In the third, unions are class actors and "schools of war" in the struggle between labor and capital. Existing unions "have tended to incline towards an often contradictory admixture of two of the three ideal types" (Hyman 2001: 4). It is almost necessary for a union to resort occasionally to a moderate level of class unionism in order to survive, although sustaining class unionism in the long run is almost impossible (Hyman 2001: 36). This is not only because of the formidable external forces class unionism has to struggle against. Movements opposing the existing order tend to either fall apart or change into rigid hierarchies (Woodcock 2014: 501). Trade union leaders become paid officials and form a bureaucracy which turns into an independent layer. Their structural conditions and hierarchical position create "a conservatizing effect" on the trade union bureaucracy (Evica 2019).

Related to their socialist orientations, TÜMTİS's leadership embraces a comparatively higher level of class unionism. Socialist orientation here means having a set of values similar to Darlington's description of the left-wing politics of the National Union of Rail, Maritime and Transport Workers (RMT) in Britain, based on "the syndicalist-type sense of a consistently adversarial attitude towards management and a commitment to the wholesale redistribution of wealth and power in society" (2009: 8). Indeed, the TÜMTİS leadership defines and imagines itself as part of a collective agency, which has the potential to change not only its members working conditions but also the entire political and economic system. It embraces a greater goal than bread-and-butter issues and aims to recompose and empower the working class against capital. The leaders express this goal through a rather sub-political discourse which resonates with workers' daily lives and problems. What motivates the average worker to join TÜMTİS is not its left-wing political stance per se. As a result of their strategy of class unionism, TÜMTİS leaders adopt a combative and mobilizing stance which leads to greater success in terms of gaining improvements.

Another subjective factor contributing to the union's success is that TÜMTİS leaders have a greater motivation and commitment than most Turkish unionists. In his account of the impact of motivation, Ganz (2000: 1014) underlines that union leaders who are committed to their job personally and/or vocationally, instead of professionally, enjoy more intrinsic rewards, which in turn brings greater motivation and creativity.

In this context, the fact that TÜMTİS leaders earn no more than the maximum wage earned by union member workers is very impressive, and the modesty of the leaders themselves and of their rooms in the union headquarters is striking. The interaction between leaders and members is not limited to the negotiation of CBAs every two years. The leaders are quite accessible to grassroots members, and visit and interact with them on a daily basis. The union leaders believe that they "share a common fate" with their members and they work hard to act accordingly. While I do not claim that all the professional leaders of TÜMTİS share this rather high level of political motivation, enthusiasm, and tenacity, I did observe that this level of commitment is the main tendency in the head office of the union.

TÜMTİS is not the only Turkish union whose leadership embraces some form of socialist ideology and class unionism. Indeed, there are at least 15 such unions. While most of them are very small and cannot exceed the 1 percent industry threshold to be authorized for collective bargaining, a few also have the authorization. In the last decade, none of these unions has achieved a growth even close to the level sustained by TÜMTİS. This is why we now need to scrutinize the power resources TÜMTİS drew on in order to explain its peculiar success.

Objectivities: Power resources that TÜMTİS tapped into

Institutional power has not been great for Turkish unions since the anti-union coup of 1980. However, this is no longer the case for all unions because those that have a leadership close to the AKP have been enjoying a certain level of institutional power since the mid-2000s. TÜMTİS is not one of them. The societal power of Turkish unions in general is not considerable either. Because most unions have become interest organizations caring only about their shrinking membership numbers, and the AKP has skillfully exploited this tendency (Buğra, Adanır, and Insel 2009; Doğan 2013: 191), the prestige of unions has eroded significantly. As a result, TÜMTİS has access mainly to two power resources, structural and associational, and the most crucial one for its revitalization has been the latter. Below I examine the union's structural power, which TÜMTİS employed secondarily, and then its associational power.

The high structural power of transportation workers

Wright (2000: 962) and Silver (2003: 13) identify two types of structural power: "Marketplace bargaining power" derives from having scarce and demanded skills within the labor market. "Workplace bargaining power," on the other hand, derives from the strategic position of a group of workers within the capitalist economy or within a workplace. As Silver notes, transportation workers "have possessed and continue to possess relatively strong workplace bargaining power," and therefore their unions tend to be stronger and more militant (2003: 98–100). For the industry in which TÜMTİS has mostly organized, namely freight logistics, Anderson underlines its "time-sensitive" nature and points to the same power resource by stating that "even minor delays can impact on revenue streams" (2015: 55). In her research on worker organizing and protests between 1870 and 1996, Silver (2003: 98) finds that transportation ranks above all other industries in terms of the number of protests. It is safe to say that this higher tendency to organize and strike is reinforced by the relatively strong workplace bargaining power enjoyed by this industry's workers. As Wright notes, "structural power may itself influence associational power" (2000: 962).

Indeed, during the extension of its membership base in small-sized delivery firms between the mid-1980s and the early 2000s, TÜMTİS organized many quite effective formal or informal strikes reinforced by the structural advantage of being transportation workers with a high level of structural power to disrupt the industry (Doğan 2015: 396; Öztürk 2010: 102–8; Selçuk 2002: 230; TÜMTİS 1998: 311). The union's efficacy in satisfying its members' demands in its stronghold of small freight companies leads to a greater identification among these members with the union. This membership base of workers identifying with the union, its goals, and activism gave TÜMTİS the core associational power on which it could build everything else.

On the other hand, workplace bargaining power based on the possibility of strike action is not automatic or generalizable in the industry. To be utilized, it seems to require the union to be organized in a significant number of firms of a similar kind and size in that industry. During and since its organizing campaigns in large companies such as UPS, DHL, and Aras, TÜMTİS has never gone on strike in these firms either formally or informally. This is not only because a strike requires much larger funds. The real problem is the nearly two dozen unorganized large-scale freight companies which would immediately take the orders of the affected firm due to the nature of the sector. "In case of a strike no company which has a contract with UPS for delivery would say let's wait for the strike to be resolved," as one union leader put it. This would be devastating for the struck firm, leading to serious downsizing or even bankruptcy. Therefore, in its revitalization process since the end of the 2000s, TÜMTİS has exploited this power resource in a quite limited way, probably only as a threat.

Associational power

In a context where all other power resources have been radically depleted, TÜMTİS had nothing but its associational power to rely on and amplify. Schmalz, Ludwig, and Webster's (2018: 118–20) identification of different bases and levels of associational power will be useful for a thorough analysis. They define five different bases of associational power: number of members, infrastructural resources, organizational efficiency, member participation, and internal cohesion. Furthermore, building on Wright (2000), they differentiate four levels at which associational power can be exercised: the workplace, the marketplace, the political system, and the transnational level.

As a small but socialist and mobilizing union since the end of the 1980s, TÜMTİS seems to have considerable associational power at the workplace level and at the marketplace level specific to small-sized freight company workers. The bases of this associational power have been member participation and internal cohesion, which compensate for the limited number of members and infrastructural resources (Öztürk 2010: 92–150).

Due to very limited financial resources, the union never had a professional staff for organizing until the ITF provided funding for the UPS campaign. Elected leaders do the job of organizing with support from grassroots members. A number of lay members tend to support the organizing drives in their area by contacting potential members. Moreover, many members working in small freight companies make additional contributions, besides their normal fees, when the union requests financial support during an organizing campaign.

Why does TÜMTİS have relatively high levels of member participation and internal cohesion? One factor is the special structural power the union has and its mastery at exploiting this resource in its stronghold of small-sized freight companies. Because of their subjectivities, the TÜMTİS leadership has also mastered framing and intermediation, two capabilities that further boost member participation and internal cohesion. As defined by Lévesque and Murray, "framing capabilities characterize a union's ability to define a proactive and autonomous agenda" (2010: 343). Class unionism serves as a strong frame which gives TÜMTİS's leadership a greater mobilizing and liberating cause. As Darlington observes, combative unionism often involves the collective mobilization of members, which boosts "members' self-confidence and their sense of collective power, and in turn encourage[s] union activism and recruitment" (2009: 20). Intermediation, on the other hand, is the ability to "arbitrate between conflicting demands and to favor the emergence of collective interest" and "collaborative action" (Lévesque and Murray 2010: 341). In neither an industry nor a workplace are workers' interests naturally commonly expressed. A group of leaders is needed to create and maintain the perception that there are common interests (Hodson

2001: 204–9; Kelly 2002: 30–6). Intermediation comes into play at this point. A relatively high level of interaction between leadership and lay members functions as a form of intermediation that builds collective interests and identities. The TÜMTİS leadership and staff work to deal with the problems of even individual workers through regular visits to workplaces. These visits serve to transmit the union's messages and to mobilize members' support for new organizing drives. They also serve to raise awareness of the fact that the maintenance of better working conditions rests on the organizing of other workplaces. Furthermore, the union tries hard to ensure internal democracy, especially during collective bargaining and organizing campaigns.

The rise of the new and more dynamic leadership in 2007 intensified the union's associational power. More importantly, due to their capability of learning, the new leaders discovered and utilized a power resource which was untapped before the end of the 2000s, namely associational power at the transnational level.

Tapping into associational power at the transnational level

Despite its distinct framing and intermediation capabilities, strong membership participation, greater internal cohesion, and the dynamism of the new leadership, by the end of the 2000s TÜMTİS could not organize in a large workplace. The Unilever and dockworker campaigns were the union's first attempts to organize at international firms. The ITF provided support to the union in both cases in more concrete ways than ever before. As a result of this closer collaboration with the ITF, a special meeting was held at TÜMTİS headquarters in Istanbul in the summer of 2009. TÜMTİS leaders came together with five key ITF officials. The subject of the meeting was how to organize at large international firms, and the meeting laid the foundations for the UPS campaign (TÜMTİS 2011: 85).

Since its 2006 Congress, the ITF has embraced an "Organizing Globally" strategy and developed union networks in the "big four" transnational logistics companies, including UPS, to support further organizing (Anderson 2015: 50). The global union federations are major players at the transnational level (Croucher and Cotton

2009). Parallel with this global trend, Turkey witnessed an increasing involvement of global labor federations in local campaigns in the 2000s (for case studies see Dinler and McGrath 2011; Dinler 2012; Korkmaz 2013; Fichter, Sayım, and Berber-Agtas 2013). In countries where domestic power resources are in decline, labor movements are more likely to apply transnational strategies (Anner 2011: 176). Moreover, Silver argues that, due to "less direct competition and less spatial differentiation among workers" (2003: 101), the material basis of labor internationalism is probably stronger among transport workers compared to manufacturing workers.

The ITF gave significant financial support to TÜMTİS to develop its infrastructural power resources. With its approach of strategic organizing, the ITF also provided the specific organizing know-how required by the task of unionizing a giant corporation and running an international campaign. Although TÜMTİS is quite experienced in organizing small workplaces using loose and informal tactics, a big corporation like UPS requires a more sophisticated and longer-term strategy. TÜMTİS's relatively quick transformation from a local union organizing in small workplaces into a respected, inspirational, and integral member of the international labor movement organizing in global corporations demonstrates that the union leadership showed significant learning capability.

During the campaigns, ITF and UNI unions, especially in Western countries, mobilized their associational power (by making the TÜMTİS campaign a bargaining issue in the firm's original country), their institutional power (through the OECD complaint in the DHL campaign), and their societal power (by holding public protests to shame the firm and alienate customers). However, one should emphasize that this international support would have been in vain if TÜMTİS had not also had the crucial and quite rare subjectivities and capabilities described above. In fact, in terms of total membership, TÜMTİS's UPS victory was "the largest organizing victory in the logistics sector in the history of ITF's Organizing Globally strategy," adopted in 2006 (Anderson 2015: 56).

As Seidman (2008) and Anner (2011: 71) have argued, transnational labor activism is not a panacea, and it can only succeed if it rests on the skillful and persistent organizing powers of local unions.

Indeed, as I confirmed with an ITF officer, the ITF's support for TÜMTİS rested on the latter's potential which ITF officers had witnessed during the campaigns in 2008 and 2009. TÜMTİS did not disappoint them.

CONCLUSION

In this chapter, I have examined an extraordinary case of class recomposition led by a Turkish union, TÜMTİS. A small local union with nearly 1,500 members under CBAs won a unionization campaign against a global giant, UPS, which led to nearly 2,700 new members with a CBA. Subsequent organizing victories at two other large corporations, DHL and Aras, proved that the UPS victory was not an accident. That the revitalization is occurring in Turkey, where the power resources of unions not aligned with the governing party have been dwindling, makes this success even more significant.

To analyze the case, I have employed the power resources approach in a critical way. The approach enables the researcher to investigate in detail the objective factors behind union agency, but it passes over the issue of subjectivity by assuming the prevalence of a particular type of subjectivity. Therefore, to the power resources analysis, I added an examination of the subjectivities of union leaders by drawing on debates about the importance of ideology and motivation for the unions. I argued that TÜMTİS's revitalization can be only explained by taking both the objectivities and subjectivities of the union leadership into account. While class unionism embraced by its leaders explains the subjective side of the process, associational power from below at the workplace level plays a key role on the objective side. In the process, this associational power converged with the associational power at the transnational level, both of which are influenced by the relatively greater structural power of transportation workers. The conjunction of these features in TÜMTİS's organizing campaigns is what has brought it the victories described in this chapter.

Beyond its recent successes, another factor which distinguishes TÜMTİS is its serious potential for growth both in membership and density in the logistics sector. Nearly two dozen large-scale freight transport companies mark TÜMTİS's potential territory for further growth.

However, the union's revitalization and successes are still fragile and reversible. There are two risks, one external, the other internal, which might hinder the realization of its potential. The external risk is the rise of right-wing authoritarian rule in Turkey. This renders not only TÜMTİS but all egalitarian and democratic forces in the country increasingly vulnerable. The internal risk is that the current leaders will experience the fate of the ex-leadership. To resist the "iron law of oligarchy" (Voss and Sherman 2000) and at the same time to sustain the idealism and dynamism required by class unionism under such formidable circumstances for many years is not an easy task. Even though, as I witnessed, there are people among the union's leadership who are unlikely to give up this mission, there are limits to individual agency and will when it comes to the struggle against institutions and structures. TÜMTİS's fate will be dependent on how it manages these two risks.

After several decades of neoliberal hegemony, we are now in a new world historical conjuncture, one in which the legitimacy of neoliberal capitalism has been undermined due to intertwined economic, social, and ecological crises which have "restored some credibility to the radical socialist case for transcending capitalism" (Panitch and Gindin 2016: 36). TÜMTİS has the potential to become part of a new global labor movement which may reshape the world in the coming decades. No matter what the future brings, the case of TÜMTİS reveals that class unionism, which brings a successful revitalization and recomposition of the working class, is not a nostalgia for the past or a possibility for the distant future, but exists here and now. It shows that hope is still alive. "The most beautiful" hope of the modern age: "the hope that we can make the ideals of equality, freedom, and solidarity real simultaneously" (Buğra 2010: 210).

NOTES

1. This chapter is a revised and updated version of an earlier article published in the *Global Labour Journal* 9(2), 2018. I am grateful to the editors for their permission to republish this revision. I would like to express my gratitude to TÜMTİS

officers and leaders Göknur Marş (ex-officer), Kenan Öztürk (president), Muharrem Yıldırım (secretary of organizing), Gürel Yılmaz (general secretary), Murat Küçükşahin (organizer), Demet Dinler (ex-project coordinator), and Terasa Conrow (Teamsters organizer), for their help and openness. I am also grateful to Michael Fichter, Jörg Bergstermann, Kenan Öztürk, Muharrem Yıldırım, Demet Dinler, Carmen Ludwig, Stefan Schmalz, Edward Webster, Ayşe Alnıaçık, and anonymous reviewers for the *Global Labour Journal* for their comments on the previous versions of this paper. This research was funded by the Friedrich Ebert Stiftung's Trade Unions in Transformation Project. I am thankful to Cihan Hüroğlu for the invitation to participate in the project.

2. Öztürk (2010) provides a detailed account of the previous leadership's performance until 2002.

3. For IG Metall in Germany, Schmalz and Thiel (2017) emphasize the importance of the election of a new national leadership for the ensuing revitalization of the union.

REFERENCES

Anderson, J. (2015). Towards Resonant Places: Reflections on the Organizing Strategy of the International Transport Workers' Federation. *Space and Polity* 19(1), 47–61.

Anner, M. (2011). *Solidarity Transformed: Labor Responses to Globalization and Crisis in Latin America*. New York: Cornell University Press.

Baydar, O. (1998). *Trade Unions in Turkey*. Istanbul: Friedrich Ebert Stiftung.

Benassi, C. and Vlandas, T. (2016). Union Inclusiveness and Temporary Agency Workers: The Role of Power Resources and Union Ideology. *European Journal of Industrial Relations* 22(1), 5–22.

Birelma, A. (2016). *In Search of the Working Class: Workers' Subjectivities and Resistance in an Istanbul Neighborhood*. Doctoral dissertation, Bogazici University, Istanbul, 2016.

Birelma, A. (2017). Subcontracted Employment and the Labor Movement's Response in Turkey. In Durrenberger, P. (ed.), *Uncertain Times: Anthropological Approaches to Labor in a Neoliberal world*. Boulder, CO: University of Colorado Press, pp. 261–86.

Birelma, A. (2018). *Trade Unions in Turkey 2018*. Berlin: Friedrich Ebert Stiftung.

Bourdieu, P. (2000). *Pascalian Meditations*. Stanford: Stanford University Press.

Buğra, A. (ed.) (2010). *Sınıftan sınıfa*. Istanbul: İletişim.

Buğra, A., Adanır, F., and İnsel, A. (2009). Societal Context of Labor Union Strategy: The Case of Turkey. *Labor Studies Journal* 34(2), 168–88.

Burawoy, M. (2010). From Polanyi to Pollyanna: The False Optimism of Global Labour Studies. *Global Labour Journal* 1(2), 301–13.

Burawoy, M. (2011). On Uncompromising Pessimism: Response to My Critics. *Global Labour Journal* 2(1), 73–7.

Çalışkan, K. (2018). Towards a New Political Regime in Turkey: From Competitive Towards Full Authoritarianism. *New Perspectives on Turkey* 58, 5–33.

Çelik, A. (2015). Turkey's New Labour Regime Under the Justice and Development Party in the First Decade of the Twenty-First Century: Authoritarian Flexibilization. *Middle Eastern Studies* 51(4), 618–35.

Çelik, A. (2017). Sendikacılığa yargı darbesi. *Birgün Gazetesi* (20 March). At www.birgun.net/haber/sendikaciliga-yargi-darbesi-151671.

Conrow, T. (2015). *Developing Strategic Campaigns*. London: International Transport Workers' Federation.

Croucher, R. and Cotton E. (2009). *Global Unions, Global Business*. London: Middlesex University Press.

Darlington, R. (2009). Leadership and Union Militancy: The Case of the RMT. *Capital & Class* 99, 3–32.

Dinler, D. (2012). *Country Trade Union Report: Turkey*. Berlin: Friedrich Ebert Stiftung.

Dinler, D. (2014). *İşçinin varlık problemi*. Istanbul: Metis.

Dinler, D. and McGrath, M. (2011). Strategic Campaigning in Multinational Companies: The Case of United Parcel Service (UPS) in Turkey. *Juridikum* 3, 373–84.

Doğan, G. (2013). 1980 sonrası sendikal hareket: Türkiye'de sendikacılığın kuğu şarkısı. In Çetinkaya, D. and Alkan, M. (eds.), *Tanzimattan günümüze Türkiye işçi sınıfı tarihi 1839–2014*. Istanbul: Tarih Vakfı Yurt Yayınları, pp. 386–406.

Doğan, G. (2015). The Deradicalisation of Organised Labour. In Akça, İ., Bekmen, A., and Özden, B. (eds.), *Turkey Reframed: Constituting Neoliberal Hegemony*. London: Pluto, pp. 188–202.

Erem, S. (2001). *Labor Pains: Inside America's New Union Movement*. New York: Monthly Review Press.

Evica, J. (2019). The Rank-and-File Strategy and the Trade Union Bureaucracy. *Jacobin* (8 September). At www.jacobinmag.com/2019/09/rank-and-file-strategy-trade-union-bureaucracy-labor-movement.

Fichter, M., Sayım, Z., and Berber-Agtas, Ö. (2013). *Organization and Regulation of Employment Relations in Transnational Production and Supply Networks. Ensuring Core Labor Standards Through International Framework Agreements?* Berlin: Friedrich Ebert Stiftung.

Frege, C. and Kelly, J. (2004). Union Strategies in Comparative Context. In Frege, C. and Kelly, J. (eds.), *Varieties of Unionism*. New York: Oxford University Press, pp. 31–44.

Ganz, M. (2000). Resources and Resourcefulness: Strategic Capacity in the Unionization of California Agriculture, 1959–1966. *American Journal of Sociology* 105(4), 1003–62.

Gürcan, E. and Mete, B. (2017). *Neoliberalism and the Changing Face of Unionism*. Basingstoke: Palgrave Macmillan.

Hodson, R. (2001). *Dignity at Work*. Cambridge: Cambridge University Press.

Hyman, R. (2001). *Understanding European Trade Unionism: Between Market, Class and Society*. London: Sage.

Hyman, R. and Gumbrell-McCormick, R. (2013). *Trade Unions in Europe: Hard Times, Hard Choices*. Oxford: Oxford University Press.

Jacobs, J. (2006). *Mobsters, Unions, and Feds: The Mafia and the American Labor Movement*. New York: New York University Press.

Katznelson, I. and Zolberg, A.R. (1986). *Working-Class Formation: Nineteenth-Century Patterns in Western Europe and the United States*. Princeton: Princeton University Press.

Kelly, J. (2002). *Rethinking Industrial Relations: Mobilization, Collectivism and Long Waves*. London: Routledge.

Korkmaz, E. (2013). Globalisation, the Global Labour Movement and Transnational Solidarity Campaigns: Three Case Studies from Turkey. *SEER Journal for Labour and Social Affairs in Eastern Europe* 1, 97–112.

Lévesque, C. and Murray, G. (2010). Understanding Union Power: Resources and Capabilities for Renewing Union Capacity. *Transfer* 16(3), 333–50.

OECD (Organisation for Economic Cooperation and Development) (2014). Joint final statement by the German National Contact Point (NCP) for the OECD guidelines for multinational enterprises, UNI Global Union (UNI) and International Transport Workers' Federation (ITF) and Deutsche Post DHL (DP-DHL) on the complaint by UNI/ITF against DP-DHL/Bonn. *Bundesministerium für Wirtschaft und Energie*. At www.bmwi.de/Redaktion/DE/Downloads/G/gemeinsame-abschlusserklaerung-deutsche-nationale-kontaktstelle-englisch-itf-dhl.html.

Ortner, S. (2006). *Anthropology and Social Theory*. Durham, NC: Duke University Press.

Öztürk, S. (2010). *Minding the Gap Between Militancy and Radicalism the Case of Topkapi Porters*. MA thesis, Bogazici University, Istanbul, 2010.

Pala, H. (1969). *Türk sendikacılık hareketi içinde TÜMTİS' in 20 yılı*. Istanbul: TÜMTİS.

Panitch, L. and Gindin, S. (2016). Class, Party and the Challenge of State Transformation. In Panitch, L. and Albo, G. (eds.), *Socialist Register 2017*. London: The Merlin Press.

Schmalz, S. and Dörre, K. (2016). The Power Resources Approach. Paper presented at the Trade Unions in Transformation Authors' Workshop, Berlin.

Schmalz, S. and Thiel, M. (2017). IG Metall's Comeback: Trade Union Renewal in Times of Crisis. *Journal of Industrial Relations* 59(4), 465–86.

Schmalz, S., Ludwig, C., and Webster, E. (2018). The Power Resources Approach: Developments and Challenges. *Global Labour Journal* 9(2), 112–34.

Seidman, G. (2008). Transnational Labour Campaigns: Can the Logic of the Market be Turned Against Itself? *Development and Change* 39(6), 991–1003.

Selçuk, F.Ü. (2002). *Örgütsüzlerin örgütlenmesi*. Ankara: Atölye.

Silver, B. (2003). *Forces of Labor: Workers' Movements and Globalization since 1870*. Cambridge: Cambridge University Press.

Thompson, E.P. (1963). *The Making of the English Working Class*. London: Victor Gollancz.

Thompson, E.P. (1991). *Customs in Common*. London: Penguin.

Tilly, C. (1995). To Explain Political Processes. *American Journal of Sociology* 100(6), 1594–1610.

TÜMTİS (1998). In *Türkiye sendikacılık ansiklopedisi*. Istanbul: Tarih Vakfı, pp. 301–12.

TÜMTİS (2011). *Olağan genel kurulu çalışma raporu 2008–2011*. Istanbul: TÜMTİS.

Voss, K. and Sherman, R. (2000). Breaking the Iron Law of Oligarchy: Union Revitalization in the American Labor Movement. *American Journal of Sociology* 106(2), 303–49.

Woodcock, J. (2014). The Workers' Inquiry from Trotskyism to Operaismo: A Political Methodology for Investigating the Workplace. *ephemera: theory & politics in organization* 14(3), 493–513.

Wright, E.O. (2000). Working-Class Power, Capitalist-Class Interests and Class Compromise. *American Journal of Sociology* 105(4), 957–1002.

Wright, S. (2002). *Storming Heaven: Class Composition and Struggle in Italian Autonomist Marxism*. London: Pluto.

3

Resisting Sexism and Racism in Italian Logistics Worker Organizing

Anna Curcio

Had Cabira[1] not come to Italy from Morocco with her parents as a teenager, she might have worked in a textile factory in her country of birth, where women get paid a pittance to sew clothes for European brands. Today, she is a point of reference for the struggles taking place in the logistics center of Bologna, Italy. There, the workers (men and mostly women) employed by the Mr. Job cooperative in charge of packaging and distribution for Yoox, a leading brand in e-fashion, demand better contractual and working conditions. Their demands include regular payslips, full recognition of hours worked including overtime, and, last but not least, an end to the blackmail, abuses, and frequent sexual harassment repeatedly inflicted on them by warehouse supervisors. While Cabira might have managed to avoid the sweatshops of the European periphery, she is nonetheless trapped in the tight web of exploitation experienced by female manufacturing workers: long working hours, low wages, no guarantees or safeguards, abuses, and often sexual violence. Women workers in the North African textile industry are subjected to the same exploitative working conditions as in the Italian logistics sector. This is an indication of the extent to which, in the Mediterranean basin between Europe and North Africa, the entire supply chain of the fashion industry is affected by deregulation and cuts to labor costs driven by the gendering and racialization of the labor process.

This chapter reflects on the experience of militant co-research in the Italian cooperative logistics sector. It will examine the tactics and strategies of a micro struggle of logistics workers at the Italian coop-

90

erative Mr. Job within a wider cycle of struggles in Italy's distribution and logistics sector, occurring between 2011 and 2014. During this cycle of struggle, contingent logistics workers successfully organized to refuse the management work regime of racialization, gendering, sexual harassment, and blackmail, not only achieving most of their demands but providing a model that threatens to disrupt the global supply chain.

RACISM AND SEXISM IN THE LOGISTICS SECTOR

Race and gender are central to the disciplining and control of workers in the logistics sector. Gender is one of the strategies used to manage and organize the entire global supply chain from weaving to sewing to distribution by using labor mobility routes between Africa and Europe. This allows the cutting of labor costs thanks to the intertwining of capitalism, colonialism, and patriarchy. Alongside gender is the use of race as a *dispositif*[2] to discipline and marginalize, one that Cabira and others like her have their first experience of in Italy.

The use of gender and race can be vividly seen in the Italian logistics warehouses where 90 percent of workers are foreign. The racialization of the labor force places migrants in the lower ranks of production where wages are lowest and safety measures and protections are often absent. At the same time, in the process of production of capital, racialization undermines the foundations of workers' solidarity, playing the game of divide and conquer between whites and blacks, Slavs and Arabs, Egyptians, Tunisians, and Moroccans, etc. As one laborer engaged in the struggle for improved contracts and working conditions in the IKEA warehouses of Piacenza put it: "Racism is a disease I learned in Italy, where the production manager kept saying that Egyptians are better than Moroccans, that Romanians steal, Arabs are lazy and things like that" (Curcio and Roggero 2013; Bortolato and Curcio 2013).

One of the key elements in the strategy to decompose worker power is the cooperative. In the Po Valley, the organization of work in distribution logistics mainly functions through the so-called system of cooperatives. These small businesses subcontract "workers-associates"—who by law are worker-owners although they do not have a share in the company's earnings—to carry out the work of managing warehouses or carriers on behalf of large, often multinational brands. This system betrays the aspirations and principles of the cooperative set up and self-managed by workers. The perversion of these cooperatives, has, in fact, allowed the circumvention of workers' rights and deepened worker exploitation. Having lost the character of worker and consumer solidarity of the cooperative movements of the nineteenth and twentieth centuries, today cooperatives are one of the main components of the local power block of the neoliberalist left parties, such as the Democratic Party (PD), and to a smaller extent the Catholic labor organizations. Today in the Po Valley region, entire productive sectors from services to logistics form a system of Chinese boxes in which cooperatives are a crucial capitalist instrument for eluding the protections and guarantees secured by the National Collective Labor Contract (CCNL), the law regulating negotiations between capital and trade unions. The supply of precarious labor by the cooperatives has made it possible to dramatically cut labor costs while worsening working conditions and massively increasing corporate profits.

In the warehouses of the Mr. Job cooperative subcontracted by Yoox, gender and race not only serve to divide and exploit, they also legitimize abuse and sexual harassment for the purposes of control and discipline. In interviews with the author, striking workers spoke of the cooperative's use of sexual harassment and racialization as a means of control. One worker on the picket line, Fatima, reported how the warehouse supervisor—who made repeated comments about her and later suspended her for alleged insubordination—told her that "had she been a bit nicer and available to him, she could have enjoyed many benefits at work."[3] Another female worker reported being annoyingly embraced and kissed on the neck by a male warehouse manager whom she struggled to get away from. Many women report attitudes that threaten their human dignity. "During Ramadan," says a woman worker, Haifa, "while we were working in these really hot warehouses, with temperatures rising to 40 degrees Celsius, it was hard to breathe. One of the supervisors kept coming around with a bottle of chilled water, only to drink it in front of us, loudly and with gusto." Another manager was reported to have said to a female worker "you must pick either me, God or your wages," in reply to her refusal to accept his sexual advances.

RACE, GENDER, AND CAPITALIST EXPLOITATION

As evidenced by the experiences of workers fighting abuses and exploitation in the warehouses managed by Mr. Job, race and gender are used together as material mechanisms for controlling the organization of work. Their use forms part of the intense exploitation made possible by the "blackmailability" of immigrant workers. Italian law clearly illustrates how blackmailability by racialization serves as a mechanism of control in the logistics sector. Law 189 of July 30, 2002, also known as the Bossi-Fini law after the two right-wing politicians who authored it, introduced a perverse mechanism relating to the issuing of immigrant visas and employment contracts.[4] As a result, logistics companies have been able to intensify the pace of work, increase productivity, and significantly raise their profits. What is more, these companies rely on female workers to carry out less physically demanding tasks which require more attention to detail such as sewing or ironing, tasks that are typical of the textile industry, which has employed women throughout its history. It recalls the reproductive work assigned to women on the basis of a presumed natural aptitude for domestic labor. In the Mr. Jobs warehouses, work is organized by juxtaposing race and gender in order to subordinate and exploit the gendered and racialized workforce.

As migrant racialized women, Cabira, Fatima, and others appear to have "privileged" access to the labor market in the textile factories managed by the cooperative's work agencies. Yet in the logistics sector in which they work there are observable processes of exploitation through the ethnicization and gendering of work along colonial lines. Migrant women, particularly from North Africa, are chosen over both other migrant and white Italian women because they can be more easily exploited as immigrants and because of the sexist presumption that they have a natural inclination to fulfil their work duties. But these workers' preferential access to logistics and distribution warehouses comes at a price: wage subordination, a hierarchy of highly deskilled tasks, dangerous working conditions, a lack of guarantees and safeguards, and a range of sexual abuse and oppression that is widely sanctioned in this sector. In other words, while migrant women have access to work in the warehouses, they experience all of the combined violence of racism and sexism within the capitalist mode of production. Capital has historically turned race and gender into an extraordinary realm of accumulation, where racism and sexism have become indispensable *dispositifs* of capitalist development. Unsurprisingly, the production of surplus value in the distribution logistics sector in Italy has been made possible by the exploitation of a racialized and gendered labor force.

THE ORGANIZATION OF WORK AND THE COMPOSITION OF STRUGGLE IN THE ITALIAN LOGISTICS SECTOR

Unlike other industrial sectors which have a higher level of investment in automation and IT systems, the Italian logistics sector is founded on the exploitation of a low-skilled and underpaid workforce (see Bologna 2013). That workforce is primarily composed of migrants or migrants' children, both of them excluded from citizenship—thanks to the perverse legislation of the *jus sanguinis* (in which citizenship is defined by the nationality of one or both parents)—who find themselves in a condition of profound political and social vulnerability. Most of them have some secondary education, some have a degree, and a number are enrolled at a university (Curcio 2015).

Immigrant workers are caught in the tight web of Italian immigration law which mainly functions as employment law. The management of migration and border controls in Italy and Europe, together with the peculiar definition and conditionality of Italian citizenship, function as a *dispositif* for the criminalization and subordination of the labor force. Immigration law segments and hierarchizes the workforce thereby increasing the levels of blackmailability and exploitation of migrants. The blackmail takes advantage of the workers' fear of losing their job, and therefore their immigrant visa, if they do not accept highly exploitative working conditions.

The cooperatives' particular form of labor management has taken root in the Italian economy with the objective of deregulating the logistics industry. The cooperatives' use of racism and sexism for discipline and control has shaped contemporary labor exploitation in the industry. Yet, the new disciplinary regime in the logistics sector has also produced an intense cycle of disruptive class struggle that has made it necessary to reorganize production. This is particularly evident in the Po Valley, the main hub of commodity circulation in Italy. The valley is carved up by a dense network of roads linking the ports of Genoa to the west and Venice to the east. These two ports are central nodes for the movement and circulation of commodities between Europe and the Middle East and North Africa. For this reason, distribution giants like Amazon and IKEA have picked the area as the main ganglion of their activities in Europe. One might say that here, given the geographical features of the territory and its infrastructures, the global large-scale distribution brands and the cooperatives that supply their precarious workforce have found a great source of valorization based on the acceleration of the circulation of capital on the one hand, and the deregulation of labor along gender and race lines on the other (see Curcio 2015). This labor regime has helped sustain the accelerated export demand in the expanding logistics sector. With expansion has come the intensification of the pace of work and processes of exploitation that have generated massive profits.

In 2011, logistics workers began opposing the worsening work conditions, launching a cycle of struggle that had been anticipated by sporadic episodes of class conflict in previous years. The struggle spread like an oil spill throughout the web of commodities circulation. Peaking between 2013 and 2014, the struggles in the logistics warehouses resonated through the whole of the Po Valley, from Milan to Bologna, Piacenza, Verona, Padua, and beyond. Picket by picket, the warehouses managed by subcontracted cooperatives acting as labor market intermediaries were organized, transforming them into powerful spaces of class struggle and political action. The outcome was the imposition of new rules and safeguards at work, marking the end of blackmailability due to the fear of losing one's job and being subject to prosecution under Italian immigration law. The struggle sought to overcome the racial hierarchies that organize work in the warehouses and resist sexual harassment and gender subordination.

The men and women working in distribution logistics gave life to an extraordinary season of struggles in 2014. In particular, when workers at the Mr. Job cooperative struck in the summer of that year to demand better working conditions, they were also simultaneously fighting against processes of racialization and gendering in the textile factory, and against the new technical composition of capital that relied on this system of cooperatives in the Italian logistics sector.

"WE HAVE NOTHING TO LOSE BUT OUR CHAINS": THE POWER OF STRUGGLE

Where race meets gender, there is not only a space of capital accumulation being defined. What is also taking shape is resistance to the material *dispositifs* of the organization of work, the current composition of capital. This was central to the strike in the warehouses from June to July 2014. The workers officially employed by Mr. Job were subjected to a climate of abuse, sexual harassment, blackmail, and threats. They were exploited by unsustainable workloads of ironing, folding, and packaging up to 110 pieces of clothing per hour rather than the 80 specified in their contract. Workers were forced to take unpaid holidays and work eight hours a day as opposed to the contracted six. In early June, they began saying no to these semi-slavery conditions with their first strike, originally organized by a small group of women. Many workers were still unsure, fearful, and scared of reprisals. However, outside the warehouses, the picket line of women workers charged the struggle with energy. The picketers mocked and ridiculed the warehouse managers, gave interviews to the press, shouted slogans, showed their strength, and encouraged other workers who soon joined the picket.

The number of strikers rose in the following days as more and more workers left the warehouse to join the struggle. While many wondered what reaction their strike might provoke, and the consequences for their immigration status, they were adamant that this was the right course of action. "We have nothing to lose but our chains," workers on the picket line shouted. Among those chanting the line from Marx and Engels was young Talita from Brazil, who had lived in Italy for ten years and worked at the Mr. Job cooperative for the past three.

The wildcat strike began on June 12, 2014, when workers engaged in autonomous self-organized activity in solidarity with others who, because of their union activity in the warehouse, had been put on forced leave or moved to other branches. Sawda, one of the workers targeted for retaliation, observed that these reprisals were "a way to scare us, to make us get our head down and be quiet." But Khadija pointed to how they had backfired because "It was impossible that some should pay for everyone, it wasn't right. So the strike began." The strike demonstrated how solidarity and active cooperation among workers in struggle functions as an extraordinary tool against exploitation and the racism and sexism that organize it. The Mr. Job workers soon invited the grassroots trade union SI Cobas—one of the most active unions in the logistics sector, which had achieved significant successes in other warehouses—to collaborate with them in organizing their strike.

The struggle at the Mr. Job cooperative allowed the workers to transform themselves into subjects who not only spoke up but also refused the *dispositifs* of command over work, thereby defining new practices of struggle that caused great disruption and harm to the brand for which they worked. It is not always possible to quantify the economic losses produced by strikes and picket lines at the gates of the warehouses where commodities enter and exit. However, there is no doubt that the damage caused by the month-long strike was considerable.

The workers' did not hesitate to escalate their struggle. Another strike day was called in solidarity with two workers suspended without legitimate reason in retaliation for disrupting production during previous weeks. This strike saw a greater level of participation with the involvement of a larger group of workers in the warehouse, around forty in all, representing 50 percent of the total workforce. On June 13, the second day of the strike, the managers brought in riot police to remove the picket line at the gates; they charged the crowd twice, injuring some of the strikers.

Such state intervention illustrates how even these relatively few workers were able to disrupt the quantity and efficiency of commodity flows in the globally linked logistics center. Over the following weeks through early July, the strikes and picket lines continued escalating when they could, to strategically disrupt the flow of commodities while avoiding further police repression. The workers had been able to create a blockage when circulation was at its most intense, thus causing greater damage throughout the global supply chain. They had played the card of unpredictability, surprising the employers with their tremendous potential for disruption at a critical choke point in the global economy.

The strike significantly raised costs for the e-commerce giant Yoox. It could not afford for its image to be tarnished by a high-profile strike over exploitative working conditions, racism, and sexual harassment in its warehouses. Furthermore, Yoox was trying to secure economic development funds in the region by partnering with government institutions that would be sensitive to the workers' grievances.

On July 7, a group of Mr. Job workers who weren't part of the strike held a press conference in front of the warehouse in which they expressed their support for the company in an attempt to bolster its image and question the negative portrayal given by the strikers. Karim, one of the leaders of the strike, explained that Yoox attempted to "clean up its image after the conflicts had uncovered how rotten the management of the work at the warehouse was." The workers were conscious of the costliness of their disruptive power, recognizing that the public support generated by negative publicity for the companies weakened Mr. Job's credibility and provided leverage for their struggle. This was their main political tool, together with the blockage at the gate during peak hours for deliveries.

In the coming months, the strength of the workers' disruptive power eventually translated into a series of victories. Mr. Job finally accepted the strikers' demands: better working conditions, safeguards of workers' rights, and the filing of charges for sexual harassment. The warehouse manager was charged with harassment and sexual violence and finally convicted and sentenced to 18 months in prison. Compensation of 80 million euros was paid to the 11 workers who had pressed charges.

SIDE NOTE

This chapter has focused on a micro struggle within a wider cycle of struggles in the distribution logistics sector in Italy occurring between 2011 and 2014. It is not the case that logistics warehouses were pacified either before or after this period. On the contrary, the unionization of warehouse workers continues to grow and strikes and pickets continue unabated to this day. However, the context of the struggle has changed since 2014. While management has introduced innovations in production and reorganized work in order to break down and fragment the struggles in the warehouses, workers and the unions have increasingly turned their attention to bargaining in response to the restructuring. This, unfortunately, has resulted in undermining the subversive power of the workers' struggles. In subsequent stages, disputes have become almost exclusively cordoned off at the shopfloor level, closing off the newly opened space for further circulating and recomposing the struggle. Meanwhile, over the past few years, the unions,[5] which up to then had been used by the workers to generalize and circulate their struggles, have partially ceased to serve this function in order to concentrate on their survival and growth by consolidating their presence in the region's logistics warehouses sector.

Much has been written on the 2011–14 cycle of struggles by comrades in Italy in recent years,[6] when strike after strike seemed to promise the possibility of generalizing the resistance to the logic of capital. This brief chapter is an attempt to systematize a series of notes on these workers' inquiries, which resulted from militant research in the summer 2014, during the pickets at the gates of the Mr. Job logistics center in Bologna, the union meetings, and the demonstrations at critical government buildings to move the negotiations forward. Militant inquiry is not only a tool of knowledge and theoretical development. Above all, it has been used for the purposes of political organization within and against the logistics industry. The logistics workers who took part in the pickets and other initiatives were joined by students and other precarious workers in struggle, who did not stop at solidarity, but bet on the possibility of forming a powerful combination by identifying common enemies within the system of cooperatives and resisting the widespread racism and sexism both in the workplace and on the campuses.

Indeed, a circulation of struggle from the logistics warehouses to the universities took place in the months preceding the strikes and pickets at Mr. Job. Porters working at the University of Bologna, subcontracted by Coopservice (another cooperative acting as labor market intermediary), were organizing too. Their forms of struggle, from wildcat strikes to pickets at the university entrances during exams, recalled practices that had already been seen in the logistics warehouses, practices that they had learned by taking part in the picket lines supporting logistic workers. What was taking form was the conflictual activation of knowledge and political practices by workers of different ages, citizenship status, and industry. This circulation defined an extraordinarily accelerated process of subjectivation that created a commonality of struggle against the cooperative system and its labor management strategies (see Curcio and Roggero 2014).

In the spring of 2014, a virtuous process of the recomposition of precarious workers was taking shape, targeting the cooperatives' system of power and organization of exploitation as a common enemy. However, this process quickly crashed as a result of the unions' choice to limit its struggles to the logistics sector, rather than extend them to the whole cooperative system, squandering the wider potential of constructing a new political composition. In this way, conflict has been constrained and redirected to strictly serve collective bargaining processes, resulting in a progressive weakening of workers' power. As a consequence, in the medium to long term, employers have been given an opportunity to reorganize and retaliate.

This is illustrated by the new CCNL passed in 2017. On the one hand, the new law reflects many of the workers' demands at the core of the warehouse struggles, including rules on work seniority, subcontracting, wage levels, and disciplinary measures such as firing practices. On the other hand, as if in a dance, the law simultaneously introduces a greater flexibility into the production cycle in terms of shift scheduling, and lengthens the work day to nine hours, including Saturdays. Above all, it introduces a series of limitations on the right to strike—the real strength of the struggles which inflicted concrete damage on the economy and the entire global logistics system. It also broadens the category of essential services in which strikes without warning are forbidden—the very kind of strike that most effectively damaged a large proportion of the logistics sector. These reforms have thus secured some short-term gains for the workers while reducing their long-term capacity to wield the disruptive power of the strike. This is a sign that despite the significant workers' victories, the game is still on.

NOTES

1. Cabira and other names used in this chapter are pseudonyms given to workers interviewed by the author.
2. By *dispositif* I refer to what Michel Foucault (1994: 299) defined as an heterogeneous whole that implies speeches, institutions, architectural structures, regulatory decisions, laws, administrative measures, scientific statements, propositions, and moral and philanthropic actions.
3. Quotations from workers throughout the chapter are from interviews conducted by the author in June–July 2014.
4. The law, which amends and restricts the national legislation on immigration and asylum, states that residence permits or immigrant visas will only be granted to foreign workers who already have an employment contract. If a migrant worker loses their job, they will have to return to their home country, or will be subject to deportation following a period of internment in a CIE (Center for Identification and Expulsion).
5. Two main grassroots unions were involved in this cycle of struggle. Adl Cobas operated in the north-east of the Po Valley in Veneto, while SI Cobas acted mainly in Emilia and Lombardia, between Milan, Piacenza, and Bologna. The strike at Mr. Job was organized by SI Cobas.
6. Many of these texts are collected at www.uninomade.org/tag/logistica and commonware.org.

REFERENCES

Bologna, S. (2013). Lavoro e capitale nella logistica italiana: alcune considerazioni sul Veneto. Paper presented at the 40 Anniversario della costituzione di Interporto Padova Spa, March 15, University of Padua. At http://it.scribd.com/doc/133176059/Bologna-Sergio-Lavoro-e-Capitale-Nella-Logistica-2013.

Bortolato, E. and Curcio, A. (2013). Facchini, la vittoria del cappuccino. *commonware* (August 14). At www.commonware.org/index.php/neetwork/32-facchini-granarolo.

Curcio, A. (2014). Practicing Militant Inquiry: Composition, Strike and Betting in the Logistics Workers Struggles in Italy. *Ephemera: theory & politics in organization* 14(3), 375–90. At www.ephemerajournal.org/contribution/practicing-militant-inquiry-composition-strike-and-betting-logistics-workers-struggles.

Curcio, A. (2015). Italy: The Revolution in Logistics. In Azzelini, D. and Kraft, M. (eds.), *New Forms of Workers Organization and Struggles: Autonomous Labor Responses in Time of Crisis*. Leiden: Brill, pp. 259–75.

Curcio, A. and Roggero, G. (2013). The Revolution in Logistics. Interview with Mohamed Arafat. *Uninomade*. At www.uninomade.org/the-revolution-in-logistics.

Curcio, A. and Roggero, G. (2014). No Coop—Dalla logistica all'università. *commonware* (April 7). At http://commonware.org/index.php/cartografia/325-no-coop.

Curcio, A. and Roggero, G. (2018). La logistica è la logica del capitale. *Primo Maggio* (March), 30–8. Translated and republished as "Logistics is the Logic of Capital," *Viewpoint*. At www.viewpointmag.com/2018/10/25/logistics-is-the-logic-of-capital.

Foucault, M. (1994). Le jeu de Michel Foucault. In *Dits et Écrits II, 1976–1988*. Paris: Gallimard, pp. 299–305.

Part II

Education, Call Centers, Cleaners, Platform Work, and Gamers

4

Making Threats: Credible Strike Threats in the US, 2012–2016

Robert Ovetz

The US teachers' strikes in eight states and the colony of Puerto Rico between Spring 2018 to Spring 2019 took many people by surprise, including the unions and the left. These strikes, most of them wildcats, sparked a debate as to whether class struggle is on the rise in the US. Most of the teachers were non-unionized and working in states where public sector strikes are illegal and union density is extremely low. Most of the strikes were preceded by threats that were mistakenly assessed as un-credible by local school districts and state officials, resulting in disruptive strikes that managed to extract surprisingly significant concessions to the teachers' demands.

For all the attention given to these strikes, many more little-reported strike threats have been made that have also successfully extracted significant concessions without strikes. The growing number of strike threats indicates that a significant rise of unreported strike-related activity has been taking place in the US even while the number of strikes remains historically low. Even as I write, the entire island colony of Puerto Rico has just concluded a general strike, autoworkers have struck GM, thousands of nurses in four states are threatening to strike, Chicago teachers are threatening to strike, and students all over the US are planning to strike for action on the climate catastrophe. It appears that US workers are using strike threats, some settled and some resulting in strikes, as a tactic to recompose their power and alter the balance of class forces.

However, issuing a threat to strike raises several critical questions. Are the workers credibly able to strike? Would the strike cause sufficient disruption costs to the employer to extract the necessary concessions to avoid the strike? Will those concessions actually represent a significant gain to the workers? Credible strike threats may offer a strategic innovation that is stimulating a revival of class struggle in the US. Understanding the necessary tactics, strategies, and objectives that make strike threats credible and their potential for disruption of the capitalist economy is essential for assessing the recomposition of working-class power.

During the five-year period between 2012 and 2016 in the US we found nearly twice as many workers made strike threats that did not result in strikes as those reported to have gone on strike. The question is how many of these strike threats were credible? This chapter is a first attempt to understand what makes a strike threat credible, and what contributions credible strike threats make to the recomposition of working-class power. To answer these questions I conducted a workers' inquiry into a strike threat made by my own union, the California Faculty Association, at all 23 campuses of the California State University system in 2016, focusing on the credibility of the strike threat on the two campuses where I taught at that time. This workers' inquiry will assess the credibility of strike threats and the degree of organizational, positional, and disruptive power they can contribute to the recomposition of workers' power.

CREDIBLE STRIKE THREATS

There is little knowledge and much confusion about strike threats. While informal or formal threats made by workers to strike are commonly mentioned in news articles, analyses of strike threats are virtually non-existent in labor studies and on the left. The recent book by Jane McAlevey, *No Shortcuts*, essentially addressed strike threats, although it too only makes a brief mention of them (2016: 61–7 and 208). What a strike threat is and what makes it credible are still unanswered questions.

A strike threat can be a formal or informal threat to strike by calling for pickets or marches at the workplace, mass sick-outs, widespread go-slows or work to rule actions. There are numerous tactics associated with strike threats, including taking an official strike vote, public warnings of the strike by the union leadership, a publicized member strike pledge, and strike-related organizing such as setting up a strike fund, a gradual escalation of tactics towards a strike, and organizing a strike committee. There is no one settled definition of what makes a strike threat, which is probably for the best because otherwise they might become regulated, regimented, and defanged.

Making a threat to strike is contingent on a range of factors including federal and state labor law, contractual stipulations, and context. Private sector workers covered by the 1935 National Labor Relations Act (NLRA) may call only two types of strikes, over economic issues or unfair labor practices (ULP). The strictly limited economic issues include wages, benefits, and working conditions. Reasons for ULP strikes include the employers' failure to respond to a request for information, illegal surveillance of organizing and unions, prohibiting the distribution of union materials, bad faith bargaining, threatening to impose penalties or discipline organizers or union leaders, restricting workers' access to the workplace, and making unilateral changes in working conditions, rules, and policies. ULP strikers are protected against being permanently fired, while workers engaging in a strike over economic issues are not (Labor Notes 2019: 12–17; National Labor Relations Board 2019a). Formal and informal strike threats often involve one of these two types of issues.

The NLRA imposes rigid windows, including 10, 30, and 60 day periods in which workers may declare their intent to strike either by a formal vote of the membership or a decision by leadership depending on the union bylaws. These declarations ordinarily occur once negotiations appear to have broken down, the employer has been notified, and federal and state mediators have been contacted (National Labor Relations Board 2019b). Unions also have to be wary of preparing strike actions before an "impasse" has been declared, to avoid being accused of engaging in bad faith bargaining. Even once an impasse is declared various kinds of mediation and fact finding may still be required by law. Labor law is pitted with innumerable obstructions impeding workers' ability to use their ultimate tactic, the strike. As a result, unions frequently strike with little advance preparation, not only out of fear of being accused of bad faith, but also because they may have hoped for a favorable fact-finders' report that would lead to a settlement without a strike. Contrary to popular belief, labor law wasn't designed to facilitate workers' collective action but, rather the opposite, to diffuse, detract, impede, manage, prevent, and repress it.

Certain kinds of strike actions such as secondary boycotts, sit-down strikes, short intermittent strikes for a common goal, blocking strike-breaking "scabs," "work to rule" slowdowns, group refusal of overtime, and sympathy strikes are also banned by law and the courts. Workers may strike over grievances once the collective bargaining agreement (CBA) expires, but then they can be permanently fired. One exception is railroad and airline workers, who may engage in secondary boycotts under the 1926 Railway Labor Act, although they are required to go through a similarly tedious time-consuming process of mandatory mediation, binding arbitration, presidential arbitration, and a cooling-off period before they can strike (Highlights of the Railway Labor Act n.d.). Federal government workers are banned from striking altogether at the risk of mass firings, as was vividly illustrated in 1981 when President Reagan fired 13,000 striking air traffic controllers. There are various limits on strike action in "critical industries," including arrests, injunctions, and a ban, can be imposed by the courts and president. Non-union strikers are free to engage in many kinds of strike action, although they can be permanently fired (Labor Notes 2019: 12–17).

Likewise, state and local public workers are covered by a myriad of state labor laws. The most regressive states ban collective bargaining and strikes altogether. But even some "union friendly" states, where bargaining and strikes are permitted, also require formal strike notices and ban strikes in "critical industries." Even where strikes are permitted, many collective bargaining agreement (CBAs) explicitly prohibit workers from striking altogether and even honoring picket lines until the agreement expires. This is common where a union is harnessed to the Democratic Party and can extract minor concessions in exchange for not embarrassing elected officials who profess to be "pro-labor."

What we have learned from the teachers' wildcat strikes in the past few years is that strike threats, even where constrained or prohibited by law, still occur among organized workers covered by a CBA as well as non-union workers. The use of the tactic, including whether a strike threat is credible or not, is used as a symbolic tactic, or is backed up by deep organizing to prepare for the strike, needs to be assessed.

WHAT MAKES A STRIKE THREAT CREDIBLE?

To be clear, not all strike threats are credible. For a strike threat to be credible it must fulfill two criteria. First, it must convince the employer not only that the workers are prepared to strike but that the costs of a strike will be higher than making a concession to settle the dispute before the strike happens.[1] Second, in order to convince the employer, it must also convince a supermajority of workers that a strike will succeed in realizing their objectives, and persuade them to get involved.

A strike threat that is credible to the employer, whether it is called as a sick-out or a walkout, is one in which the preparations are perceived by the employer to likely result in a strike that, first, will be more costly than conceding to all or some of the workers' demands in order to avoid it. The employer must be also convinced of a second aspect, that a supermajority of workers have publicly expressed a willingness to participate and are actively preparing to strike. As labor educator Dr. Helena Worthen puts it,

> the "threat" is in the eyes of the employer. That's the importance of the word "credible." Does the employer believe that the union and the workers will really strike? If the employer believes the threat, it is credible. So a statement that workers will strike may, technically, be a threat to strike, but a "credible" strike threat is something that is believed in—credited—by the employer.[2]

In short, when a strike threat is credible to the *employer* it may result in concessions to the workers' demands. If the workers reject the concessions and strike, either the employer miscalculated the risk or found the risks of a strike to be lower than the costs to avoid it, as in the case of many of the recent US teacher wildcat strikes. If the workers strike and gain nothing more than the previous offer of concessions to end their strike then their threat was not credible and the

Table 4.1 Credible Strike Threat Matrix

	Low Disruptive Power	*High Disruptive Power*
Low Organizational Power	Not credible strike threat	Not credible strike threat
	Strike threat will fail	Strike threat may fail
	No strike likely	Short strike possible
	No concessions likely	Small or modest concessions expected
High Organizational Power	Credible strike threat	Credible strike threat
	Strike threat will succeed	Strike threat will succeed
	Strike likely	Strike extremely likely
	Low to modest concessions expected	High concessions expected

strike was defeated. The different possible outcomes of a strike threat are portrayed in Table 1. While it is hard to generalize without the specific details of each strike threat, strike, and outcome, understanding what makes a strike threat credible is critical for the fortunes of worker organizing today. Identifying what makes a strike threat credible is certain to have significant lessons about the resurgence of class struggle in the US and elsewhere, where CBAs, law, and policy constrict or prevent the use of the strike as a tactical weapon.

Whether a strike threat is credible to the *workers* depends on several important factors. First, if the workers are unionized, the workers and not the union staff or officers are in charge of the strike and have the resources and support to withstand a tough and long fight. Second, as McAlevey argues (2016: 4, 20), whether unionized or not, a supermajority of workers will engage in strike-related action when they are convinced of their power to withstand the risks of striking and to win.

We know so little about how strike threats are used and when they are credible because they have been mostly either ignored or feared by both employers and unions. Much of the US left and the field of labor studies ignores, doesn't understand, or outright opposes the use of strike threats as a strategy. A thorough search of my university's databases found only a handful of articles published in the past three decades entirely devoted to them. Becker, for example, observed that the National Labor Relations Board and court rulings have weakened the credibility of strike threats by banning the use of tactics such as secondary boycotts and strikes that can provide added leverage to a threat (Becker 1994: 362; 1998: 9). Without credible strike threats workers and unions lack effective means to compel employers to negotiate (Lindbeck and Snower 1987: 762; Kilgour 1990: 269).

Nevertheless, the cost of an actual strike is central to establishing the credibility of the threat. A 1985 ruling by the Supreme Court of California found that a credible strike threat can alter the balance of power preventing an illegal public sector strike from taking place. "Without the right to strike, or at least a credible strike threat, public employees have little negotiating strength. This, in turn, produces frustrations which exacerbate labor-management conflicts and often provoke 'illegal' strikes" (*County Sanitation Dist. No. 2 v. Los Angeles County Employees' Assn.*). The court concluded that a credible strike threat can "equalize" power between workers and employers, raising the costs to employers of not settling, and reducing the incidences of strikes. Although they do not take into account the cost of an actual strike, Lindbeck and Snower (1987: 761, 781) argue that a union must accurately estimate a wage demand lower than the expected cost of a strike to the employer to keep the strike threat credible.[3]

One of the best analyses of credible strikes that is relevant to strike threats was published in 1950, but even that was only offered in passing. John Steuben's little-known book *Strike Strategy* warned that employers are constantly assessing the credibility of a strike while engaged in preparations to defeat it. Although Steuben is talking about strikes, the same assessment by management is applicable to preparations to strike. Steuben warned:

> carefully observe the degree of participation of the rank and file. When management comes to the conclusion that the workers are passive, show lack of interest, and merely "sweat it out," it is greatly encouraged to initiate back-to-work movements and other steps based on the notion that the workers are not solidly behind the union. (Steuben 1950: 98)

Steuben also precisely captured an analogy between a credible strike threat and an actual strike:

> By the same token, active participation on the part of the strikers has just the opposite effect on management. When the employer sees his workers taking active part in the strike and that among them are key people in each department, without whom the plant cannot run, he becomes aware of the strength of the strike. Also, when the workers actively participate in the strike and management observes it, the strikers commit themselves to the union and realize that from then on their future depends almost entirely on the victorious outcome of the battle. (Steuben 1950: 98)

How do workers obtain the necessary power to demonstrate the credibility of their strike threat to the employer and prove it to their fellow workers? And what do they then do with it?

THREE TYPES OF WORKERS' POWER

The few existing studies of credible strike threats are impaired by their viewing of unions, workers, and employers through the stagnant lens of *homo economicus*, the idea that humans are rational cost-calculating beings, a fundamental assumption of capitalist economics. An exception to this framing is Adăscăliței and Guga's study of Romanian *Dacia* autoworkers' strike activity in which they define a credible strike threat as one that is credible to the employer based on the record of previous strikes and strike-related activity, as well as the autonomy and credibility of the union. The credibility of the threat is an outcome of what they describe as

> "labor interest representation," which, when unpacked, adds up to establishing whether unions simultaneously achieve effectiveness (unions defend workers' interests), autonomy (representation is independent from the employer), and legitimacy (the outcomes obtained correspond to the demands of the rank and file). (Adăscăliței and Guga 2015: 476)

Adăscăliței and Guga sought to understand why the *Dacia* auto workers had a higher rate of wage increases relative to other Romanian industrial workers. The reason, they argue, is that the union was able to effectively "calibrate its threats" by increasing the aggressiveness of the mobilization and adversarial and confrontational threats (from protests to slow downs to short, sudden work stoppages) in the course of the collective bargaining to demonstrate the credibility of the strike threat (Adăscăliței and Guga 2015: 485). Because the union's record of previous strike action had established its autonomy and legitimacy, it achieved a high level of associational power which translated into a high level of structural power. This allowed it to use calibrated tactics which translated into potential disruptive power and demonstrated the credibility of their strike threat to management, who then conceded higher wage increases to avoid a costly strike.

Adăscăliței and Guga demonstrate the relationship between Wright's (2000: 962) concepts of the "associational"[4] and "structural"[5] power of workers. Workers situated in strategically placed locations in the plant, company, or the global division of labor—thereby having structural power—can make a compelling threat of disruption to the employer. Associational and structural power have a feedback effect on one another. Solidarity from related sectors and communities outside the workplace increases associational power. Combined with high levels of structural power, a strike threat becomes even more credible to the workers and attracts commitment from previously uncommitted workers. High levels of both types of power threaten to raise the economic and social costs of a potential strike to the employer and result in a higher level of concessions to avoid a more costly strike.

Most interestingly, Adăscăliței and Guga (2015) observed that even a failed strike raised the credibility of the next strike threat for the workers. During the next round of struggle the union was able to draw on the experience of the previous failed strike to raise the credibility of the strike threat and achieved their objectives of higher wages and stopping the expansion of contingent labor. They did this by calibrating the intensity of their tactics to take advantage of their structural power, thereby deepening their associational power by bringing in less or uncommitted workers by convincing them of the promise of exercising their structural power.

What threatens to raise the costs of a strike to the employer? For this, Perrone offers a third power, what he calls the "disruptive potential" of workers, which is of primary interest here. "Disruptive power," Perrone demonstrated in his analysis of strike threats and strikes, is "derived from [workers'] position within the hierarchy of the system of economic interdependencies" (1984: 413–14). Due to their strategic position in an economy characterized by complex interconnections and dependencies, even small numbers of workers can wield great disruptive power by interrupting or withholding critical goods or services across multiple sectors and drawing the state and other political actors into the conflict (see Glaberman 1947; Wallace, Griffin, and Rubin 1989: 197–8; Womack 2006: 67). While the costs of striking may be minimal for any particular striker, firm, or sector, these complex interconnections and dependencies serve as an effect multiplier on the larger national and even global economy. The greatest impact may not be merely between sectors, but between a single sector and the global system. For this reason, Perrone saw disruptive power as integral to and inseparable from structural power (1983: 232–3, 235, 238, 240–1).[6]

Recent work by Moody (2017), Alimahomed-Wilson and Ness (2018), and Sowers, Ciccantell, and Smith (2018) have attempted to apply Perrone's notion of disruptive power to choke points in the global logistics supply chain.[7] As Sowers et al. explain, "positional power is thought to be greatest when it has *disruptive* potential beyond the local context of work" (2018: 22, emphasis added). According to Alquati, the interdependence revolves around dominant firms or sectors. Targeting them can provide leverage at the choke point:

> the new carousels of the assembly line tend to align all the tempos, types, tolerances and quantities of the phases of the cycle, which are linked to it (inside and outside the firm) in a more or less rigid way, to its new rhythm, to its depreciation, to the rigidity of its investment, etc. The interdependence tightens, but the propulsive moment belongs to the large firm, of the most advanced technolog-

ical level, as power, as the concentration here of the profit motive. (Alquati 2013: 19)

Today the global logistics supply chain has become the dominant form of complex interconnections and dependencies. Emerging as a strategy to decompose working-class power during the last cycle of struggle, logistics has in turn become the terrain of class struggle to which workers must adapt their organizational forms, tactics, strategies, and objectives in order to recompose their class power (see Moody 2017; Benvegnù and Cuppini 2018: 230; Olney 2018: 244).

According to Moody, this new technical composition of capital has concentrated larger numbers of workers "linked together in vulnerable technology-driven supply chains, themselves organized around enormous logistics clusters that concentrate tens and even hundreds of thousands of workers in finite geographical sites" (2017: 41, see also 66–7). Industrial, logistics, communications, IT, and transport clusters are fixed to discreet geographical locations impairing them from being dismantled and relocated. And as they grow ever bigger and increasingly rely on down- and upstream firms and sectors, they are becoming ever more vulnerable to disruption by workers with high levels of organizational and positional power (see also Alimahomed-Wilson and Ness 2018: 2–7).

Workers with high levels of positional and disruptive power can press for gains in a single shop or firm without resorting to a strike, extracting concessions from employers to buy labor peace and avoid disruption. However, rather than using their positional and disruptive power for their own particular interests, such workers may use their power as leverage for the working class as a whole. Workers located in strategically critical choke points in a firm, industry, or global commodity chain, on the other hand, can reject becoming a new "aristocracy of labor" by turning their positional power used to achieve gains on the shopfloor into a disruptive power that threatens the very operations of a critical global sector, the relations of production, and capitalism itself to the benefit of workers along the entire supply chain. As Olney (2018) reminds us, the International Longshore and Warehouse Union (ILWU) has on occasion played this role on behalf of workers down- and upstream along the global logistics supply chain.

Analyzing choke points, positional power, and disruptive power becomes a critical factor in determining the credibility of a strike threat. Workers with high levels of positional power strategically located at a choke point simultaneously have a high level of threatening disruptive power. According to John T. Dunlop, such workers have "strategic power" because in

> any technological process for producing and distributing goods and services, there are some workers who have [a] greater strategic position than others; that is, these workers are able to shut down, to interrupt, or to divert operations more easily than others ... The term strategic ... is not identical with skill. It means sheer bargaining power by virtue of location and position in the productive process... (Dunlop 1948, cited in Womack 2006: 82–3)

A credible strike threat is one which the employer expects will exceed or raise the costs of not settling because it will disrupt operations. Employers are clearly aware that variable levels of positional power correspond to varying levels of disruptive power (Perrone 1984: 420). Perrone found that, for this reason, workers' positional power is correlated to wage gains due to this disruptive potential which allows them to achieve their demands without having to strike.[8] As he explained, "groups seem to be able to secure high wages on sheer positional grounds, with little or no necessity to resort to strike action" (1983: 253–4). In other words, a strike threat succeeds because the workers' power to disrupt is expected to raise the costs of not conceding, making the threat credible to the employer.[9]

In essence, positional power is positively related to disruptive power—a key conclusion missed by many who cherry-pick Perrone's concepts. Labor studies scholars and union strategies tend to favor a limited focus on organizational power while rarely addressing positional power, let alone the implications of disruptive power that are integral to it. What made the Association of Flight Attendants president Sara Nelson's threat to launch a general strike that ended the federal government shutdown in 2019 so extraordinary is that it was clearly motivated by the objective of using the disruptive power of flight attendants to cripple the US and global economy. The same cannot be said for the 2015 United Steelworkers oil refinery strike that used disruptive power just enough to inconvenience the US economy to extract the demanded concessions while minimizing the contagion of global disruption.

The implications of Perrone's notion of disruptive power is that it is system changing, even revolutionary. As Womack reminds us:

> Well-combined operations, if they included technical stoppages in the right order at the right time, could change the entire structure of power; technically strategic workers could change the legal, moral, and economic rules ... Unless the labor movement will use labor's technical power, its major power now, it will not gain the political power to force its legal changes, which moral appeals will then justify. (Womack 2006: 15)

The potential power to disrupt the existing global logistics supply chain due to its complex interconnections and dependencies is extremely high. Choke points can create widespread disruption if a single shop or firm produces an input, finished good, or service critical to down- and upstream firms and sectors, or to an entire nation or even the global economy.[10] Specific sectors such as logistics, transport, oil and gas, steel, rare earth mineral mining and processing, and IT infrastructure can provide even workers who have low or modest organizational power with sufficient positional and disruptive power to create an "unmanageable supply chain" (Alimahomed-Wilson and Ness 2018: 4). However, the effects of such disruptive power will likely be minimal if the global working class is not sufficiently recomposed. Workers elsewhere in the global division of labor must have sufficient organizational and positional power to continue circulating and amplifying the disruption.

SCORING THE CREDIBILITY OF A STRIKE THREAT

While the number of strikes has continued to steadily decline over the past few decades, the evidence points to there being more workers

Table 4.2   Credible Strike Threats Scorecard

Power Type	1 Point Each Max	Notes
Organizational Power Criteria		
complete inquiry of technical composition: division of labor, relations of production, outsourcing, automation, deskilling, integration, dispersal, reorganization, employer responses to previous & existing grievances/complaints		
complete inquiry of current class composition: wage/benefit/status/authority, skill hierarchies, job classifications & responsibilities, departments, turnover, tenure, promotion, internal unions		
identification of organic leaders, key influencers & unknown committees		
recent forms of worker cooperation, collective action & strike action (banking model)		
worker self-directed organizing		
worker-controlled strike organizing committees		
80-100% worker support for strike		
workers use tactical escalation of strike-related action to prepare for strike		
strike fund established		
numerous non-worker allies & public stakeholders participating in public strike-related activity		
frequent & large public actions by workers, allies & public stakeholders *before* the strike		
frequent & large public actions by workers, allies & public stakeholders *during* the strike		
large public events of support prior to strike		
numerous influential allies & public stakeholders making public expressions of support		
extensive mainstream & other media coverage		
TOTAL SCORE/PERCENT Organizational Power (15 max)		
Positional Power Criteria		
nearly unanimous support for the strike in a practice strike vote		
nearly unanimous participation of different racial, ethnic, genders & nationality groups		
near unanimity of shops/locals participate (where more than one union in workplace exists)		

Table 4.2 continued

Power Type	1 Point Each Max	Notes
outcome of current tactical escalations on employer/firm/ industry/economy		
near unanimity of internal locations participate in strike-related action (where multiple workplaces in one firm exists)		
strike-related action in downstream choke points of external related employers/sectors		
strike-related action in upstream choke points of external related employers/sectors		
TOTAL SCORE/PERCENT Positional Power (7 max)		
Disruptive Power Criteria		
single firm critical to national (or state) economy		
multiple firms in one sector critical to national (or state) economy		
single sector critical to national (or state) economy		
multiple sectors critical to national (or state) economy		
single firm critical to international economy		
multiple firms in one sector critical to international economy		
single sector critical to international economy		
multiple sectors critical to international economy		
strike-related action in other firms/sectors/geographic locations by location & time		
disruptive impact on supplier firms		
disruptive impact on receiving firms		
single firm in one sector with organizational power score of 12-14		
multiple firms with organizational power score of 12–15		
single sector with organizational power score of 12–15		
multiple sectors with organizational power score of 12–15		
strike-related activity spread to/disrupt additional firms		
strike-related activity spread to/disrupt additional sectors		
government intervention to settle strike		
high level of expected costs to employer		
open-ended duration		
TOTAL SCORE/PERCENT Disruptive Power (20 max)		
TOTAL SCORE/PERCENT (42 total)		

ready and willing to strike. We call the willingness to strike, and the capacity to do so, a credible strike threat, and argue that it should be counted as strike activity. Threatening to strike can be measured along a continuum of willingness and capacity to strike that determines whether a threat is more or less credible. Organizational, positional, and disruptive power play a crucial role in assessing just how credible a strike threat really is.

The problem is that we don't have a good measure to how many strike threats are actually made because, until we began to count them, there had been no prior effort to do so.[11] Counting strike threats would allow them to be assessed on whether they accomplish the objectives of the workers who make them, be they demands for wages and benefits, better working conditions, or more control.

Strike threats that achieve the majority of their objectives could be considered credible strike threats. If they do achieve their goals it must be asked what made them credible. Inversely, if they failed, it must be asked what necessary characteristics they lacked that would have made them credible. Understanding the credibility of a specific strike threat means conducting a qualitative analysis of the workers' organizational, positional, and disruptive power.

This chapter will not attempt to assess the credibility of all strike threats but rather provide a tool for workers to assess their own threats as part of a workers' inquiry. For this we can draw on McAlevey's "structure test" to assess how employers weigh what she calls the "concession cost" for settling versus the "disruption cost" that creates a crisis (2016: 61–7, 208). A workers' inquiry needs to assess the extent to which the workers' have recomposed their organizational, positional, and disruptive power so as to know how to adapt their tactics, strategies, and organizational form to achieve their objectives. The higher the cost to the employer settling, the higher the level of all three types of workers' power will be needed, with the exception of a minority of workers with sufficient positional power to cause costly disruption.[12]

Table 4.2 provides a credibility scorecard based on these three types of power that can be used as criteria in a workers' inquiry. While each power factor overlaps with elements of a workers' inquiry, they are not entirely the same. Rather, we can use class composition theory to inform how we assess the three power factors, so that organizational power corresponds to the workers' recomposition of power in a particular workplace, positional power corresponds to the workers' recomposition of power across multiple workplaces, firms, or industries, and disruptive power corresponds to the effectiveness with which the recomposed working class is able to apply its strength.

Organizational power

First, the workers' inquiry needs to assess the level of organizational power: What is the technical composition of capital and the current class composition of the workers? Have key influencers, organic leaders, and unknown committees currently engaged in various forms of collective action been brought in and committed to the strike? Who is organizing the workers—the workers themselves or union officers? Who is making the decisions about the strike preparations—workers or a union officer-controlled strike committee? Are the workers using tactical escalation to assess their own strength? Are more un- or less committed workers joining in strike-related actions? Are workers reaching out to obtain support through their social networks outside the workplace and how extensive is the support? What was the outcome of previous collective action? Is there a strike fund?

Positional power

Second, what is the status of the workers' positional power? Are there self-organized strike groups with a supermajority commitment in every shop, department, office, and location of the firm or industry? Are workers in up- or downstream workplaces, firms, or industries along the global supply chain also engaged in cooperative strike-related action? Are the workers escalating the intensity of each tactic drawn from their tactical repertoire to build the confidence and solidarity of the workers across these workplaces, firms, or industries in collective strike-related action (McAlevey 2016: 35; Ovetz 2019)? Is there a supermajority public commitment and participation in strike-related action among all the different ethnic, racial, national, gender, and other groups among the workers across these workplaces, firms, or industries?

Disruptive power

Lastly, do the workers have any potential disruptive power? Does the workers' positional power provide an opportunity to acquire disruptive power? Even if the workers have low organizational power—for example if they lack commitment from and participation by a supermajority of the workers—do they potentially have high positional power by virtue of being situated at a choke point in the shop, firm, industry, or the national or global economy? Is the strike open ended? What is the expected cost to the employer, sector, country, or global economy? Is government intervention expected?

THE RISING NUMBER OF STRIKE THREATS

While there has been much handwringing over the historical decline in the number of strikes over the past several decades, our research has found a greater number of strike threats translating into more strike-related organizing than previously reported. The rising level of strike-related activity demonstrates the need for taking strike threats seriously as a tactic for recomposing working-class power.

In our survey of published news and government reports on strike-related activity we found 134 strike threats in the US between 2012 and 2016. Of these, 97 were settled without a strike in firms of any size, involving in total 701,700 workers. We did not investigate the remaining 37 threats that resulted in a strike, or compare them to the reported strikes. As we explain below, due to the Bureau of Labor Statistic's (BLS) limited criteria for what strikes are reported, some of these 37 cases may not have even been counted in the official figures.

More than half of the strike threats, 73 of the 134, occurred in workplaces with fewer than 1,000 workers. Of these 73, 20 resulted in strikes, involving 8,573 workers in total; six strike threats had an unknown outcome at the time of the study; and the remainder resulted in no strike. In contrast, the 97 strike threats settled without a strike was 134.7 percent higher than the BLS report of 72 strikes in firms with 1,000 or more employees, involving 352,000 workers in total. The number of workers involved was 199 percent—nearly double—the number that went on strike.

What we measured is different from what the BLS measures in several important ways and may account for our substantially different outcomes. The BLS only measures strikes involving 1,000 or more workers. Although only 0.3 percent of US businesses have 500 workers or more, those large employers account for around 50 percent of the national workforce (Kiersz 2015). By contrast, our study counted all threats to strike in workplaces with *any* number of workers. Because of the BLS's high threshold, we cannot be certain how many strike threats—or even strikes—actually occurred during these five years or any other time period in which this threshold has been used. In effect, any estimate of how many strikes there are or how many workers are going on strike will be subject to the shifting baselines fallacy and should be used with caution.

We also identified a steady number of strike threats made between 2012 and 2015, increasing substantially in 2016 (see Table 4.3). While the number of workers involved in the threats fluctuated wildly, the number in 2016 was more than three times higher than in 2012. Although this time range is extremely short, it illustrates that while the number of strike threats was steady between 2012 to 2015, the number of workers involved grew overall during this entire period.

Table 4.3   Settled Strike Threats 2012–2016*

Years	# Settled Strike Threats*	# of Workers Involved
2012	18	86,755
2013	16	147,742
2014	19	109,585
2015	16	92,323
2016	28	265,295
Total *Settled* Strike Threats	97	701,700
Average per year	19.4	140,340
% of average strikes**	134.7%	199.3%

Source: Ovetz, R., 2017.
* Only strike threats resulting in a settlement without a strike were counted
** Total strikes recorded. See BLS, Work stoppages of 1,000 or more workers,
1947–2016, accessed June 26, 2016: https://www.bls.gov/news.release/wkstp.t01.htm

Although we had not yet restarted our count of strike threats, the growth we documented was shortly followed by the many teacher strikes noted above. If we compare our strike threats data to the strikes reported by the BLS (Table 4.4), our annual average number of strike threats (19.4) was also about one third higher than the annual average number of strikes measured by the BLS (14.4).

Table 4.4   Strikes 2012–2016*

Years	# Work Stoppages	# of Workers Involved
2012	19	148,000
2013	15	55,000
2014	11	34,000
2015	12	47,000
2016	15	99,000
Total	72	352,000
Average per year	14.4	70,400

Source: Ovetz, R., 2017.
*See BLS, Work stoppages involving 1,000 or more workers, 1947–2016, accessed June 26, 2017: https://www.bls.gov/news.release/wkstp.t01.htm

Our preliminary attempt to measure the number of strike threats is not comprehensive. Although we were able to identify a total of 134 reported strike threats made during these five years we cannot be certain how many were actually made for several reasons. The BLS does not and will not collect data on them, even turning down my request that they do so as noted above. Furthermore, some strike threats may not have been reported by the union or included in the databases we searched. We may have also been unable to find participants who were involved in unreported strike threats. In short, we do not yet know what we do not know about how many strike threats occurred during these five years.

It should also be emphasized that we did not attempt to assess how many of the strike threats were credible.[13] In total, 72 percent (97 of 134) of the reported threats were settled without a strike. Further study is needed to adequately assess the reason for the resulting strikes, whether the strike threats were credible, and the possible differences in the outcomes of settled strike threats and those that resulted in strikes. That could be attempted in real time using our Credible Strike Threats Scorecard (Table 4.2), when strike threats are reported to us at www.strikethreats.org.

Further investigation is also needed to determine if the strike threats prompted employers to make concessions that were advantageous for the workers involved. This information is hard to obtain for many reasons, including that not all contracts are made publicly available, union leaders do not disclose the full details of settlements to members, and members may not be fully informed of the details of a settlement and how to assess whether it resulted in gains. Moreover, we cannot argue against the silence of what never happened. It is extremely difficult to make a confident assessment that a concession obtained without a strike is an improvement over what could have been obtained by a strike that never occurred. However, a recent strike could be compared to a settled strike threat. Whatever the assessment attempted, it will ultimately be left to the workers themselves to decide on whether it was an effective outcome and what contribution it makes to their next cycle of struggle.

Despite these limitations, we will now attempt to assess the credibility of a strike threat in which the author was involved.

A WORKERS' INQUIRY INTO THE 2016 CSU STRIKE THREAT

In spring 2016 about 26,000 tenured and non-tenured faculty, counselors, coaches, and librarians of my union, the California Faculty Association (CFA), threatened to go on strike across the entire 23 campuses of California State University (CSU) system for five work days interrupted by one weekend. A couple of days before it was to begin the strike was called off. The CSU system moved towards meeting the wage demands of the faculty and a new contract was settled and soon overwhelmingly ratified by the membership, who also later voted to extend it.

Did the faculty make a *credible* strike threat that ultimately served to avoid the costs and disruption of a strike? As a CFA member who participated in strike-related activity at both the San Francisco State University (SFSU) and San José State University (SJSU) campuses, which are about an hour's drive apart, I have conducted a workers'

Table 4.5 Credible Strike Threats Scorecard for CFA 2016 (SFSU and SJSU)

Power Type	1 Point Each Max	Notes
Organizational Power Criteria		
complete inquiry of technical composition: division of labor, relations of production, outsourcing, automation, deskilling, integration, dispersal, reorganization, employer responses to previous & existing grievances/complaints		unknown because no structure test conducted
complete inquiry of current class composition: wage/benefit/status/authority, skill hierarchies, job classifications & responsibilities, departments, turnover, tenure, promotion, internal unions		unknown because no structure test conducted
identification of organic leaders, key influencers & unknown committees		unknown because no structure test conducted
recent forms of worker cooperation, collective action & strike action (banking model)	1	
worker self-directed organizing		
worker-controlled strike organizing committees	1	
80-100% worker support for strike	1/2	% voting is unknown
workers use tactical escalation of strike-related action to prepare for strike	1	
strike fund established		
numerous non-worker allies & public stakeholders participating in public strike-related activity	1	
frequent & large public actions by workers, allies & public stakeholders *before* the strike	1/2	only the Sacramento rally & SFSU public strike vote were large
frequent & large public actions by workers, allies & public stakeholders *during* the strike	1/2	while frequent, the actions were extremely small
large public events of support prior to strike	1	
numerous influential allies & public stakeholders making public expressions of support	1	
extensive mainstream & other media coverage	1	
TOTAL SCORE/PERCENT Organizational Power (15 max)	8.5/57 percent	
Positional Power Criteria		
nearly unanimous support for the strike in a practice strike vote	1	
nearly unanimous participation of different racial, ethnic, genders & nationality groups		
near unanimity of shops/locals participate (where more than one union in workplace exists)		

Power Type	1 Point Each Max	Notes
outcome of current tactical escalations on employer/firm/industry/economy		
near unanimity of internal locations participate in strike-related action (where multiple workplaces in one firm exists)		
strike-related action in downstream choke points of external related employers/sectors		
strike-related action in upstream choke points of external related employers/sectors		
TOTAL SCORE/PERCENT Positional Power (7 max)	1/14 percent	
Disruptive Power Criteria		
single firm critical to national (or state) economy	1	
multiple firms in one sector critical to national (or state) economy		
single sector critical to national (or state) economy		
multiple sectors critical to national (or state) economy		
single firm critical to international economy		
multiple firms in one sector critical to international economy		
single sector critical to international economy		
multiple sectors critical to international economy		
strike-related action in other firms/sectors/geographic locations by location & time		
disruptive impact on supplier firms	1	
disruptive impact on receiving firms		
single firm in one sector with organizational power score of 13–15		
multiple firms with organizational power score of 13–15		
single sector with organizational power score of 13–15		
multiple sectors with organizational power score of 13–15		
strike-related activity spread to/disrupt additional firms		
strike-related activity spread to/disrupt additional sectors		
government intervention to settle strike	1	Numerous state legislators intervened to prevent the strike
high level of expected costs to employer		
open-ended duration		
TOTAL SCORE/PERCENT Disruptive Power (20 max)	3/15 percent	
TOTAL SCORE/PERCENT (42 total)	12/28.5 percent	

inquiry that attempts to assess whether the CFA strike threat was credible by completing our Credible Strike Threats Scorecard (Table 4.2). There are a number of key questions I will ask as part of my workers' inquiry into the strike threat. Was it member or staff led? Did we draw in and motivate more inactive members to get involved? Were new allies on and off campus recruited to help support the faculty, coaches, counselors, and librarians? Was public perception of the strikers and the strike threat favorable? Did we gradually increase the intensity of our tactics as we approached the strike date? The results are reported in Table 4.5.

What follows is the result of my workers' inquiry into the recomposition of academic workers' power prior to and following the strike threat and the settlement. It should be noted that I was able to assess the strike threat at only two of the 23 campuses, which sets some limits to my workers' inquiry. I have not been able to definitively determine whether CFA conducted an analysis of the strike threat for all 23 campuses. Even as an actively involved rank-and-file member of the CFA I do not have sufficient information to definitively answer the questions above—which is central to the reason I find that the strike threat was not credible. I relied on first-hand observations, interviews, and participation in strike-related actions over a period of several months at SFSU and SJSU, the two campuses where I taught as a one-year contract lecturer. I also received comments on an earlier draft of this chapter from senior unnamed CFA chapter officers, active executive committee members, and strike organizers at both campuses, and have incorporated their responses into this chapter.

Strike preparations

In the seven months prior to the announced dates of the strike, CFA staff and activists issued four major CFA systemwide reports on racial and gender equity, privatization, funding and pay (CFA 2015a and b), and the SFSU chapter released a financial analysis of the campus administration written by an outside expert (CFA 2016). CFA staff sent out weekly Wednesday website posts and emails to members who had opted in. The timeframe of the different events are telling for conducting a workers' inquiry into the organizational, positional, and disruptive power of the strike threat.

After three days of bargaining in the summer of 2015, with no movement at the table, the CFA declared an impasse and mediation began on August 31. The executive board then announced the strike vote on September 23, 2015, and the membership voted online and in person between October 19 and 28 to authorize the strike.[14] The 94.4 percent vote in favor was announced at a press conference at SJSU on November 4, 2015. Fact finding began on November 23.

At this point CFA strike-related action began in earnest. Picket lines, flyering, and strike organizing meetings began, and marches took place at the next few Board of Trustees meetings in Long Beach and at the state capitol beginning in December. Protests were organized at several events attended by the system Chancellor, strike sanctions were requested and given by several labor councils and the California Labor Federation, campus and student senates and campus employee unions expressed support, a hardship fund for members was created in March 2016, and members were asked to wear their red strike-threat T-shirts during the first week of spring 2016 classes. The strike was endorsed by the California Democratic Party. The CFA generated significant press coverage of the strike across the state and nationwide.

The April 13–15 and 18–19, 2016 strike dates, during which all the campuses would walk out simultaneously, were announced on February 5, just nine weeks prior to the first day of the strike, and the membership were informed in the February 10 website posting and email. The CFA announced on February 17 that "Strike Schools" were being held on the campuses to inform the membership of the strike plans. Online strike pledge forms for each campus were announced on February 24 and a single form for the entire system made available on March 2. The March 28 fact-finders' report was reported to the membership the same day as granting the union the "legal right to strike" under the state Higher Education Employer-Employee Relations Act by suspending Article 9.1 of the CBA which prohibits "strikes or other concerted activity that would interfere with or adversely affect the operations or the mission of the CSU." The CBA also mandates: "9.2 The CFA shall not promote, organize, or support any strike or other concerted activity. 9.3 The CFA shall endeavor to prevent faculty unit employees from participating in a concerted activity which would interfere with or adversely affect the operations or the mission of the CSU."[15] No weekly website posting or email newsletter was produced between March 30 and April 13, the day the strike was scheduled to begin, although on April 8 a press release and email were sent out announcing the tentative agreement. 97 percent of the faculty voted to ratify the new CBA in an online vote held between April 22 and 29.

From a review of my own experience, emails, and the CFA newsletters, most of the communications came from local chapter officers, staff, and activists. The SFSU chapter communicated with members far more frequently than did the SJSU chapter.

Organizational, positional, and disruptive power at SFSU

SFSU had a core strike committee including approximately 20 active faculty organizers engaged in regular strike organizing. The committee used many kinds of tactics, including a Welcome Back message for fall and spring semesters that addressed bargaining and the strike, monthly newsflashes, four Strike Bulletin Updates issued between February and March 2016, daily flyering, picketing, coalition building, obtaining statements of public support, generating media coverage, holding strike organizing and members meetings, raising the strike in department meetings, robo-calls from the chapter president to faculty, hall walking, three silent vigils, a mock trial of the Chancellor, strike updates to the Academic Senate to gain its support, informational picket lines, general member and department meetings, commitment cards, participation at the Board of Trustees action in Long Beach, and campus rallies that gave the strike preparation regular publicity.

The chapter president was a lecturer, as were many of the most active strike committee organizers. The committee met several times a week in the CFA chapter office and was supplied with flyers, signs, banners, T-shirts, door hangers, informational lawn signs which were displayed on the campus, posters for bulletin boards, and other necessary organizing supplies. Organizers and interns also did faculty-to-faculty phone banking from the office and stored the materials for the weekly morning informational tabling.

The strike organizing committee was composed of contingent lecturers and tenure track professors, including myself, as well as librarians and coaches. About 5–10 members attended the weekly organizing meetings that began at the start of the spring semester. We did a barebones structure test by dividing up between us a list of members and their offices, who we then personally visited to gauge their support for the strike and to distribute door hangers. It is unclear whether online and contingent faculty who don't come to campus or use their offices, and faculty located at satellite campuses, were contacted. However, the only concrete in-person actions for them to engage in were putting a strike hanger on their door and signing a strike pledge card in person or online. It is also unclear if follow up to identify and bring over "No" votes to our side was ever attempted.

There was no comprehensive attempt to identify key influencers or unknown committees in each department and have them organize a strike action group. And it was well known that chairs and tenured faculty opposed to the union dominated several departments and reportedly retaliated against activists, taking down door hangers and signs. No effective effort was made to counter their influence. The organizing committee had the advantage of an active paid student internship program directed by a lecturer who was also a strike committee member. These students had been receiving training in advocacy and mobilizing as members of the CFA-funded Students for Quality Education, but had little training in strike organizing. They played an important role in generating student support on campus, but did not play a central role in organizing the strike, which was done by the members.

Passive organizing was done by posting organizers near the foot entrances and the parking lots in the early morning and mid afternoon to gauge members' support and give them a strike flyer to distribute in their department and put on their door. Signs were made and distributed at the strike committee meetings and each morning at an information table set up on a main mall near several key entrances to the campus. Strike-threat T-shirts were also distributed to members to wear on a designated day each week. Door signs and doorknob hangers were widely distributed and displayed around campus.

On the first day of the official strike authorization vote there was a long line of waiting members supported by representatives of many other campus and city unions and community groups expressing solidarity. The event was widely covered in the media. However, only the percentage voting to strike systemwide was reported. We never learned the proportion of members who actually voted and the breakdown of the vote by campus, job classification, or department—information that would be essential for conducting a structure test to see where we were weak and strong in order to know where to direct our organizing efforts.

The public strike vote generated a significant turnout but the momentum could not be sustained. Even at SFSU there were insufficient numbers of people signing up for strike duty, which included picketing all the entrances of our busy urban campus. One of the main strike committee members informed me shortly after the vote to approve the settlement that the strike would have failed, and that the settlement averting the strike was the best possible outcome, because too few members were involved in the organizing or had signed up for picket duty, and some faced retaliation in their departments.

SFSU academic workers were not sufficiently able to recompose either their organizational or their positional power. Although preparations began months in advance, there was still insufficient lead time to engage in deep organizing, or identify key influencers and have them brought into the effort. The four Strike Bulletin Updates issued between February and March 2016 were produced too late to inform, inspire, and organize a supermajority of the faculty to participate in the strike set to begin on April 13. Despite the many tactics used to actively and passively inform the membership about the strike and motivate them, public displays of commitment were extremely low. Furthermore, the tactics did not seem to be used as part of a concerted strategy of gradual escalation. Although well-organized, the preparations promised little to no disruptive power from either the strike-related actions or an eventual strike. The finite duration of the strike and the limited period any one campus would be on strike likewise promised little to no disruption. The strike threat thus had *very little* credibility.

Organizational, positional, and disruptive power at SJSU

In contrast, preparations at SJSU offered *no* credible strike threat at all. New to the campus, I spent weeks emailing the lecturer representative, the person who sent out the chapter newsletter, and the chapter president. Although I received a response from the chapter president and the lecturer representative informing me how to get on the strike committee email list, I didn't receive any specific details about how to get involved until only a few weeks before the strike date. I was unable to attend the strike committee meetings and received little advance or follow up information about what was planned.

Strike organizing at SJSU was in vivid contrast to the efforts at SFSU. Although there was a strike committee there appeared to be no publicly announced meetings, no office visits, no flyering, and no person-to-person communications about the strike. I was later informed that there were several phone banks to call members, although I did not receive a call. The chapter distributed strike commitment cards but there was no public signing event, such as the one held by the SFSU CFA chapter. My department discussed whether to inform our students of the threatened strike, but no effort was made to gauge support. Although signs and stickers could be found in many buildings, few members wore the red strike-threat T-shirt. There were two rallies, one in October, and another just prior to the strike date. The first, which I did not participate in, had about 200 in attendance in the center of campus, but the second rally, in which I did participate, was attended by only a few dozen people, some of whom were students. The South Bay Labor Council granted strike sanction to the SJSU CFA chapter; local California Teachers Association (with which CFA was affiliated until 2019) members committed to walking picket lines; local members of the state Assembly and Senate pledged their support; and significant local media coverage was generated.

Only a few weeks before the strike date, the chapter hired paid student interns to do door-to-door visits to engage support for the strike. However, the only action they requested supporters to do was put on a door hanger and wear the T-shirt. Follow-up visits were conducted but my experience was that the information obtained by the interns was not shared with the membership or even those on the strike committee email list. No structure test was conducted on the campus despite information that opposition to the strike was concentrated in the Business and Engineering departments. The strike committee began to prepare for the strike very late and communicated poorly or not at all, even with members who wished to be involved such as myself.

Overall, SJSU academic workers were woefully unprepared to strike. Nearly all the strike preparations were driven by union officers and staff, and carried out by student interns, with little genuine member involvement in organizing, although the number of activists was reportedly between 20 and 25 people. Members were not trained to organize one another, and additional trained temporary staff were brought in very late. There was no sustained daily strike-related activity, few of the tactics employed by the SFSU CFA chapter were used, and, as with its sister chapter, those that were used were not part of any concerted strategy of escalating intensity. What little strike-related activity that did occur at SJSU promised to cause no disruption.

Assessing the credibility of the CFA strike threat

Five days before the strike was to begin the union staff and officers notified the membership that the strike would not start as scheduled because a tentative agreement had been reached. A strike vote took place soon after and the agreement was nearly unanimously approved, although neither the percentage nor any details about the composition of members voting was reported.

While this workers' inquiry covers only two of the 23 CSU campuses, from my participant observation in the strike organizing I conclude that the strike threat was hardly credible. Strike organizing at these two nearby campuses were polar opposites of one another, and yet even the more active effort at SFSU demonstrated extremely low levels of organizational and nearly no actual disruptive power.

However, overall the strike threat had a very high level of potential positional power. As the second largest public university system in the country, in the largest state with the largest state economy—playing a central role in the global logistical supply chain, particularly at SJSU in the center of the Silicon Valley—a strike could have resulted in substantial disruptive power even during its planned limited duration. Lacking a structure test not merely of the two campuses evaluated in this workers' inquiry but of all 23 in the system, there is no way to accurately gauge what level of disruption might have resulted from a strike.

There are several critical reasons for the low levels of organizational and potential disruptive power. Preparations for the strike trailed behind bargaining, a strategic mistake common with contract unionism (Ness 2014: 269–78). As is common with many other unions, leadership and staff issued an anonymous survey about bargaining issues, but never reported back the results to the membership, let alone those who answered it, nor revealed the composition of the respondents. As a result, the survey was not used as an organizing tool but only to inform bargaining.

Information given to members on bargaining, strike strategies, and organizing was inadequate, other than in passive email bulletins such as that of September 23, 2015, when bargaining had broken down, an impasse was declared, and the CFA threatened to strike. The strike authorization vote took place five to six weeks after that critical moment at which bargaining had collapsed. Because the spring semester started in late January and the first strike bulletins were not issued at SFSU, for example, until February, a mere ten weeks remained to organize the strike even at the better organized of the two campuses.

During these long intervals between the end of bargaining and the beginning of strike organizing, little to no organizing took place. Rather, CFA officers, leaders, and activists focused on media relations, lobbying, mobilization, and coalition building which proved to be quite effective. As one of the chapter officers commenting on this chapter concluded, "a threat involves creating an impression of power, and gaining allies among powerful institutional players in the political field. CFA succeeded in creating such an image at three levels." These three levels included "creating the impression among the administrators at each campus that the faculty were organized," "lobbying legislators and gaining commitments from legislators" to support the strike, and the "the symbolic fight over legitimacy in the media." Because the Chancellor replaced the CSU bargaining team two days before the start of the strike, this officer argues that "the performative characteristics of threats" demonstrated that "CSU feared CFA's capacity to embarrass them and win public opinion."

This interpretation of the CFA strike threat is analogous to the *Game of Thrones* character Lord Varys telling an adversary "Power resides where men believe it resides. It's a trick, a shadow on the wall. And a very small man can cast a very large shadow." There is, however, a critical difference between the *appearance* of power and its actual presence. Once an adversary realizes they are inside Plato's cave the strike threat loses its credibility.

In addition to the tactical and strategic limitations, CFA's bargaining objectives were also problematic. There were no demands that could effectively motivate a supermajority of members to commit to striking. CFA's rallying cry was an underwhelming "Fight for 5 [percent]," hardly a basis for a "fight" or inspiring organization and commitment after years of wage freezes and austerity, especially since many of the CSU campuses are in some of the most expensive metropolitan areas in the country. "Fight for 5" came across as paltry and insufficient, although the CSU's wage concession nearly matched it.

Because there was no structure test, workers' inquiry or deep organizing, the CFA went into bargaining and strike preparations virtually blind about its own power. It knew very little about the technical composition of the CSU system or the class composition of the academic workers. Although the CFA's reports provided a wealth of useful information about the composition of its own members, working conditions, CSU finances, and existing problems, the information did not appear to be used to inform tactics and strategies for collective strike action other than to build some community linkages and make a moral case that could help us in the fight.

For example, more than half the faculty are part-time lecturers. Between 2013 and 2016, the number of part-time lecturers grew by 56 percent, far faster than tenure-track and tenured professors whose numbers shrank (CSU n.d.). In 2013, 34 percent of full-time faculty were non-white and 45 percent were women. The CFA neither organized around issues specific to the composition of the faculty nor knew the extent of each group's support for the strike.

The mistitled report *The Price Students Pay* didn't focus on the actual price but attempted to connect the costs to the students by connecting them to the fact that half the faculty made less than $38,000 per year. This focus on faculty pay garnered little interest among students, who either didn't receive the message or heard it as members of working-class families that earned even lower wages. The other three reports, such as *Race to the Bottom*, were also overly focused on the erosion of faculty pay and the growth in management and management pay relative to faculty pay (CFA 2015a and b). The CFA did not have comprehensive information about the composition of the student body, let alone the thousands of administrative staff, who were sought out for support.

The four detailed reports were used to make the case for striking strictly on pay and funding issues. But they lacked a comprehensive understanding of the technical composition (for example, the growth of online classes and in productivity), other than the growing size of management, and the class composition (management's erosion of faculty control over academic decision making). As a result, CFA was not prepared to organize the members to strike on issues other than pay. Rather, it used the reports to generate moral support for impoverished professors while lobbying the recalcitrant administration and legislature, mobilizing supporters and allies, and engaging in media promotions in order to advocate for the 5 percent pay increase. The reports were not used to *organize* but to *mobilize* around a moral argument about impoverished professors that, while shocking and becoming more prevalent, seems to run counter to common belief.

One chapter officer I interviewed emphasized mobilizing rather than organizing by pointing to the end result, a modest concession in pay. McAlevey (2016: 1–70) argues that the nearly universal movement of unions away from deep organizing to advocacy and mobilizing is the cause of the decades of defeats for workers in the US. This emphasis on mobilizing is illustrated by the minimal organizing that took place at any period after bargaining had begun on

May 19, 2015, or after the strike threat was made on September 23. It didn't begin in earnest until the spring semester another four months later. No structure test was conducted, and even if one had been, there was no clear strategy, little organizing, and no tactical escalation. The members were not ready or able to strike.

Another reason for the low level of organizational power may have been that the main demand was for a long overdue but uninspiring 5 percent wage bump. There were no other demands related to the growing numbers of faculty and librarians hired as contingent workers (half the faculty), growing class sizes, efforts to standardize the curriculum through departmental and student "learning objectives," the growth of online classes, the lack of office space, attacks on ethnic studies programs, austerity, and other issues concerning healthcare, pensions, evaluations, campus safety, the spike in student hunger and homelessness, and work control issues.

CSU conceded the 5 percent demand just five days before the strike was to begin, leading the CFA to call it off. The ratification vote was very high but we do not know the percentage of CFA members voting or its composition. Overall, members received a small wage gain totaling between 10.5 and 13.15 percent over the following two years, no cuts to healthcare (although as I write they are expected in the new round of bargaining), and a few other minor adjustments. The new CBA provided for a 5 percent increase on June 30, 2016, a 2 percent increase on July 1, 2016, a 3.5 percent increase on July 1, 2017, and a 2.65 percent step increase during the fiscal year 2017–18 for eligible faculty. Ninety-eight percent of the faculty voted between October 30 and November 2, 2017 to approve a two-year extension of the contract until June 30, 2020. This added an additional 3.5 percent increase in 2018, and a 2.5 percent increase in 2019. In total, the salary increase amounted to between 16.5 and 19.15 percent over the four years following the strike threat—which is below the annual 5 percent demanded. Ranging between 4.13 and 4.79 percent, the strike threat failed to even achieve it's underwhelming demand of 5 percent.

This modest pay rise was exchanged for continually growing class sizes (productivity increases) and a doubling in the number of years for new hires to vest in the retiree medical coverage. During the 2019 state legislative session, CFA shifted to a class collaborationist model by partnering with the CSU to successfully lobby the legislature for more state funding. This resulted in the further 6 percent pay increase in 2018 and 2019, in exchange for extending the contract until June 30, 2020 without reopening negotiations.

While modest wage gains were made, the CFA's strike threat was not credible and the settlement was a wash because the wage gains were canceled out by the concessions in higher productivity, the two-tiered retiree medical coverage, the growth of contingent lecturers, and the lack of action on other critical issues. The contract has since been extended with no strike-related activity at all. The threat promised to cause little to no fiscal cost to the CSU, certainly less than the potential non-monetary costs of minor disruption for a limited duration, bad publicity, and a political backlash against the CSU system administration if the strike had taken place. The CSU's expected material and intangible costs for the threatened strike from minor disruption and bad publicity were likely only slightly higher than the costs of making a monetary concession offset by the members' tangible concessions in higher productivity and delay in accessing retiree medical coverage.

CONCLUSION

The rising number of strike threats made by workers in the US may be an indicator of the emerging recomposition of working-class power. However, the story is incomplete as long as we don't know whether these strike threats had sufficient organizational, positional, and disruptive power to convince employers of the higher cost of a strike than conceding to some or all of the workers' demands. We do not yet know whether strike threats are merely a strategy for avoiding a strike that the workers demand but that the union is unprepared for, unwilling to organize, and expects to lose. There is great uncertainty as to whether strike threats are a potentially powerful new strategy to bypass the paralyzing harness of labor law to achieve workers' objectives.

However, the larger number of strike threats than actual strikes might point to a rumbling from below by workers anxious to recompose their power and apply their leverage against the disciplinary role of both contract unionism and capitalism. The 2018–19 teacher strikes were mostly carried out by self-organized workers who didn't belong to unions. Their strikes were made all the more possible because if there are no unions then there are no rules and no limits. As capital and the state depart from the tripartite relationship with unions that characterized the Fordist era, self-organized workers are no longer restrained or harnessed to CBAs and labor law. Carrying out strike threats may be a way for workers to test and expand their own organizational, positional, and disruptive power.

The lessons of the CFA strike threat

There are several important lessons to be drawn from the CFA strike threat in 2016, one of the largest during the five-year period we documented. First, a credible strike threat must be preceded with a thorough workers' inquiry as outlined in the introduction to this book. An in-depth analysis of both the technical composition of capital and the current composition of the workers will inform the tactics, strategies, organizational form, and objectives for workers to recompose their power and make a credible strike threat.

Once the tactics and strategies are put into practice, various structure tests, such as calibrating the intensity of the threat, will be critical to producing a credible strike threat (see Adăscăliței and Guga 2015). To escalate the tactical intensity of the struggle workers must expand the commitment of fellow workers to strike-related organizing in order to raise the level of organizational power. This maximizes the potential concessions from a strike threat for the workers in inverse proportion to the employers' perception of the rising costs from the strike.

Yet, a strike threat with a high level of organizational power but lacking positional power is likely to be a credible nuisance rather than a credible threat of disruption. Assessing whether a concession that avoids a strike is a gain to the workers is a qualitative and subjective observation that can best be made by the workers themselves in the context of their specific demands, whether those demands were achieved by the concessions, and the level of support for the settlement by the workers. Even a modest gain will provide a deposit in the bank on which workers can draw in the next cycle of struggle to increase the credibility of their strike threat for both their fellow workers and the employer.

We should be cautious about strike threats which achieve their demands because they were set so low as to impose a fiscal cost on the employer lower than the expected intangible and tangible costs in terms of bad publicity and political consequences. Such strike threats might appear to be performatively credible but lack the organizational power to potentially inflict disruptive costs. This was the case with CFA's strike threat.

Turning an un-credible strike threat into a symbolic victory will not contribute to recomposing working-class power. Rather, if it results in another CBA that represents a short-term gain but a long term-defeat, then the union will have maintained its role as a brake on class struggle. As Glaberman (1947) observed in his study of the United Autoworkers Union, "the unions control and limit the class struggle in the factory and make possible longer or short periods of class peace."

The CFA was unable to organize the necessary organizational power because it lacked a strategy that used tactical intensity. Although it had a potentially high level of positional power it lacked the organizational power to deploy it. As a result, the CSU did not take the strike threat as credible, thereby prompting the CFA to settle six days before the strike began. The CFA's lack of organizational power translated into an incapacity to take advantage of its positional and disruptive power, and so it cut its losses and took a small pay increase that was likely a wash in light of the concessions the workers made. Without a credible strike threat the CFA lacked the power to disrupt one of the nation's largest public university systems, and thereby the national supply of educated skilled labor and the numerous corporations doing business with the university system in the very heart of the global IT industry.

The lessons of strike threats

Alongside the larger questions about the recomposition of working-class power, the CFA strike raises a critical question about whether a credible strike threat is sufficient to achieving a successful outcome for the workers. Is a strike threat merely a form of Lord Varys's shadow of power with the limited objective of extracting limited concessions? There are two possible ways to address this question in future workers' inquiries.

First, did the credible strike threat actually increase the potential gain for the workers? Further workers' inquiries should ask whether the concessions were less or greater than the gains from previous collective action, or what might have been achieved if the strike had taken place. This can be done by comparing the details of specific strikes in similar or related sectors with analogous organizational, positional, and disruptive power. Various strikes that settled before a strike occurred, after a strike, or where the strike failed to result in a settlement could be contrasted. This would give workers the ability to make a comparative analysis of the factors that make a strike threat credible and a strike successful in achieving the workers' demands.

Second, did the workers tilt the balance of power sufficiently to extract a concession that strengthens them for the next round of struggle and creates the capacity to circulate their struggle? Again, a workers' inquiry in preparation for strike-related activity may transcend the specific concerns about the organizational power of a particular struggle by connecting to its positional power. The coordinated use of credible strike threats spread across multiple workplaces, employers, and industries in distant geographical areas has the potential to generate a high level of disruptive power through hit and run strikes, for example.

A workers' inquiry into strike threats is not merely an exercise in carrying out a structure test to win some particular demand in bargaining. The objective is to bring about a decisive end to the class struggle against capitalism. As Panzieri observed, the class struggle "expresses itself not as progress, but as rupture; not as 'revelation' of the occult rationality inherent in the modern productive process, but as the construction of a radically new rationality counterposed to the rationality practiced by capitalism" (1980: 54). That rupture is contagious, spreading into all of society, connecting the waged and unwaged workplaces. As Tronti reminds us, "When the development of capital's interests in the factory is blocked, then the functioning of society seizes up: the way is then open for overthrowing and destroying the very basis of capital's power" (1980: 28–9).

ACKNOWLEDGMENTS

I am deeply indebted to Dr. Helena Worthen, who initially encouraged me to study credible strike threats and provided incisive feedback on an early version of this chapter. I also would like to thank Gabriela Crowley for her invaluable assistance as my Research Assistant. I am grateful to my colleagues in the SJSU Political Science department for their thoughtful feedback at my colloquium presentation of this research, and to the College of Social Science for two invaluable grants to support it. SJSU does not endorse the findings of this study which are exclusively that of the author. Please record your US strike threat at our website: www.strikethreats.org

NOTES

1. Dr. Helena Worthen defines a credible strike threat as this first type: credible to the employer.
2. Email from Dr. Helena Worthen, September 20, 2017.
3. Maranto and Fiorito (1987: 327–8) disagree, suggesting that a union's record of striking and making credible strike threats may produce bad publicity and negative public opinion thereby increasing the cost to the union during a representation election if workers perceive possible income loss from potential strikes.
4. There is much confusion about the origin of the ideas of associational and organizational power. In his postscript to Perrone (1984), Wright introduces the concept "organizational power," but then drops it in favor of "associational power" in a later related piece (Wright 2000). I prefer the term organizational, rather than associational, power.
5. Here too I prefer to use the term "positional," rather than Wright's concept of "structural" power (in Perrone 1984: 421–3, and Wright 2000: 962), throughout this chapter. Wright's use of structural power is confusing and questionable for two reasons. First, Perrone used positional and structural power interchangeably throughout his English translated works, although concluding with the latter. "Positional" is also used in the title of the article: "Positional Power and the Propensity to Strike" (1983). Second, Wright's later piece exclusively uses "structural" in an identical manner to Perrone's meaning of "positional" power without citing or crediting Perrone, an issue that should be rectified by the

three journals that published their pieces. When I raised this issue in an email (October 21, 2018) with Wright shortly before he passed away, he disagreed that Perrone should have been credited, citing the fact that he helped have Perrone's work translated and published in English after he died unexpectedly in an auto accident. Today, many labor theorists either use the two terms interchangeably or mistakenly cite Wright as the author of the influential concept of "structural" power. Because some of my fellow authors in this book are divided on this issue I have allowed them to continue using structural.

6. Note that in this article the translators appear to be substituting "structural" for "positional" power in the text despite the fact that the title of the article is "Positional Power and the Propensity to Strike" (1983). This use of these two terms in the Perrone's two articles (1983, 1984) is further confused by Wright's substitution of his own terms for Perrone's in his single-authored article which has been mistakenly widely accepted by later writers as the origin of the concept of structural power. Some of this may be attributed to problems with the translation. For example, much of the theory and conclusion in Perrone (1983) is repeated with minor changes in Perrone (1984), such as the nearly identical texts on page 240 (Perrone 1983) and page 420 (Perrone 1984).

7. Womack's (2006) fascinating history of disruptive tactics and strategy focuses on the disruptive power of workers in what he calls "strategic positions" at different stages of the past century.

8. Perrone's study confirmed an earlier observation by John T. Dunlop that "The bargaining power of wage earners depends on their strategic position in dealing with the firm" (cited in Womack 2006: 79).

9. Wright elaborates: "with high organizational *and* positional power, strikes are entirely unnecessary to win demands, and thus propensity would be low" (in Perrone 1984: 421–2).

10. Wallace, Griffin, and Rubin (1989: 199) refer to this as three levels of positional (I prefer disruptive) power: the ability of workers to disrupt their own industry, "upstream" industries (which receive), and "downstream" industries (which supply).

11. In 2018 the US Bureau of Labor Statistics formally rejected my proposal that it begin recording the number of strike threats (Monthly Labor Review 2018).

12. McAlevey's (2016: 61–7, 208) structure test does not account for two possibilities. First, it is possible that well-organized workers have little positional power and cause little to no disruption. Second, a small group of workers with low organizational power but strategically located at critical choke points may have a high level of positional and disruptive power. One reason for these absences may be the limited objectives of the structure test in contrast to that of the workers' inquiry.

13. I want to thank my colleagues in the SJSU Political Science department who pointed this out to me when I presented my research in a colloquium in 2018.

14. The in-person strike vote took place at all the campuses on varying days, including a kick off event and three days of voting at SFSU and seven days at SJSU. See www.calfac.org/post/strike-vote-411.
15. See www.calfac.org/headlines/cfa-headlines-march-28–2016 and www.calfac.org/resource/collective-bargaining-agreement-contract-2014–2017#article-9.

REFERENCES

Adăscăliței, D. and Guga, S. (2015). Negotiating Agency and Structure: Trade Union Organizing Strategies in a Hostile Environment. *Economic and Industrial Democracy* 38(3), 473–94.

Alimahomed-Wilson, J. and Ness, I. (eds.) (2018). *Choke Points: Logistics Workers Disrupting the Global Supply Chain*. London: Pluto.

Alquati, R. (2013 [1961]). Organic Composition of Capital and Labor-Power at Olivetti. *Viewpoint* 19. At www.viewpointmag.com/2013/09/27/organic-composition-of-capital-and-labor-power-at-olivetti-1961.

Becker, C. (1994). "Better Than a Strike": Protecting New Forms of Collective Work Stoppages Under the National Labor Relations Act. *University of Chicago Law Review* 61(2), 351–421.

Becker, C. (1998). Elections Without Democracy: Reconstructing the Right to Organize. *New Labor Forum* 3, 97–109.

Benvegnù, C. and Cuppini, N. (2018). Struggles and Grassroots Organizing in an Extended European Choke Point. In Alimahomed-Wilson, J. and Ness, I. (eds.), *Choke Points: Logistics Workers Disrupting the Global Supply Chain*. London: Pluto, pp. 230–42.

CFA (California Faculty Association) (2015a). *The Price Students Pay*. At www.calfac.org/sites/main/files/file-attachments/race_to_the_bottom--the_price_students_pay_final.pdf.

CFA (California Faculty Association) (2015b). *Race to the Bottom: CSU's 10-year Failure to Fund its Core Mission*. At www.calfac.org/race-to-the-bottom.

CFA (California Faculty Association) (2016). Financial Analysis of San Francisco State University by Prof. Howard Bunsis. (April 7). At www.calfac.org/special-report/financial-analysis-san-francisco-state-university.

County Sanitation Dist. No. 2 v. Los Angeles County Employees Assn., Local 660, 699 P.2d 835, 847 (1985). At https://scocal.stanford.edu/opinion/county-sanitation-dist-no-2-v-los-angeles-county-employees-assn-28417.

CSU (California State University) (n.d.). Headcount of Full-Time Faculty by Rank and Campus, Fall 2018. At www2.calstate.edu/csu-system/faculty-staff/employee-profile/csu-faculty/Pages/headcount-of-full-time-faculty-by-rank.aspx.

Dunlop, J. T. (1948). *The Development of Labor Organization: A Theoretical Framework*. Indianapolis: Bobbs-Merrill.

Glaberman, M. (1947). Strata in the Working Class. *Internal Bulletin of the Johnson-Forest Tendency* (August). (Originally published under the name Martin Harvey.) At www.marxists.org/archive/glaberman/1947/08/strata.htm.

Highlights of the Railway Labor Act ("RLA"), and the US Department of Transportation's ("DOT") Role in RLA disputes (n.d.). Office of Rail Policy and Development, Federal Railroad Administration.

Kiersz, A. (2015). The Impact of Small Business on the US Economy in 2 Extreme Charts. *Business Insider* (June 16). At www.businessinsider.com.au/us-employment-by-firm-size-has-a-fat-tailed-distribution-2015-6.

Kilgour, J. (1990). Can Unions Strike Anymore? The Impact of Recent Supreme Court Decisions. *Labor Law Journal* (May), 259–69.

Labor Notes (2019). How to Strike and Win. *Labor Notes* 488 (November).

Lindbeck, A. and Snower, D. (1987). Strike and Lock-Out Threats and Fiscal Policy. *Oxford Economic Papers: New Series* 39(4), 760–84.

McAlevey, J. (2016). *No Shortcuts: Organizing for Power in the New Gilded Age*. Oxford: Oxford University Press.

Maranto, C. and Fiorito, J. (1987). The Effect of Union Characteristics on the Outcome of NLRB Certification Elections. *Industrial and Labor Relations Review* 40(2), 225–40.

Monthly Labor Review (2018). Counting Strike Threats. (May). At https://www.bls.gov/opub/mlr/2018/letters-to-editor/pdf/strike-threats.pdf.

Moody, K. (2017). *On New Terrain: How Capital is Reshaping the Battleground of Class War*. Chicago: Haymarket.

National Labor Relations Board (2019a). The Right to Strike. At www.nlrb.gov/strikes.

National Labor Relations Board (2019b). Collective Bargaining (Section 8(d) & 8(b)(3)). At www.nlrb.gov/rights-we-protect/whats-law/unions/collective-bargaining-section-8d-8b3.

Ness, I. (2014). *New Forms of Worker Organization: The Syndicalist and Autonomist Restoration of Class Struggle Unionism*. Oakland, CA: PM Press.

Ness, I. (2015). *Southern Insurgency: The Coming of the Global Working Class*. London: Pluto.

Olney, P. (2018). Beyond the Waterfront: Maintaining and Expanding Worker Power in the Maritime Supply Chain. In Alimahomed-Wilson, J. and Ness, I. (eds.), *Choke Points: Logistics Workers Disrupting the Global Supply Chain*. London: Pluto, pp. 243–58.

Panzieri, R. (1980). The Capitalist Use of Machinery: Marx Versus the Objectivists. In Slater, P. (ed.), *Outlines of a Critique of Technology*. London: Inks Links.

Perrone, L. (1983). Positional Power and Propensity to Strike. *Politics and Society* 12, 231–61.

Perrone, L. (1984). Positional Power, Strikes, and Wages. *American Sociological Review* 49(3), 412–21.

Sowers, E.A., Ciccantell, P.S., and Smith, D.A. (2018). Labor and Social Movements' Strategic Usage of the Global Commodity Chain Structure. In Alimahomed-Wilson, J. and Ness, I. (eds.), *Choke Points: Logistics Workers Disrupting the Global Supply Chain*. London: Pluto, pp. 19–34.

Steuben, J. (1950). *Strike Strategy*. New York: Gaer Associates Inc.

Tronti, M. (1980 [1965]). The Strategy of Refusal. In *Italy: Autonomia, Post-Political Politics*. New York: semiotext(e), pp. 28–35.

Wallace, M., Griffin, L.J., and Rubin, B. (1989). The Positional Power of American Labor, 1963–1977. *American Sociological Review* 54, 197–214.

Winslow, S. (2015). Supreme Court Will Take Case That Could Make Public Sector "Right to Work." *Labor Notes* (June). At http://labornotes.org/2015/06/how-unions-are-preparing-public-sector-right-work-threat.

Womack, J. (2006). Working Power Over Production: Labor History, Industrial Work, Economics, Sociology, and Strategic Position. XIV International Economic History Congress, Helsinki 2006, Panel 56: The Economics of Latin American Labor. At www.helsinki.fi/iehc2006/papers2/Womack.pdf.

Wright, E.O. (2000). Working-Class Power, Capitalist-Class Interests, and Class Compromise. *American Journal of Sociology* 105(4), 957–1002.

5

The Self-Organization of the Mexican Multitude Against Neoliberal State Terror: The CNTE Dissident Teachers' Movement Against the 2013 Education Reform

Patrick Cuninghame

> *"El maestro luchando también está enseñando"*
> ("The teacher in struggle is also teaching")
> —CNTE slogan

This chapter will analyze the class recomposition of the Mexican multitude. The multitude is large and diverse, incorporating many segments of the Mexican working class. It includes the precarious urban proletariat trapped in the informal economy, the smaller industrial working class—some of which has formed quasi-independent trade unions or self-organized into cooperatives in the "solidarity economy"—and the growing service sector of highly qualified but low paid "cognitariat." We could also include the rural working class such as the landless peasantry and agricultural day workers forced off the land and into neo-slavery or migration by agribusiness and transgenic corporations like Monsanto. But it is also necessary to include the increasingly insecure and proletarianized urban middle classes, hit by stagnation since the 2008 global economic meltdown. Using concepts drawn from contemporary autonomist Marxist theory, this chapter examines the Coordinadora Nacional de los Trabajadores de la Educación (CNTE/National Coordination of Educational

Workers) dissident teachers' struggle against the 2013 education counter-reform, involving different sectors of the recomposed urban and rural multitudes engaged in resistance to the violent imposition of neoliberal education policy.

Since 2006 the Mexican neoliberal state has launched a social war against its own population in the name of the "war against drugs and organized crime," but in reality to establish an undeclared state of exception and a political climate of generalized terror in order to force through deeply unpopular neoliberal structural counter-reforms. This social war can be seen as part of capital's "global civil war" to fragment humanity and consume nature which has intensified since the 9/11 terrorist attacks in the US (Berardi 2016). The results of this prolonged operation in deep social engineering, or class decomposition in autonomist Marxist terms, have been 202,000 Mexicans killed (Calderón et al. 2019: 38), up to 37,400 forcibly disappeared (Human Rights Watch 2019), and hundreds of thousands wounded, tortured, kidnapped, falsely imprisoned, and displaced. Yet, despite being the seventh most violent country in the world in 2018 (Human Rights Watch 2019), international criticism of the Mexican regime has been minimal, while the principal architects of this genocidal offensive, such as ex-president Calderón (2006–12) of the Partido de Acción Nacional (PAN/National Action Party)[1] and ex-president Peña Nieto of the Partido Revolucionario Institucional (PRI/Institutional Revolutionary Party)[2] (2012–18), were feted by world leaders and dignitaries as exemplary democratic reformers and courageous crime fighters. President Andrés Manuel López Obrador (commonly known as AMLO) of the centrist Morena (Movimiento Regeneración Nacional/National Regeneration Movement)[3] promised to swiftly reduce violence as part of his electoral landslide victory of July 2018, which he hailed as the start of a "Fourth Transformation" (with the independence movement of 1810–21, the mid-nineteenth-century liberal reforms and civil war, and the 1910–20 Mexican Revolution being the previous three). However, 2019 is slated to be one of the most violent years since records started in 1997, with over 17,000 homicides at its mid-point (Telesur 2019).

Nevertheless, the high levels of resistance and autonomous self-organization among sectors of the urban and rural working classes, or the "multitude" (Hardt and Negri 2004), and above all the dissident teachers of the CNTE,[4] have forced the "Pact for Mexico" authoritarian neoliberal coalition government[5] and its eleven structural counter-reforms into crisis.

The CNTE's existence is due to decades of betrayal and repression by *charro*[6] trade unions in collaboration with the PRI, its corporate partners, and nominally center-left but objectively pro-neoliberal parties like the Partido de la Revolución Democrática (PRD/Democratic Revolution Party).[7] As a result, the Mexican multitude has increasingly distanced itself from these duplicitous institutional actors and has chosen instead to self-organize and self-defend itself to resist the social war. This is a war launched by the parties, national and global business interests, the corporatist unions, the repressive apparatus of the state bureaucracy, and the "armed entrepreneurs" of the narco drug-trafficking cartels (Fazio 2016), with the tacit support and complicit silence of the US and European Union governments and the global capitalist institutions.

THE SELF-ORGANIZATION OF THE MULTITUDE

What is the "multitude"? And what is the class composition of the Mexican multitude? Why is it turning to autonomy, self-organization, and self-management and away from the political parties, unions, and the institutions of the state? Can they halt the "necropolitics" of the crisis-ridden "neofeudal" state[8] (Negri and Cocco 2006; Fazio 2016)? What is the significance of these struggles, in terms of constituent power, for the deepening crisis of Empire, now under the sway of the radical right populist US President Trump? Can the countertendency of the autonomous struggles of the Mexican multitude reignite the anti-neoliberal social movements in Latin America and work closely with the autonomous struggles of the multitude in the US against "alt-right" neofascism, the latest metamorphosis of stagnating global capital? These are some of the theoretical and political questions this section seeks to answer before moving on to the issue of neoliberal state terrorism and its necropolitics during the struggle over neoliberal education policy.

Hardt and Negri redefine their heterogeneous concept of "multitude" in relation to poverty and the commons as follows:

The poverty of the multitude ... does not refer to its misery or deprivation or even its lack, but instead names a production of social subjectivity that results in a radically plural and open body politic, opposed to both the individualism and the exclusive, unified social body of property. The poor, in other words, refers not to those who have nothing but to the wide multiplicity of all those who are inserted in the mechanisms of social production regardless of social order or property. And this conceptual conflict is also a political conflict. Its productivity is what makes the multitude of the poor a real and effective menace for the republic of property. (Hardt and Negri 2009: 39–40)

Here, the authors place the multitude as a networked body politic of antagonist subjectivity that embraces all the previous antagonist class formations. Above all, the multitude embraces the old industrial working class, once considered by both orthodox Marxism and Italian workerism as *central* to the class struggle. It merges them with the new class formations of antagonist subjectivity, above all the *poor*, including the precarious, informalized, and unsalaried cognitarian urban worker of production and reproduction as well as the expelled and expropriated landless peasant or day laborer forced into migration.

According to Negri and Cocco (2006), the Latin American multitude has evolved from the working class since the mid-twentieth century. The first stage was the "ECLAC [Economic Commission for Latin America and the Caribbean][9] period" (1950–60), when usually isolated struggles by limited sectors of the industrial working class, mainly in Brazil, Argentina, and Mexico, were confronted by stable conservative regimes, and resolved themselves as either "desperate insurrectional movements" or as "organizational forms functional to developmentalism" with only a limited capacity to impact national institutions and the wage relation. The second phase (1960–80)—the period of military dictatorships and authoritarian regimes, such as in Mexico—witnessed the consolidation of the struggles of the central strata of the urban proletariat, which produced transitory forms of armed struggle based on a "confusion between the ideological instances of metropolitan small groups and intellectuals and the expression of mass proletarian interests and desires." These defeated struggles nevertheless had the crucial effect of dissolving corporatist identities and political forms in order to realize the "social autonomy of the proletariat [which] opened up the political recomposition of the multitudes" (Negri and Cocco 2006: 217–19). In the final phase, 1980 to today,

> after the fall of the dictatorships and with the first glimpse of the democratization of the conflict, the struggles presented themselves as constituent. They submerged themselves in the structure of society and in the global set of populations. They are class struggles, which however spread themselves and become social struggles, which begin to outline a transformational project and include the beginnings of programmed demands. The commons anticipate and dissolve partiality, identity and corporatism. They are new struggles in the new global tissue—the struggles of the multitude. (Negri and Cocco 2006: 218–19)[10]

One of the main characteristics of the multitude, at least the multitude in movement, is its capacity for self-organization; that is, its capacity to organize autonomously at a distance from political parties, trade unions, non-governmental organizations, civil society organizations, civic associations, and pressure groups that have become absorbed into, are functional to or dependent upon state power. These also include those "revolutionary vanguard" organizations whose objective is state construction and which therefore fall finally into the same abstract logic as capitalist state-centric organizations (Holloway 2002). This does not exclude the possibility that the multitude may choose at some point to organize itself through these organizational forms, but it will always do so independently of the imperial state and in opposition to those recuperated organizational forms that may have at one point been autonomous and constituent themselves. So what are the principles and practices underlying and informing autonomous self-organization?

The self-organization of the movements and instances of the multitude imply autonomy, self-management, self-determination, self-government, intersubjectivity, responsibility, morality, cooperation, and communication. In discussing the relationship of the multitude with democratic resistance to war and empire, Hardt and Negri remind us that:

> In the era of imperial sovereignty and biopolitical production, the balance has tipped such that the ruled now tend to be the exclusive producers of social organization ... Correspondingly, the ruled become increasingly autonomous, capable of forming society without the rulers. We spoke earlier of the newly hegemonic forms of "immaterial" labor that rely on communicative and collaborative networks that we share in common and that, in turn, also produce new networks of intellectual, affective, and social relationships. Such new forms of labor ... present new possibilities for economic self-management, since the mechanisms of cooperation necessary for production are contained in the labor itself. Now we can see that this potential applies not only to economic self-management but also political and social self-organization. (Hardt and Negri 2004: 336)

While this may apply in the metropolis of Empire, does it still apply to rural and urban struggles in the semi-periphery, such as Mexico? Here we need to consider the importance of migration as a movement in the multitude in breaking down both territorial and technological frontiers, permitting what were once isolated rural struggles to network with the rest of the deterritorialized global social space despite racism, barriers, and exclusion. The example of Chiapas is also relevant in this aspect, as many Zapatistas have emigrated to and some have returned from the US since their revolt began in 1994.

However, in the Mexican context we need to consider other practices as part of self-organization: the mobilization and coordination of labor for the production and defense of the common, and the option of guerrilla warfare against state terrorism or else a democratic use of violence as self-defense. This is again illustrated by the example of the Zapatistas, who have so skillfully steered a course between these two options, magnifying the benefits while avoiding the pitfalls, unlike other guerrilla armies or self-defense groups in other parts of Mexico which have been repressed. Or do we need to see these uprisings against neofeudal biopower in San Salvador Atenco, Ostula, and Cheran[11] as more spontaneous peasant *jacqueries*, following Hardt and Negri's (2009) use of the term? Either way the questions of self-organization, direct democracy, and the use of organized violence in self-defense cannot be avoided. Finally, self-organization involves the incorporation of significant cultural values, imagination, and practices in order to root it in the community's everyday life as an urgent and vital social reality and not just mere abstract politics (Shukaitis 2008).

THE NEOLIBERAL TERRORIST STATE

Against the self-organizing, autonomous movements of the multitude stands the increasingly violent, often terrorist, late neoliberal state. The neoliberal state is determined to control and, when necessary, exterminate resistance in its protection and promotion of the new wave of primitive accumulation through ethnic and social cleansing that has accelerated as a result of the global economic crisis (Harvey 2003).

The modern nation state has a long history of practicing terrorism, understood as the extralegal use of lethal violence for political ends, against certain social, ideological, religious, and ethnic groups considered to be "undesirable." The state claims that its terrorism is legitimate since it bases its claim to authority on the political necessity for order, and that only it can exercise violence legitimately, over which it claims to have a monopoly. All others who use political violence without the justification of the state's authority and role in the production of order are therefore subversives, outlaws, and terrorists. As Agamben (2005) points out, the state itself can be a terrorist through an unreasonable or unjustified use of its physical force against certain groups when it claims that it itself is under threat. It therefore makes claims to self-defense from external and, above all, internal threats through the declaration of a "state of exception," imposing martial law or introducing emergency laws that remove or suspend some or all human, political, and civil rights, including that to life. According to Walter Benjamin (1986), the nature of this state violence is "divine," or unquestionable and beyond reason. The state's self-defense clause has been used to commit mass terrorism on various occasions, from the eighteenth-century French Jacobins, from whom the term "terrorism" was derived, to European imperialism, and Nazism, fascism, and Stalinism in the twentieth century.

In Latin America, following the independence movements of the early nineteenth century that inspired liberal nationalist revolutions in Europe, the national oligarchies quickly abandoned their liberal ideals, returned to economic feudalism, and governed through genocide, racism, and military dictatorship. In Mexico, the Porfirian dictatorship led to revolution and civil war from 1910 to 1920, which left 10 percent of the population dead. More recent examples include the US-sponsored military dictatorships in Chile— the bloody birthplace of the Chicago Boys' neoliberal shock doctrine (Klein 2007)—Paraguay, and Argentina in the 1970s. Despite partial democratization in Latin America since the 1980s, and the Pink Tide of the first decade of the twenty-first century, state terror has continued and even increased, particularly through the wars against drugs and organized crime in Colombia and Mexico, the civil war in Colombia since the 1960s, and the terrible race war conducted by the Brazilian neofeudal oligarchy and its special forces against the marginalized populations of the favelas, above all Afro-Brazilians, that kills around 50,000 a year (Amnesty International 2017). Neoliberalism has combined with violent authoritarianism to produce a state terrorist response to the antagonist movements of the multitude:

> Social violence is inherent to the iron logic of the development of capital; it is part of its historical nature. It is in its genetic code, as organic DNA for its economic and social reproduction. And the most important and highest expression of this structural violence resides in the state, the political instrument to exert repression as a form of domination of one class over another. Violence is consubstantial to capitalism, especially to the process of the development of the neoliberal savage capitalism of our day. It is true that social violence has existed since ancient times, from when society became historically divided into social classes. But it is also very true that violence unleashes its annihilating potential with capitalism. It is in this bourgeois society that historically it deploys all its destructive

energy against both humanity and nature itself. Capital is a social relation of the exploitation of one class by another. In the capital wage labor relation is the origin of all possible forms of social violence. It is the essential nucleus that detonates all the violence that has taken place ... Extreme violence is the crime, physical annihilation in its different manifestations, and genocide is the most terrible violence of extermination, among which is found state terrorism in its diverse forms. (Munguía Huato 2015: 101–2)

Drawing on Traverso's (2003) idea of violence having a genealogy, Munguía Huato (2015: 108) traces the historical development of the present violence in Mexico as a process which began in 1958 with the violent suppression of a national rail strike and reached its culmination in 1968 in Mexico City's Plaza Tlatelolco, where around 300 demonstrating students and other participants were massacred by the army and the Olympic Battalion paramilitary death squad. Revueltas (1958) describes this as a "state crime with all the impunity of the political power of a *barbaric democracy*" (in Munguía Huato 2015: 108). Also important to this genealogy of violence are Gunder Frank's (1972) notions of "lumpendevelopment" for a "lumpenbourgeoisie," as part of the "development of a lumpen underdevelopment" by a "lumpen state," similar to the contemporary idea of the "narco failed state." At the core of this lumpen narco-terrorist "failed" state is the collusion between the global institutions of capital that have imposed neoliberalism, the Mexican oligarchy, the security forces, the US state, and the cartels of organized crime, a collusion which has led to the explosion in state and social violence since 2006:

The state, in order to apply neoliberal policies that privatize public goods, to carry out its "structural reforms," requires a greater authoritarianism with its concomitant violence, and this presupposes diverse forms of repression against the dissident, oppositional working population, including the criminal practice of the forced disappearance of leftist political activists. Of course, this state violence intersects with the violence of the narcos; furthermore, the same mafia cartels are criminal experts in the practice of the forced disappearance of innocent citizens who are uninvolved in political activism. (Mungía Huato 2015: 109)

Thus the self-organizing autonomous movements and communities of the Mexican multitude have to confront one of the most violent terrorist states; a state that is determined to dispossess them of their lands, resources, public resources and services, communities, culture, freedom, rights, dignity, and even their lives. All these human attributes are up for sale to national and international enterprises, attracted to Mexico not only by the low-wage and minimal tax regime but also by a state that has historically developed for the purpose of repressing dissident leftist working-class movements and communities who struggle to defend and advance their collective interests and social needs and are therefore objectively opposed to capitalist interests.

THE CNTE'S STRUGGLE AGAINST THE 2013 EDUCATION REFORM

One of the most important movements resisting neoliberalism, dispossession, and state terrorism is the cognitariat multitude of the CNTE dissident teachers' movement. The CNTE was founded in 1979 as a separate oppositional caucus within the Sindicato Nacional de los Trabajadores de la Educación (SNTE/National Union of Educational Workers), the main teachers' union but part of the pro-capitalist, anti-worker Congreso de los Trabajadores de México (CTM/Congress of the Workers of Mexico), which has been closely allied to the PRI since it was founded in 1936 by then President Cardenas. The CNTE was part of the growing independent union movement of the late 1970s, the main form of worker opposition to the PRI authoritarian regime that had launched a "Dirty War" first against the 1968 student movement, then against the urban and rural guerrilla movements, and in general against the rural and urban proletariat. This all took place as the "economic miracle" of the 1960s ended and was replaced by the prolonged crisis of the 1970s, with growing national debt, hyperinflation, devaluation of the peso, and the collapse of oil prices and living standards. This compounded the growing legitimacy crisis of the PRI regime, which launched a "political opening" in 1977 to further split the left opposition by legalizing its most moderate sector, above all the Stalinist Mexican Communist Party (PCM).

The CNTE has been particularly strong in the poorest, least developed (in capitalist terms) and most indigenous southern states of Oaxaca, Chiapas, Guerrero, and Michoacán. From the start, it had to contend with fierce internal repression from the leadership of the SNTE, particularly from Elba Esther Gordillo, the most powerful union leader in Mexico and one of the most corrupt. Gordillo was arrested by Peña Nieto's government in early 2013 as a political move to placate his national and international critics, and certainly not to clean up the endemically corrupt pro-government unions of the CTM. Several militants of the CNTE were assassinated by Gordillo's *pistoleros* and shock groups during the 1980s and 1990s (Hernández Navarro 2011). The dissident union's most important moment came in 2006, as the largest and most important organization within the Asamblea Popular de los Pueblos de Oaxaca (APPO/Popular Assembly of the Peoples of Oaxaca) and the Oaxaca Commune. This occurred when the strike of its local branch, Section 22, and the occupation of the main square of Oaxaca City in June 2006, triggered a popular rebellion against the PRI-PAN authoritarian neoliberal regime, the first since the 1994 Zapatista uprising. Unfortunately, the rebellion was militarily crushed five months later under the orders of then PAN President Fox. The crackdown on the Frente de Pueblos por la Defensa de la Tierra (FPDT/Peoples' Front for the Defense of the Land)[12] movement against the construction of a new international airport on the communally held lands of the small rural community of San Salvador Atenco, near Mexico City, in May 2006, and that of the Oaxaca Commune in November, created the political conditions for the coming slaughter of "Calderón's War" (2006–12), followed by "Peña's War" (2013–18) (Fazio 2016).

Although many CNTE members had been arrested and some killed during the Oaxaca Commune—which ended in repression after it had forced out the particularly despotic PRI state governor, Ulises Ruiz—the CNTE grew as a social movement trade union. The union gained the solidarity and support of ample sections of the population and crucially among teachers and parents outside its historical support base. According to La Botz (2016), its growth in political influence and power has been critical in the fight against Peña Nieto's 2013 education reform, which was in reality a disguised neoliberal counter-reform of labor:

> It directly attacked the largest employment sector in Mexico, more than a million basic education teachers, among the lowest paid in the country, which in effect reduces them to second-class workers with even less rights than those still protected under the reformed 2012 Federal Labour Law. Now teachers will be forced to endure continuous control and monitoring by the state's new educational [assessment] agency the INEE.[13] The youngest teachers now face the constant threat of summary dismissal and the more experienced teachers of being reduced to bureaucrats and of losing their rights attached to the number of years of service they have accrued as teachers. This has all been done in the name of "improving" basic education (that is, preparing for privatization, uncritically copying the disaster in the USA which led to the closure of … 50 … schools in Chicago [in 2013]), and under constant international criticism and pressure from the Organization for Economic Cooperation and Development and the World Bank. (Cuninghame 2015: 245–6)

The CNTE teachers consider the compulsory annual testing to be racist and classist, as teachers in rural areas and the poorer southern states of Mexico, where the CNTE is mainly based, have far fewer resources and facilities than those who work in schools in cities and in the richer central and northern states:

> Already, the reform has had many debilitating effects for Oaxacan teachers. The most obvious are the precarious contracts and employment instability created by a standardized, nationwide evaluation, which will make it easier for teachers to be dismissed. Teachers in the states of Michoacán, Chiapas and Oaxaca have thus far largely resisted the execution of the evaluation. They defend their position by calling attention to how the reforms ignore the many cultural differences in a country as large and ethnically diverse as Mexico.

"We aren't against the evaluations," said a teacher from the rural town of Tuxtepec. "We just want it to be a fair and contextualized one, that gives us a chance." (Hess 2016)

CLASS COMPOSITION IN EDUCATION

The large number of teachers gives the CNTE tremendous potential power in the Mexican economy. To understand that power it is necessary to examine the current class composition in public education in Mexico. There are nearly 2 million education workers at all levels of the education system in Mexico, making them the largest single group of workers in Mexico and Latin America. 75.3 percent of these teachers work in basic primary and secondary education, 12.1 percent in high school education, and 12.6 percent in higher education; 62 percent are women and 38 percent are men, and 73.9 percent have degrees (Notimex 2019). Of the SNTE's 1,673,623 members, approximately 100,000 basic and high school teachers are members of the dissident CNTE. The SNTE is divided into 61 regional sections or local and state unions, all of which are corporatist (Islas 2018). The education system is controlled by the Secretario de Educación Pública (SEP or Secretary of Public Education).

The SNTE has nearly all public school employees among its membership, giving it great leverage over education policy. The official census of schools, teachers, and pupils in elementary, secondary, and special education taken in September 2013 (FLACSO Mexico 2014), found that there are 23,562,183 students served by 236,973 schools, of which 87.6 percent (207,682) are basic and special education schools serving 81.4 percent of all students. Of these, 86.4 percent of all schools are public. The Mexican education system employs 1,949,105 staff, of which 88.1 percent work in basic and special education schools, and a little more than half, 1,128,319 of the total workforce, are teachers.

The conditions of schools in Mexico are highly uneven. The survey found that only 51.6 percent of public schools have drainage for sewage, 69 percent had drinking water, 87.2 percent had toilets, and 88.8 percent were electrified, while every private school has all of these basic services. According to the SEP, the government rates

9.2 percent of these schools as "negative," which is another way of saying they are "failing," according to the US neoliberal education policy model. The states with the largest number of schools classified as "negative" were Chiapas (41 percent), Oaxaca (27.4 percent), and Michoacán (27.3 percent).

The technical composition of Mexican public education is critical to understanding the intense resistance to neoliberal education reform policy. Mexico's education system is an example of shared federalism in which the schools are partly run by the 32 states while coordinated at the federal level by the SEP. The system is composed of state schools and federal schools. The teachers in state schools only need a degree in any subject, while those in federal schools are required to have full teaching qualifications obtained at a teacher training college. This is critical because "Almost 90% of pupils enrolled at the three educational levels are studying in public institutions, which mostly depend administratively on state governments (about 70% of public schools) and the rest on the federal government" (INEE 2009: 35).

The key component of the neoliberal reform was to restructure the public education system by deskilling the teaching workforce in order to decompose the power of the organized teachers, especially CNTE, which strongly opposed this policy. The 2013 reform would no longer have required teachers to have full teaching qualifications and no longer have reserved places in the federal schools for the more qualified teachers. This measure was contrary to the recommendations of the OECD and the World Bank which promoted the need for a neoliberal reform of education on the grounds that, although Mexico has the fifteenth largest economy in the world by GDP and has a relatively large education budget, its teaching standards and educational achievement were the lowest among the 35 OECD countries. The resulting neoliberal policy was less about improving educational standards than disciplining a recalcitrant education workforce and privatizing schools.

It is also no accident that the three states with the highest percentage of so-called "failing" schools—Chiapas, Oaxaca, and Michoacán—are all in the poorer south and are the main strongholds of the CNTE. Not surprisingly, 2014, the year this survey of the condition of public education was published, marked the highpoint of the CNTE's struggle against the neoliberal education counter-reform. The classification of schools as "failing" is evidence of the way the SEP and the INEGI (Instituto Nacional de Estadistica y Geografia/National Institute for Statistics and Geography) has stigmatized these states as "failing." According to the logic of neoliberalism, this justifies targeting public education and teachers that resist repression and mass firings as targets for "reform." CNTE activists in these states faced severe repression due to organizing and strikes led by the majority of dissident teachers in states whose schools were suffering disproportionately from the lack of basic services such as toilets and electricity. The CNTE was targeted in these states because the Mexican state sees them as the main obstacle to its plan for the privatization of basic education. The CNTE teachers' power as a class agent over the classroom, schools, and curriculum is based on the fact that, according to Beltrán et al., "the most important intellectuals of a country are elementary school teachers, because they are the ones who build the capacity to learn; then, those of us on other levels, we ride on the shoulders of those giants to be able to advance the knowledge of society" (2016: 200).

The 2013 neoliberal reform attempted to introduce various anti-worker-solidarity, pro-individualist, and meritocratic measures, to the detriment of teacher and parent control of the schools and to their bargaining power and work contracts. Above all, the intention was to end the state-union pact which had long characterized the organization of education, and to remove the predominant influence of the SNTE, whose leader, Elba Esther Gordillo, was imprisoned, despite her enthusiasm for neoliberalism and its corrupt benefits, a few months before the reform was introduced. By using the unpopular and discredited image of the corrupt pro-boss SNTE, the aim was to attack the autonomous power of the dissident CNTE by first tarring it with the same brush as the SNTE, i.e. presenting it as equally corrupt and responsible for low educational standards. The second line of attack and repression was through the use of punitive teacher assessments which were used to justify mass sackings when the CNTE teachers refused to participate in the reforms. This heightened the conflict with the Peña government, leading to the Nochixtlan massacre in June 2016, and the effective shelving of the reform thereafter. However, despite being an evident political attack on workers' rights and control over the workplace, the reform also contained a plethora of neoliberal-type educational and technical changes, many of which have been incorporated into the new educational reform of September 2019 passed by AMLO, which returns to the previous state-union pact of yore and was supported by most of the Morena deputies close to the CNTE, although probably not by the CNTE rank-and-file:

> Once the political issue to be resolved was identified, the second factor to be solved were those particular problems that result in poor educational quality, identifying four: 1) the suitability of teachers and managers; 2) school infrastructure; 3) school organization, and 4) educational materials and methods. Based on these problems, the government proposed a strategy that would address each of them, resulting in, first, the professional teaching service in which income, promotion, permanence and recognition were defined by performance and not only by political or seniority factors. Secondly, the Certificados de Infraestructura Educativa Nacional (CIEN/National Educational Infrastructure Certificates) schools program was created with the purpose of addressing the problem of educational infrastructure, providing greater investment in this area and generating National Educational Infrastructure Certificates. Thirdly, the School Plan was pushed to the center, from which lines of action were derived, such as the flexible school calendar, strengthening of school technical councils, resources for schools and the promotion of full-time schools. And, fourthly, a new educational model was designed that took into account a curricular approach with a humanistic approach, focused on the development of key learning. (Faustino Zacarías 2018)

These attempted changes were all resisted as they would have decomposed teachers and parents' power by depoliticizing educational organization and by introducing individualist criteria and bourgeois values into the teacher training and educational provision service. These reforms would have removed union control over the workplace and fragmented teachers at different levels of neoliberal "performance," as well as ending teacher-parent solidarity by imposing so-called educational criteria over social class solidarity and co-organization. The new 2019 reform partially restores the CNTE's power over schools in its areas of influence, thus obtaining the support of most of the CNTE's leadership. However, the neoliberal educational assessment and organizational criteria and values still exist, continue to threaten the social and cultural base of the CNTE teachers' power, and promise yet further necessary struggle against so-called "post-neoliberal" social policy.

Since its foundation in 1979 at the end of the surge of independent unions during the 1970s, the CNTE has organized several cycles of struggle through strikes, blockades, boycotts, and marches. It has always sought to go beyond the limitations of mere unionism by allying itself with other radical working-class movements such as the Popular Metropolitan Movement during the successful strikes of 1980; with other independent unions and student movements during the actions against neoliberal structural adjustments in the 1980s; with other public sector workers and mass revolutionary movements such as APPO in 2006; and with armed self-defense organizations such as the Community Police in the state of Guerrero during the first decade of the millennium. During the cycle of struggles between 2013 and 2016 the CNTE allied itself with an even broader range of autonomous movements and independent unions seeking to unshackle themselves from undemocratic and sometimes corrupt leadership (Márquez 2013).

As a result of this experience the CNTE's forms of organization have been close to the theoretical model of the multitude proposed by Hardt and Negri and Virno. It is an illustration of the new form of the autonomous working class in struggle, always looking for alliances with other grassroots struggles to go beyond its immediate class composition. In doing so, it seeks to short circuit the authoritarian regime's use of corrupt corporatist union leadership combined with state terrorism to maintain the Mexican working class in a state of permanent repression and division.

This process of class composition, decomposition, and recomposition was best illustrated by the battle and massacre of Nochixtlan. In June 2016 the entire population of this small town blockaded the main road between Oaxaca City and Mexico City and repulsed several armed attacks by the federal police and gendarmes, who used helicopters to drop tear gas on hospitals and schools, resulting in the death of eight people, none of whom were teachers, and injury to 226 more. The CNTE's struggle had spread to the entire multitude, who were determined to halt the neoliberal counter-reform and defend their school system and their relationship of co-organization with dissident autonomous teachers. This struggle occurred in three phases which will be explored in detail.

THREE PHASES OF THE STRUGGLE

In the first phase, the CNTE declared a national mobilization against the reform in August 2013 to disrupt the start of the school year. The most militant teachers gathered in Mexico City to occupy the Zocalo, the symbolic main square, where they remained until mid-September, converting it into a tent city. Discussions and meetings took place in the tent city to explain to the public why they were taking action, since the media, with very few exceptions, are pro-government and simply amplified its propaganda about "lazy," "irresponsible" teachers.

The CNTE was also building an alliance with the student movements of UNAM and UAM, the two main state universities, during this phase. Neoliberal business interest groups like Mexicanos Primeros (Mexicans First), led by Claudio X. Gonzalez, an entrepreneur close to President Peña Nieto, placed advertisements in the media demanding the government repress the movement and arrest the leadership of the CNTE. Their ire was further raised by the daily marches that left the Zocalo main square to picket government offices, also blockading the main avenues of the city center, causing significant disruption and impacting the economy, forcing the government to negotiate. Strikes were only used later in 2016 and only in the southern state and CNTE bastion of Oaxaca. However, the regime changed track without warning in September, and the PRD mayor of Mexico City, an ally of Peña Nieto, ordered the violent clearance of the Zocalo by riot police, leading to dozens of arrests.

The second phase consisted of creating a new but smaller mass open-air occupation and tent city, this time in the Plaza de la

Republica, built to celebrate the Mexican Revolution. Circulating the struggle, teachers flocked there in solidarity from all over Mexico, including from states, particularly in the more conservative north, where the CNTE was not previously strong. This time the teachers covered their tents with photos of the terrible state of many schools, particularly in the poorer rural areas where buildings either did not exist or were missing walls or roofs or concrete floors, while others had no toilets, desks, or chairs. Money budgeted by the Secretary of Public Education simply never arrived. The gendered nature of the movement became increasingly clear as the majority of the occupiers were women teachers who had introduced a system whereby they could continue to protest while regularly returning to their regions to be with their families and work in their schools.

This phase lasted from late 2013 well into 2014, when the CNTE, along with the more radical social movement sector and the activist base (but not the centrist leadership) of Morena, had to switch their attention to the worst act of state terrorism since the "Dirty War" of the 1970s. On September 26, 2014, three students from the Ayotzinapa rural teacher training college and three others were killed—probably by a combination of the local and federal police, the army, and the PRD-linked Guerreros Unidos drug cartel—in Iguala, Guerrero, one of the most violent states. At the same time, 43 other students were shot at, dragged from buses, and forcibly disappeared by the same state and parastatal elements. They have remained disappeared for the last five years despite a powerful national and international movement, led by the parents of the disappeared students, which effectively destroyed the legitimacy of the Peña government, one of the most corrupt as well as violent in Mexican history, and so considerably helped AMLO's landslide electoral victory in 2018, although the parents have always maintained their autonomy from all political parties.

This massacre and mass disappearance provoked one of the most important mass mobilizations in recent Mexican history, which included the CNTE. Its principal demand, apart from the immediate reappearance of "The 43" alive, was the resignation and impeachment of Peña Nieto, considered responsible for this and several other state crimes. While it failed to achieve this, it certainly destroyed Peña Nieto's international image as the "democratic reformer" that

Time (2014), and other mass media and neoliberal governments, had carefully contrived. The Coordinadora Estatal de Trabajadores de la Educación en Guerrero (CETEG/State Coordination of Educational Workers in Guerrero)—a radical dissident teachers' movement in Guerrero which has recently united with the CNTE—played a prominent role, along with students from the Ayotzinapa college, in direct actions against the Guerrero state government, which helped to bring down its corrupt PRD governor, Angel Aguirre, who was strongly suspected of complicity in the Iguala massacre. Peña Nieto became the most unpopular president in Mexican history and the head of a lame duck government, weak and vacillating before Trump's open racism against Mexican and Central American migrants (Hoosten 2016).

The third phase of the CNTE's struggle took place between May and September 2016, consisting of a national strike and the occupation of another important square in Mexico City, with extensive use of marches, pickets, and blockades, including of motorway toll booths, again in alliance with the student movement (Dillingham and González Pizarro 2016). Among the CNTE's demands was that the government cancel the much-hated *evaluaciones* (punitive assessments) (Aboites 2016).

The main innovation of these three phases was the organization of three National Forums on Education, to which a wide variety of experts, militants, activists, and intellectuals, not necessarily in agreement with the CNTE, were invited to speak as a valid alternative to the government's heavily criticized and rejected educational reform. In June, many working-class parents, along with teachers, occupied some 300 primary and secondary schools throughout the country in protest, often on their own initiative rather than that of the teachers.

Once again the government resorted to state terrorism to repress this growing and increasingly radical national movement. This time the repression was instigated by a new SEP minister who publicly committed himself to forcing all teachers to undergo assessment and conducted mass dismissals in Oaxaca and Chiapas, the main centers of the movement. Several state leaders of the CNTE were arrested and absurdly charged with money laundering and organized crime, activities more usually associated with the PRI. The culmination of the Mexicanos Primeros-instigated state repression and media vilification of the teachers and their working-class supporters came with the massacre in Nochixtlan in June 2016, a town situated on the main route to Oaxaca City, which the local population had blockaded in solidarity with the CNTE. The PAN-PRD governor of Oaxaca, Gabino Cue, invited the federal government to send heavily armed police and gendarmes to attack and clear the blockade. The police opened fire on the demonstrators and then began a manhunt throughout the town, using helicopters to drop tear gas on homes, schools, and hospitals. At least eight people were killed (Resumen Latinoamericano y del Tercer Mundo 2016). Nochixtlan is the latest of 16 massacres of unarmed civilians by federal, state, and municipal police, the army, the gendarmes, the Marines and/or by organized crime cartels since January 2010.

However, this tactic of using state terrorism to intimidate and pacify opposition and force through neoliberal structural reforms following the 2008 global economic crisis has proved to be a failure. Levels of popular mobilization remain high, as was shown by the widespread protests and vociferous opposition, including by the normally conservative and passive middle classes, to the *gasolinazo* (over 20 percent hike in gasoline prices) in January 2017 (Rangel and María 2017).

In September 2016, following the Nochixtlan massacre, some state leaders of the CNTE made opaque deals with local state governments, after returning to work without having gained concessions from the government. These under-the-table deals were made over the heads of the CNTE members and without respecting the assembly and direct participation methods of decision making. As a result, the leaders forced their members back to work at the beginning of the school year without having gained any major concessions from the government on the punitive assessments. The more authoritarian and corrupt aspects of Mexican trade union culture, including the more politically independent sector, are dying hard even in the CNTE (Dillingham and González Pizarro 2016).

On the other hand, the CNTE has successfully resisted any attempt by Morena or other center-left parties to opportunistically ride their electoralist tigers, and has remained autonomous from all political parties. Morena and AMLO cozied up to the CNTE during the electoral campaign of 2018, but once in power soon switched their allegiance to the notoriously corrupt SNTE, even releasing Gordillo from prison to resume her control of the union. Contrary to AMLO's promise during the election campaign to completely repeal the reforms, in May 2019 the Morena government forced through a new education reform which was described by critics as being 80 percent the same as Peña Nieto's, partially maintaining the hated punitive assessments and plans for the eventual privatization of basic education.

Although the exact details of the new reform are, perhaps deliberately, unclear, the aim continues to be to impose a special labor regime on teachers. Teachers have been a central target of the state, compared to other sectors of the working class and the public sector, due to the historical legacy of the radical teachers who founded some of the guerrilla groups of the 1960s, such as teacher Lucio Cabañas's Partido de los Pobres (Party of the Poor). Teachers leading the main opposition to neoliberal state terrorism continue to be seen as a class threat which must be carefully managed and surveyed through "testing," while smoothing the path for the privatization of a vital and highly lucrative public service for business interests such as Mexicanos Primeros.

Nevertheless, it has to be said that where state terrorism failed, duplicitous populism seems to have prevailed. While AMLO may have won this round, the CNTE have said they will oppose any attempts to reimpose punitive assessments or privatize education with the same highly effective tactics they used against Peña Nieto.

CONCLUSION

This chapter has focused on the struggle of the CNTE against Peña Nieto's educational counter-reform as an important example of the Mexican multitude's capacity to resist the attempts by the oligarchy and its political class to force through unpopular neoliberal policies using state terrorism. However, the collapse of the PRI-PAN *ancien regime* at the polls in 2018 resulted in the dramatic rise of Morena, a new centrist political party legitimized by the 53 percent vote it received. As party leader and president, AMLO has proven to be a charismatic populist who declared neoliberalism dead in March 2019 while simultaneously pursuing "austericide" neoliberal policies. This poses even greater challenges.

The CNTE offers a combative example of an urban and rural working class—the cognitarian and proletarian singularities of the multitude—who are able to articulate their struggles locally, nationally, and globally to thwart the most violent efforts of an authoritarian state. The next phase of the struggle, now against Mexico's first legitimately elected democratic but still authoritarian neoliberal government,[14] will test the CNTE, the Zapatistas, and other self-organized autonomous movements of the multitude to a far greater extent.

NOTES

1. A neo-conservative clerical party with fascist origins.
2. An authoritarian neo-conservative party with "post-revolutionary" origins.
3. A center-left party founded by AMLO and registered as a political party in 2014 following a split from the neoliberal centrist Revolutionary Democratic Party (PRD) in 2012.
4. A dissident left caucus inside and against the corrupt corporatist SNTE (National Union of Educational Workers).
5. It was formed in December 2012 and dominated by the PRI and the PAN, while including the PRD and the PVEM (Partido Verde Ecologico Mexicano/Mexican Green Ecological Party) as junior partners.
6. Used to describe pro-business corporatist unions with government-appointed leaders, after one 1950s-era union leader who liked to dress as a traditional *charro* cowboy.
7. A centrist neoliberal, formerly center-left party, formed in 1989 from the national-popular Cardenist wing of the PRI and the ex-Mexican Communist Party.
8. According to Negri and Cocco (2006), the Latin American neoliberal state (and those of other similarly "semi-peripheral" regions such as China, India, and Russia) is counterintuitively "neofeudal" since its oligarchies and elites continue to use feudal strategies of violent wealth concentration and authoritarian state development. This was first identified by dependency theory as a consequence of the failure to develop a properly capitalist mode of production after independence in the early nineteenth century. In the twenty-first century, elites have returned to what can now be called "neofeudalism" after attempts at democratization and even "progressive post-neoliberalism" in Brazil and Argentina.

9. A regional development organization of the United Nations founded in 1948 against the wishes of the US government.
10. All translations are mine.
11. For the uprising in San Salvador Atenco near Mexico City see footnote 12. Ostula and Cheran are two indigenous communities in the state of Michoacan which set up forms of directly democratic self-government and armed self-defense in 2009 and 2011 respectively, involving the expulsion of all political parties and the police, along with organized crime cartels who are considered to be in collusion with local authorities as a result of their attempts to deprive those communities of any access to or control over their natural resources such as forests and unspoilt beaches, respectively.
12. The FPDT was created in 2001 in the small town of San Salvador Atenco where the majority of the land is collectively owned. Despite severe repression in 2006, it is still campaigning against the new international airport near Lake Texcoco first proposed by President Fox in 2001 and then by Peña Nieto in 2013, and which was finally cancelled to the dismay of international investors and neo-liberal ratings agencies like Standard and Poor's. The cancellation followed a disputed consultation organized in September 2018 by AMLO, who prefers to build the airport in Santa Lucia where a community-based anti-airport movement similar to the FPDT is also organizing.
13. The Instituto Nacional por la Evaluación de la Educación (INEE/National Institute for the Assessment of Education) was established by the neo-conservative President Vicente Fox in 2002. It was used by the 2013 Education Reform Act with the main objective of introducing the punitive annual assessment of teachers in basic education to "justify" the arbitrary dismissals of hundreds of dissident CNTE and radical left teachers. It was abolished by the 2019 Education Reform—a victory for the CNTE—and has been replaced by the Centro Nacional para la Revalorización del Magisterio (National Center for the Reevaluation of Teachers), which, however, maintains the potential to reintroduce punitive assessments of teachers.
14. At least 20 environmental and political activists, community leaders, and critical journalists were murdered by paramilitary death squads or narco hitmen during the first half of 2019, an increase since 2018. Furthermore, the AMLO government has massively and provocatively increased military patrols of Zapatista areas in Chiapas.

REFERENCES

Aboites, H. (2016). Evaluación: 100 años de devastación. *Ponencia en el Foro del CNTE sobre la Reforma Educativa* (August 9). At https://cnteseccion9.wordpress.com/2016/08/14/ponencia-hugo-aboites-en-el-foro-9-de-agosto-2016/#_ftn1.

Agamben, G. (2005). *State of Exception*. Chicago: University of Chicago Press.

Amnesty International (2017) *Amnesty International Report 2016–17: The State of the World's Human Rights*. London: Amnesty International.

Beltrán, M.R., Ordorika, I., Gil, M. and Rodríguez, R. (2016). Reforma educativa y evaluación docente: el debate. *Perfiles Educativos* 38(151), 190–206.

Benjamin, W. (1986). Critique of Violence. In *Reflections: Essays, Aphorisms, Autobiographical Writings*. New York: Schocken Books.

Berardi, F. (2016). The Coming Global Civil War: Is There Any Way out? *e-flux* 69. At www.e-flux.com/journal/69/60582/the-coming-global-civil-war-is-there-any-way-out.

Calderón, L.Y., Heinle, K., Rodríguez Ferreira, O., and Shirk, D. A. (2019). Organized Crime and Violence in Mexico. Analysis through 2018. *Justice in Mexico*, Department of Political Science and International Relations, University of San Diego, CA.

Cuninghame, P. (2015). Self-Management, Workers' Control and Resistance Against Crisis and Neoliberal Counter-Reforms in Mexico. In Azzellini, D. (ed.), *An Alternative Labour History: Worker Control and Workplace Democracy*. London: Zed Books, pp. 242–72.

Dillingham A. and González Pizarro, R. (2016). Mexico's Classroom Wars. *Jacobin* 24. At www.jacobinmag.com/2016/06/mexico-teachers-union-cnte-snte-oaxaca-nieto-zapatistas-strike.

Faustino Zacarías, O.H. (2018). La reforma educativa de 2013 y lo que está por venir. *Nexos* (September 26). At https://educacion.nexos.com.mx/?p=1520.

Fazio, C. (2016). *Estado de emergencia: de la Guerra de Calderón a la Guerra de Peña Nieto*. Mexico City: Grijalbo.

FLACSO Mexico (2014). Presenta INEGI resultados del Censo de Escuelas, Maestros y Alumnos de Educación Básica y Especial. *FLACSO México*. At www.flacso.edu. mx/noticias/Presenta-INEGI-resultados-del-Censo-de-Escuelas-Maestros-y-Alumnos-de-Educacion-Basica-y.

Gunder Frank, A. (1972). *Lumpenbourgeoisie, lumpendevelopment*. New York: Monthly Review Press.

Hardt, M. and Negri, A. (2004). *Multitude: War and Democracy in the Age of Empire*. New York: Penguin.

Hardt, M. and Negri, A. (2009). *Commonwealth*. Cambridge, MA: The Belknap Press of Harvard University Press.

Harvey, D. (2003). *The New Imperialism*. Oxford: Oxford University Press.

Hernández Navarro, L. (2011). *Cero en conducta. Crónicas de la resistencia magisterial*. Mexico City: Fundación Rosa Luxemburg and Para Leer en Libertad A.C.

Hess, S. (2016). Oaxaca's Teachers Movement Not Thwarted By State Terror. *Common Dreams* (June 27). At www.commondreams.org/views/2016/06/27/oaxacas-teachers-movement-not-thwarted-state-terror.

Holloway, J. (2002). *Change the World Without Taking Power: The Meaning of Revolution Today*. London: Pluto.

Hoosten, J. (2016). The "Colossal Failure" of Trump's Mexico Visit. *Politico* (September 3). At www.politico.eu/article/the-colossal-failure-of-donald-trumps-mexico-visit-wall-immigration-nieto

Human Rights Watch (2019). Mexico Events of 2018. *World Report 2019*. At www.hrw.org/world-report/2019/country-chapters/mexico.

INEE/Instituto Nacional por la Evaluación de la Educación (National Institute for the Assessment of Education) (2009). Panorama Educativo de México 2009. At www.inee.edu.mx/wp-content/uploads/2019/04/2009_Ciclo2008-.pdf.

Islas, L. (2018). ¿Cuántos integrantes tiene el SNTE? UNiÓN, *El Universal* (February 26). At www.unioncdmx.mx/articulo/2018/02/26/educacion/cuantos-i ntegrantes-tiene-el-snte.

Klein, N. (2007). *The Shock Doctrine: The Rise of Disaster Capitalism*. Toronto: Random House of Canada.

La Botz, D. (2016). Mexican Teachers' Long History of Struggle for Democracy. *Mexican Labor News & Analysis* 21(7). At www.ueinternational.org/MLNA/ mlna_articles.php?id=247.

Márquez, C. (2013). El magisterio mexicano y su larga trayectoria de lucha. *In Defense of Marxism* (October 1). At www.marxist.com/el-magisterio-mexicano-y-su-larga-trayectoria-de-lucha.htm.

Munguía Huato, R. (2015). Desaparecidos. Violencia, impunidad y terror del estado, "México es una fosa clandestina." In Aguilar Mora, M. and Albertani, C. (eds.), *La noche de Iguala y el despertar de México. Textos, imágenes y poemas contra la barbarie*. Mexico City: Juan Pablos Editor, pp. 99–122.

Negri, A. and Cocco, G. (2006). *Global: Biopoder y luchas en una América Latina globalizada*. Buenos Aires: Paidós.

Notimex (2019). ¿Cuántos maestros hay en México? *La Silla Rota* (May 15). At https://lasillarota.com/nacion/cuantos-maestros-hay-en-mexico/285281.

Rangel, L. and María, E. (2017). Mexico's *Gasolinazo. Jacobin* (January 23). At www.jacobinmag.com/2017/01/mexico-gasolinazo-amlo-nieto-pri-morena-prd.

Resumen Latinoamericano y del Tercer Mundo (2016). 12 muertos, 25 desaparecidos y decenas de heridos por represión en Oaxaca/Se extienden las protestas de maestros en otros Estados. *Resumen Latinoamericano y del Tercer Mundo* (June 20). At www.resumenlatinoamericano.org/2016/06/20/van-8-muertos-22-desaparecidos-y-decenas-de-heridos-por-represion-en-oaxaca.

Revueltas, J. (1958). *México: una democracia bárbara*. Mexico City: Ediciones Era.

Shukaitis, S. (2008). Dancing Amidst the Flames: Imagination and Self-Organization in a Minor Key. In Bonefeld, W. (ed.), *Subverting the Present, Imagining the Future: Insurrection, Movement, Commons*. New York: Autonomedia, pp. 99–113.

Telesur (2019). Mexico: Homicides in First Half of 2019 Reach Record Numbers. *Telesur* (July 24). At www.telesurenglish.net/news/Mexico-Murders-in-First-Half-of-2019-Reach-Record-Numbers-20190724-0029.html.

Time (2014). The Committee to Save Mexico. *Time* (February 13). At http://time.com/7058/the-committee-to-save-mexico.

Traverso, E. (2003). *The Origins of Nazi Violence*. New York: The New Press.

6

Notes from Below: A Brief Survey of Class Composition in the UK

Callum Cant, Sai Englert, Lydia Hughes, Wendy Liu,
Achille Marotta, Seth Wheeler, and Jamie Woodcock

Notes from Below is a workers' inquiry project that we, as authors and editors, have been involved with in the UK since the start of 2018. This piece is collectively written by the editors of the journal, drawing on our previous work, as well as that of our co-authors. As we have stated in the publication:

> We draw our methods and theory from the class composition tradition, which seeks to understand and change the world from the worker's point of view. We want to ground revolutionary politics in the perspective of the working class, help circulate and develop struggles, and build workers' confidence to take action by and for themselves. (*Notes from Below* 2019)

A part of this has been attempting to update and rearticulate workers' inquiry as a method. This has involved us seeking to write about and with groups of workers that we have already been in contact with. Since the start of 2018, we have increasingly come into contact with other authors—both workers and researchers of various kinds. The process has therefore involved a survey of the changing class composition in the UK, albeit weighted towards examples that we have already been active around—or the most visible examples, mostly focused on London.

We situate our analysis of these surveys as learning from and updating the class composition tradition. Class composition has its roots in Italian Workerism, but has been updated in various ways for today (Woodcock 2017, 2019; *Notes from Below* 2018a; Cant 2019). In this sense, class composition is tied to workers' inquiry, as a practice of both research and organizing. Workers' inquiry has a longer history, starting with Marx (1880) and his famous postal study, while it was later developed by Italian Workerists from the 1960s. Class composition is a framework for making sense of workers' inquiries, putting theory into critical conversation with the experiences of workers. Broadly speaking, it is a theory of how classes are composed—and decomposed—under capitalism. The earlier formulation interrogates the technical composition (that is the organization of work) and the relationship to political composition (forms of workers' struggles). At *Notes from Below*, we have expanded the framework to include a third dimension of social composition. Class composition is therefore comprised of:

a material relation with three parts: the first is the organisation of labour-power into a working class (technical composition); the second is the organisation of the working class into a class society (social composition); the third is the self-organisation of the working class into a force for class struggle (political composition). (*Notes from Below* 2018a)

We use this threefold analysis of class composition in this chapter to make sense of the inquiries featured in *Notes from Below*.

Before getting into these different inquiries, it is first worth sketching out the overall contours of class composition in the UK. The UK labor market is marked, broadly speaking, by low official unemployment, low wages, and low productivity. This has even been remarked on with the emergence of a productivity paradox following the 2008 financial crisis. Despite the introduction of new technologies and more workers into employment, productivity remains low. Despite this, there remain large areas of absolute surplus value extraction—alongside the continuing dominance of global finance in London. Since 2008, the public sector has been under sustained assault of austerity, shrinking the size of the workforce, and intensifying the work of those that remain. The most recent years have been shaped by uncertainty around Brexit, with a continuing certainty of an intensified border regime and continuing exploitation of migrant workers—with or without legal papers. Official levels of trade union organizing have trended downward, with density standing at 23.4 percent (13.2 percent in the private sector and 52.5 percent in the public sector) (BEIS 2019). It is from this context that we have started these inquiries to make sense of class composition at different points across the economy.

This chapter is therefore divided into six sections. The first is education (including higher education—in which a significant part of the editorial board is based) but is not limited to just teachers or academics; second, platform capitalism, covering the gig economy in food delivery and transportation; third, hospitality, focusing on service work in restaurants and bars; fourth, the tech industry and videogames; and fifth, housing, as part of social composition. We then conclude the chapter by reflecting on the changing class composition in the UK from these examples, along with future predictions.

SECTOR ONE: EDUCATION

The first sector in which we have conducted sustained inquiries, analysis, and organizing is education. Jamie and Sai work as university researchers, Callum is a PhD student, Achille is an English language teacher, and the trade union that Lydia works for organizes within this sector. This has meant the editorial board is close to the sector, with inquiries being an ongoing part of the board members' engagement with their own work. This makes the co-research particularly close, as these are mainly inquiries led by workers "from below," rather than instigated from the outside, or "from above."

The education sector as a whole had the highest union density of any sector in the UK in 2018 at 47.6 percent, with 48.4 percent of workers covered by a collective bargaining agreement (BEIS 2019). However, there are important differences in this sector. Education is broadly divided into three different parts in the UK. First, school education, which covers the 5–16 age range and is available for free (apart from the option of private, paid-for education that represents around 6.5–7 percent). Second, further education, which covers colleges (16–18 years old) and other continuing education and private provision (which we will not discuss in this section). The third is higher education, mostly university provision for undergraduate and postgraduate education.

The first aspect of class composition that we want to cover in this section concerns academics in higher education. In 2018, the University and College Union (UCU) engaged in fourteen days of strike action over changes to the pension plan covering a portion of universities in the UK. Higher education, like much of the public sector in the UK, is in the throes of widespread transformation, from the introduction of tuition fees in 1998—which was not met with widespread opposition—to the tripling of fees in 2010—which was met with a wave of mass student demonstrations and limited strike action. Since then, academic pay has fallen annually, with a series of unsuccessful instances of industrial action. However, in 2018, the union prepared for serious industrial action to oppose changes to the pension scheme. It was the largest higher education strike in a generation, involving 42,000 academic and non-academic workers in 64 different universities striking for fourteen days. We intervened regularly into the dispute as *Notes from Below* through the *The University Worker* bulletin, making arguments for different tactics and strategy (Woodcock and Englert 2018).

The strikes in higher education—or more accurately, parts of higher education—ended in neither defeat nor victory. The UCU membership accepted a deal by ballot that essentially froze the dispute, proposing a year-long investigation by a joint expert panel. At the time of writing this year is over, with no further details about what will happen to the campaign. The pension dispute was followed by a strike ballot over pay, precarity, and equality. However, this ballot failed to meet the legal threshold of 50 percent for a vote turnout. One reading of this is that many members are more concerned about (and prepared to take action over) pensions than they are about the demands that many younger/early career and minority academics have been organizing for. Another reading might be that risking another strike and lost wages with the existing union leadership did not look like a good bargain. The union then held a leadership election. The incumbent general secretary (the only one the union had ever had) was unseated in a surprise victory for an activist from the pension campaign. However, as Sai Englert has pointed out, while Jo Grady's election is clearly a success, it also points to another problem:

> the lack of any real rank and file movement within the UCU. Indeed, despite the repeated description of Grady as a rank and file candidate on social media by her supporters, this is not an accurate depiction of the situation … there is no organised rank and file in the UCU and all attempts to form one since last year's strike have failed to attract more than the usual suspects. (Englert 2019)

The union has previously been dominated by two factions. The first is the Independent Broad Left—which is neither "independent, broad, or on the left. The IBL is a Communist Party led, highly conservative faction in the union that has consistently opposed industrial action or confrontation with employers or the government" (Englert 2019). The other is the existing UCU Left which has failed to relate to new layers of activists from previous disputes. Beyond these bureaucratic shifts in the union, there have been moments of potential rank-and-file organizing within and beyond the union. Grady's election offers the potential to open up spaces in which this kind of organizing could bloom, but this risks taking agency away from the academic workers fighting against local managers still set on a privatization agenda in higher education.

The second part of the sector involves other workers on academic campuses. In particular, the struggles of cleaners in central London has provided an important example of precarious migrant workers successfully organizing, as well as an inspirational example for academic workers (Woodcock 2014). The Independent Workers Union of Great Britain (IWGB) started in 2012 as a breakaway from the mainstream trade union Unison at Senate House, University of London. The branch was comprised of Spanish-speaking Latin American migrants fighting against outsourcing. Due to the proximity of these struggles to both students and academic workers, the union has drawn in a layer of activists who have engaged in militant trade unionism alongside cleaners. The IWGB organizes strike action with vibrant picket lines (something of a rarity in the UK), as well as targeting outsourcing companies outside the workplace with protests. The union brought together these different sections of workers and students, acting as a point of recomposition separate from the crushing bureaucracy of the mainstream trade unions, while also bringing vibrant traditions of organizing from Latin America. The role of the IWGB in providing a focus for unorganized or so-called "unorganizable" workers has since spread out from the university, which will be covered in subsequent sections.

SECTOR TWO: PLATFORM CAPITALISM

The sectors of food delivery and taxi transportation have been significantly transformed in the UK in recent years. While this has been most marked in London, it has also spread across major cities. This sector, which we call here platform capitalism, has been a focus of *Notes from Below* since the launch of the journal. Following higher education, this is the next closest sector to the editorial board. Jamie has been engaging in inquiries with platform workers since 2016, Callum worked for Deliveroo (which has been written up in Cant 2019), Achille has organized with UberEats riders, as has Lydia both directly and through the IWGB. There are no comparable statistics about trade union membership for this sector, as the platform companies claim not to employ any drivers, instead relying on the bogus self-employment categorization of independent contractor status.

Despite this lack of trade union data, platforms have been an important site of struggle in the UK since 2016. The strikes of Deliveroo workers in London (Woodcock 2016) were a powerful and visible example of how such workers can organize across the city and take coordinated strike action. While there were claims at the time that this new technical composition of work would make it either too hard or impossible to organize, workers found new ways to resist. A layer of the activists from this first strike reached out to the IWGB, having seen the recent successes of bicycle couriers campaigns, and formed a branch of the union. Deliveroo workers published a regular bulletin called *The Rebel Roo* (2016), an archive of which can be found at *Notes from Below*. Following that action, there was a strike wave in food delivery platforms across Europe, with "three sporadic peaks of mobilization ... the first [in] summer 2016, the second [in] spring 2017, and the third [in] winter 2017" (Cant 2018a).

In the UK, the campaign became locked into a long-running legal dispute over employment status. A similar process has unfolded with Uber drivers, who began organizing almost as soon as UberX had been launched in London. Uber drivers first formed the London Private Hire App Based Drivers Association (LPHADA) in 2014, later joining the large mainstream union GMB in 2015, which led to the forming of United Private Hire Drivers (UPHD) in the GMB. They left in 2017 to join the IWGB as an autonomous branch.

These networks clearly show that any claim that platforms prevent workers from meeting and organizing is misguided. The lack of employment status prevents the recognition of a union, but it also stops anti-trade union legislation being used to prevent action by these workers. Platforms have not been prepared to negotiate with workers at all (as this risks making it look like they are engaging in an employment relationship), so there is little ability to contain or mitigate workplace struggles. The use of social media, both in local organizing on WhatsApp as well as international connections, has also accelerated the circulation of struggles. For example, in 2018, food platform workers from 12 countries and 34 organizations met in Brussels for the founding meeting of the Transnational Federation of Couriers (*Notes from Below* 2018b).

The result has been an explosive growth of workers' struggles in the platform economy. For example, in 2018 UberEats riders went on strike over a shift in payment rates that meant earnings for a delivery would drop from around £4.26 to £2.62. In just over two years following the Deliveroo strikes, there were actions in Bristol, Leeds, Brighton, Cardiff, Glasgow, Plymouth, and Southampton. There was also strike action in central London in September 2018 (Cant and Hughes 2018). This was then followed up with strikes organized with the Industrial Workers of the World (IWW), limited to local areas in London and across the country. This was "a potential mutation of the tactics, spreading the action wider as drivers actively picket and build the strike across what is effectively their workplace," often outside the busy McDonalds (Hughes and Tippet 2018). The same month, this was followed by the UPHD, now a branch of IWGB, calling a 24-hour strike at Uber in London, Nottingham, and Birmingham. Unlike the previous action, this was not a defensive action. Instead, workers went on strike to demand an increase of fares to £2 per mile, and that Uber reduce its commission to 15 percent, end unfair deactivations and bullying, and respect workers rights (Woodcock and Hughes 2018). This highly visible action—accompanied by a call for users to respect the digital picket line by not using the app—fed into the internationally coordinated action, including strikes and protests, in the run up to Uber's IPO.

We have focused on platform workers for two key reasons. First, platforms act as a capitalist laboratory in which new techniques of management, algorithmic control, worker exploitation, and extraction of value are experimented with and tested (Cant 2019). If successful, these are likely to be exported into other sectors. Second, these are important examples of workers experimenting with new forms of organizing—with relevance not just for workers in these sectors. The recent popular attention that the platform economy has received has meant that many of these stories of worker resistance are now being documented. In this light, Callum and Jamie have argued that "we need to stop talking about resistance as emerging in platform work," and instead start an analysis based on the evidence that:

> Resistance is clearly already happening, from Deliveroo riders in London, Uber drivers in Bangalore, to Meituan workers in Guangzhou. A working class recomposition is rapidly under way. The key question now is understanding what forms of struggle can be successful beyond the short term and how these can be generalised more widely by the working class, both logging off platforms and breaking away from capitalism more broadly. (Cant and Woodcock 2019)

SECTOR THREE: HOSPITALITY

The UK hospitality sector (which includes hotels, pubs, restaurants, and so on) expresses some of the most profound symptoms of a wider working-class decomposition. In 2016, trade union membership in the sector hit rock bottom, with density reaching just 2.5 percent—the lowest of any sector in the UK economy. This compares to retail, which has a similar technical composition in many ways, with an overall density of 11.9 percent. Overall, trade unions were present in 30.5 percent of workplaces and 14.7 percent of workers were covered by collective bargaining agreements. However, there has been a slight recovery in hospitality over the last few years. Membership in the sector has risen slightly from 40,000 in 2017 to 49,000 in 2018, with 3.3 percent of workers in the sector belonging to trade unions. A similar 3.5 percent of employees had their wages and conditions impacted by a negotiated agreement between their employer and a union. Perhaps most revealingly, trade unionists were only present in 9.6 percent of workplaces, meaning that in the other 90 percent, not a single worker was a member of a union (BEIS 2019).

Trade union membership is, of course, not an exact measure of working-class self-organization. Like in the platform capitalism sector, workers can rely on predominantly non-union forms and still take very significant collective action. But in hospitality, that scenario remains highly optimistic. Despite a technical composition characterized by long and precarious hours, low pay, work intensification, severe disciplinary control, and rampant harassment, workers in the sector largely rely on individual resistance strategies such as skiving (missing work), stock shrinkage (stealing from work), and turnover rather than collective forms of organization (see Mullholland 2004).

However, new opportunities also arise from changes in the technical composition. For example, Wetherspoons has transformed the British pub through the centralization of capital, creating bigger and more connected workplaces. Rather than the individual landlord who is either an owner or rents from a brewery, Wetherspoons operates a chain of 900 pubs across the UK. As workers explained in the first issue of *The Spoons Striker*:

It can be hard to live on the money we make. We spend most of our wages on renting damp flats, we have to walk to work when we can't afford the bus, and we have to choose between dinner and a haircut. We're forced to work as fast as we can for long shifts with barely any breaks, even when we're sick or injured. We've seen the people we work with struggling to make ends meet, sofa surfing and scraping by. Meanwhile, Tim Martin [the owner] is worth £322 million. Our work has made him, the bosses, and the shareholders rich beyond our wildest dreams, but we're left a few weeks' pay away from poverty. We won't take it anymore. That's why we're fighting back. (The Spoons Striker 2018)

While there have been struggles of pub workers before, the centralization of capital in the pub sector driven by Wetherspoons has greatly increased the opportunities for workers to self-organize. Building on this, over the past two years we have seen visible examples of a counter-tendency emerging within the sector. For example, in September 2018, there were strikes at Uber/UberEats, Deliveroo, Wetherspoons, McDonalds, and TGI Fridays.

Across these different workplaces there were a range of unions involved, "from huge Labour Party and TUC [Trade Union Congress] affiliates Unite, to small Labour Party and TUC affiliates the Bakers Food and Allied Workers' Union (BFAWU), to the syndicalist IWW and grassroots IWGB" (Cant 2018b). Each of these represents a different political composition, both in organizing practices and perspectives. As Cant has observed, the BFAWU McDonalds campaign, "the McStrike model," has been closely modelled on the Service Employees International Union's "Fight for $15" campaign in the US. This campaign was translated in the UK into union recognition at £10 per hour. In practice, this has meant a centralized team of paid staff, the orientation of strike efforts towards media representation, and the calling out of only a very small number of workplaces on strike. The focus here is on what Beverly Silver (2003) calls "associational power" rather than "structural power." This narrows the scope of the campaign, while also not leading to the systematic organizing of workers at McDonalds—indeed workers' agency remains mostly in the background. Cant contrasts this model with that of the "Couriers Network" used by IWW (see Fear 2018), in which networks of workers are supported by external trade unionists.

What can be lost in the critique of mainstream trade union organizing are the processes through which these campaigns are started. For example, workers at the international chain TGI Fridays began organizing in response to changes in how tips were handled at the restaurants. Workers in the "test" restaurant that trialed the new payment system were able to find other workers through Facebook to start organizing against the changes. Without union experience, they started agitating for a strike and then reached out to BFAWU. However, once that happened they increasingly lost control of their campaign. After joining BFAWU, they were then quickly incorporated into the much larger Unite, which has not shown a willingness to continue supporting the campaign. However, what this highlights is that beyond the general low level of visible resistance and trade union organizing in the sector, there are likely to be many of these initial conversations, starting of WhatsApp groups, and searching for potential allies on Facebook happening across the country, even if these may not lead to a strike like those discussed above. The key question is whether the changes in the technical composition outlined here are laying the basis for a more disruptive political recomposition on a larger scale.

SECTOR FOUR: TECH INDUSTRY

We have regularly featured pieces about the Tech Workers Coalition (TWC) in *Notes from Below*, including an issue specifically on workers and technology. This has involved sketching out potential areas of inquiry, as well as tracing the formation and activities of the TWC as a workers' network. We have also documented the new unions like Forum for IT Employees (FITE) that are organizing workers in South India (Balaji and Woodcock 2019). Much of the organizing has been focused on the US, which has seen a process of recomposition in which tech workers have begun to challenge management at work.

R.K. Upadhya (2018, 2019), a TWC organizer, has argued that the struggles of tech workers can be broadly characterized as stemming from three different types of grievances. The first are "standard workplace issues" related to the technical composition of work, involving issues like wages and benefits. The second are "social composition issues" which relate to discrimination in the workforce. Lastly, there are "ethical and political issues" relating both to the politics of corporate executives as well as the production of technologies with unethical or oppressive outcomes. The most notable of the latter have been the struggles against contracts with the military to build drone technologies, or the use of facial recognition by immigration enforcement. The organizing has also explicitly drawn upon the workers' inquiry as a method to identify and organize around these issues. As Upadhya (2019) notes, "All three of these grievance areas have entered into mainstream consciousness in the past year, with increasingly visible and militant actions being taken by tech workers across the industry," particularly at Google. While this has been taking place, a London branch of the Tech Workers Coalition has also been formed, showing the potential start of an organizing project with tech workers more broadly in the UK.

While most of these actions may not appear to have a direct connection to the UK, they have shown a moment of visible and highly publicized workplace resistance within a sector that has previously not been seen as a site of struggle. Due to the international nature of the technology industries, the stories and experiences have circulated widely. The overlap, whether directly in terms of relationships or indirectly in terms of publicity, between tech and games workers was also an important factor leading up to the birth of Game Workers Unite (GWU). This international network to unionize the games industry began in early 2018, following a confrontational panel on the topic at an industry conference in San Francisco. Following this, the network gained a global profile within the games industry, rapidly introducing the idea of unionizing to a workforce that has previously had no experience with organizing of this kind. Local chapters of GWU have been started across the world. Woodcock reached out to the first worker to join GWU in the UK, working with him on the early stages of organizing (Woodcock and Declan 2018). Over a period of less than a year, game workers in the UK formed a branch of the IWGB, becoming the first trade union to be established out of this movement (preceded only by the French Le Syndicat des Travailleurs et Travailleuses du Jeu Vidéo [STJV], which had been formed before GWU).

What is notable about the movement of GWU in the UK is how rapidly the political recomposition of these workers has taken place. *Notes from Below* supported game workers as they established organizational structures while learning what a union means in their sector. Similar to what Upadhya has noted about the tech industry, the concerns of the game workers are focused around similar issues in the workplace that involve more than the technical composition. There are two main issues that the union is organizing around. First, the widespread culture of long working hours (known as "crunch"), and second, discrimination and inequality in the workplace. The first is a traditional workplace demand around limiting the working day (something that would have been familiar to Marx), as well as payment for work, while the second involves challenging management over practices that have shaped both the workplace and videogames culture more broadly (Woodcock 2019).

Like the tech workers, game workers are quickly moving to questions of workers' control, rather than, as in the higher education sector, limiting organizing to economistic demands (which are in many sectors still incredibly important). However, the game worker network began outside of the workplace, which has meant many of the activists are drawn into organizing from outside the workplace. The continuing recomposition of game workers needs to spread within particular workplaces and involve concrete campaigns if the organizing over the past year is to translate into worker power.

SECTOR FIVE: HOUSING

The British working class is experiencing a profound and ongoing housing crisis with its roots in the transformation of the social composition initiated during the neoliberal turn (see Robertson 2017). The private rented sector (PRS) is currently characterized by high rates of turnover and mobility, with 62 percent of households having spent under three years in the same accommodation. In general, rents are expensive, the quality of stock is low, and abusive practices such as revenge evictions and harassment are common. In 2013, a UK renters' union movement began to develop in reaction to these conditions. In the years since, this movement has taken on increasing significance although renters' unions remain relatively tiny. While there are 4.5 million UK households in the PRS, housing organizers report that the ACORN union has 1,700 members across England

and Wales, Living Rent has 720 members in Scotland, and the London Renters' Union has 1,700 members in the capital.

Despite its small size, this movement has punched well above its weight. These unions have all successfully defended many members against private landlords, housing associations, companies, and councils. Some evictions have been blocked, repairs made, and compensation won. At the municipal level, ACORN Bristol defeated the local (Labour-controlled) council's attempt to remove council tax exemptions from 16,000 of the city's poorest residents. Working with the London Renters' Union, they have also applied the necessary pressure to lead Sadiq Kahn, Labour Mayor of London, to discuss rent controls. Nationally, the Conservative government has been under pressure to be seen as acting against the excesses of the housing crisis and to win back young voters who have increasingly sided with Labour (Millburn 2019). As a result, they have made gestures towards amending existing legislation in favor of renters. In 2016, the then Chancellor Philip Hammond announced that they would ban letting agents (or real estate agents) from charging unjustified fees. In 2019, then Prime Minister Theresa May announced that they would abolish Section 21 "no fault" evictions.

These victories, although they were not won by renters' unions alone, are highly significant. At every level, from single local cases won through direct action to national legislative changes won through wider campaigns, renters' unions are part of a significant process of self-organization which is rapidly increasing the "associational power" (Wright 2000) of workers in their communities.

The strategy applied to build this power has been characterized as "community syndicalism" (Cant 2018c). In essence, it is a structure-based approach which uses cycles of inquiry, organization, and mobilization to develop and exercise class power on the terrain of social composition.

Some participants in these unions are more explicitly experimenting with forms of "territorial inquiry," as a modified form of workers' inquiry (Living Rent 2018). All of them use some form of participatory research in the early stages of their organizing cycle in order to identify antagonisms, organic leaders, and power resources within communities. The information gathered through this research is then applied to organize a specific neighborhood, and this new structure is then used to take direct action over the immediate structurally grounded concerns of members (Cant 2018c).

Significantly, a core "militant minority" (Uetricht and Eidlin 2019) has been heavily involved in the expansion and campaigning of these unions. This minority largely shared the dissatisfaction of key early participants with the social movement approach of the left that was dominant in the period following 2010–11. In some instances, they have theorized their role as part of a strategy of "Corbynism from Below," in which renters' unions are seen as part of the organizational structure from which a combative extra-parliamentary power can be developed to defend and extend a potential left-wing Labour government (Blackburn 2017; Brand, Williams and Cant 2017). However, this has not precluded renters' unions from having a combative relationship with Labour councils, which often continue to act as the managing committee of the developer bourgeoise despite protestations to the contrary.

Transnational discussions with the housing movement in Berlin have demonstrated the potential for this movement to scale up. The social composition of the urban working class in Germany is shaped by a housing market with two defining features: first, housing assets are significantly centralized and financialized; second, 85 percent of households are tenants. This has proven to be an explosive mixture. Over the course of years, a block-by-block organizing approach has created the basis for a housing movement which has won mass working-class support for demanding the expropriation of housing owned by large corporate landlords and putting it under public ownership (Guttierez 2019; Jungwirth and Guttierez 2019). While this is dissimilar in a number of ways to the social composition of workers in the UK, it proves the enduring political potential of struggles over access to the means of subsistence, as well as the means of production.

Our inquiries with these emergent forms of community self-organization began with discussions of how to theorize class antagonisms in the sphere of reproduction using a workerist framework. The concept of "social composition" (*Notes from Below* 2018a) emerged from these discussions. Social composition is a conceptual addition to a classical workerist framework which proposes that in addition to the working class being technically composed into a productive workforce, it is also socially composed into a class society. Just as inquiry into technical class composition allows for the emergence of strategies of refusal that seek to break the domination of capital in the workplace, so too might inquiry into social class composition allow for the emergence of strategies that can tip the balance of forces between classes as it manifests beyond production. However, there remains much more work to be done to conceptualize the link between the forms of power which emerge from the social composition of the working class and other forms of power which emerge from the technical composition of the working class—and the way in which both operate to impact a wider balance of class forces.

In his history of the European socialist movement, Geoff Eley (2002: 57–8) has demonstrated how the rise of the urban working-class neighborhood led to the emergence of a second front of class formation and struggle. Mike Davis (2018: 77–95) has developed this point to argue that socialist politics was not only born in the factory, but also in the factory district where struggles over issues of rent and consumption—usually led by women—constitute a largely forgotten but extremely important component of the history of class struggle. The emergence of renters' unions in our contemporary context demands that we inquire into these struggles as they take place today and develop the theoretical tools necessary to conceptualize them—rather than relegating rent to a secondary concern.

WHERE NEXT?

We present this survey not as a full account of class struggle in the UK, but as snapshots of struggles that we have been involved with or featured in *Notes from Below*. It is a partisan account—and one that misses out many sectors of work, including farming, logistics, factory work, healthcare, retail, office work, and so on. However, we present these case studies to show the important dynamics, both in what is featured and what is not, of the current class composition in the UK. The formal levels of organization of the working class are low: strike numbers remain some of the lowest they have ever been, shop stewards are aging, and the ratio of stewards to members continues to grow. The working class is clearly in an advanced stage of decomposition. Despite the trends of low unemployment and significant political—or at least parliamentary—contestation, real wages are falling and working conditions are deteriorating.

The case studies presented here also show another dynamic. The last period of political turmoil preceding 2010 was contested primarily by social movements, not by workplace or community movements based on a structural antagonism to capital. However, these examples show that unorganized or so-called "unorganizable" workers can take action—and can be successful when they do. The profiles of these workers are often different from those in the established trade union movement, and they organize in different ways or in new types of organizations. Many are migrants, have insecure employment status, or are younger and new to organizing. For example, trade union membership amongst 16–19 year olds rose by a third in 2018 (BEIS 2019). These counter-dynamics are still emerging, as this rise still only equates to 3.2 percent as members. However, they could form part of a wider recomposition of workers in the UK. At *Notes from Below* we will continue to engage with, document, and support these struggles as and when they happen.

REFERENCES

Balaji and Woodcock, J. (2019). FITE and IT Worker Organising in India. *Notes from Below* (January 26). At https://notesfrombelow.org/article/fite-and-organising-it-workers-india.

BEIS (Department for Business, Energy and Industrial Strategy) (2019). Trade Union Membership: Statistical Bulletin. *Trade Union Membership Statistics 2018*. At https://assets.publishing.service.gov.uk/government/uploads/system/uploads/attachment_data/file/805268/trade-union-membership-2018-statistical-bulletin.pdf.

Blackburn, T. (2017). Corbynism from Below? *New Socialist* (June 12). At https://newsocialist.org.uk/corbynism-from-below.

Brand, D., Williams, P., and Cant, C. (2017). 3 Ways You Can Build Corbynism from Below. *Novara Media* (October 19). At https://novaramedia.com/2017/10/19/3-ways-you-can-build-corbynism-from-below.

Cant, C. (2018a) The Wave of Worker Resistance in European Food Platforms 2016–17. *Notes from Below* (January 29). At https://notesfrombelow.org/article/european-food-platform-strike-wave.

Cant, C. (2018b). McNetworks: Two Current Modes of Struggle. *Notes from Below* (October 11). At https://notesfrombelow.org/article/mcnetworks-two-current-modes-struggle.

Cant, C. (2018c). Taking What's Ours: An ACORN Inquiry. *Notes from Below* (August 16). At https://notesfrombelow.org/article/taking-whats-ours-an-acorn-inquiry.

Cant, C. (2019). *Riding for Deliveroo: Resistance in the New Economy*. Cambridge: Polity Press.

Cant, C. and Hughes, L. (2018). "No Money, No Food!" London UberEats Workers on Strike. *Notes from Below* (September 21). At https://notesfrombelow.org/article/no-money-no-food-london-ubereats-workers-strike.

Cant, C. and Woodcock, J. (2019). The End of the Beginning. *Notes from Below* (June 8). At https://notesfrombelow.org/article/end-beginning.

Cleaver, H. (1979). *Reading Capital Politically*. Brighton: Harvester Press.

Davis, M. (2018). *Old Gods, New Enigmas: Marx's Lost Theory*. London: Verso.

Eley, G. (2002). *Forging Democracy: The History of the Left in Europe, 1850–2000*. Oxford: Oxford University Press.

Englert, S. (2019). After Grady's Election: Where is the Rank and File? *Notes from Below* (May 31). At https://notesfrombelow.org/article/after-gradys-election-where-rank-and-file.

Fear, C. (2018). "Without Our Brain and Muscle Not a Single Wheel Can Turn": The IWW Couriers Network. *Notes from Below* (August 16). At https://notesfrombelow.org/article/without-our-brain-and-muscle.

Guttierez, D. (2019). 5 Theses on Movement Building from the Berlin Housing Movement. *Notes from Below* (October 9). At https://notesfrombelow.org/article/5-theses-movement-building-berlin-housing-movement.

Hughes, L. and Tippet, B. (2018). "Uber, Uber You Can't Hide! We Can See Your Dirty Side!" A Report from the Uber Strike 9th October. *Notes from Below* (October 11). At https://notesfrombelow.org/article/uber-uber-you-cant-hide-we-can-see-your-dirty-side.

Jungwirth, M. and Guttierez, D. (2019). Expropriate the Big Landlords: An Interview from the Frontlines of the German Housing Movement. *Notes from Below* (October 9). At https://notesfrombelow.org/article/expropriate-big-landlords-interview-frontlines-ger.

Kelly, J. (1998). *Rethinking Industrial Relations: Mobilization, Collectivism, and Long Waves*. London: Routledge.

Living Rent (2018). Territorial Inquiry: Living Rent Public Walk in Partick and Whiteinch. *Notes from Below* (August 16). At https://notesfrombelow.org/article/territorial-inquiry.

Marx, K. (1880). A Workers' Inquiry. At www.marxists.org/archive/marx/works/1880/04/20.htm.

Milburn, K. (2019). *Generation Left*. Cambridge: Polity Press.

Mulholland, K. (2004). Workplace Resistance in an Irish Call Centre: Slammin', Scammin' Smokin' an' Leavin'. *Work, Employment and Society* 18, 709–24.

Notes from Below (2018a). The Workers' Inquiry and Social Composition. *Notes from Below* (January 29). At www.notesfrombelow.org/article/workers-inquiry-and-social-composition.

Notes from Below (2018b). The Transnational Couriers Federation. *Notes from Below*. At https://notesfrombelow.org/issue/the-transnational-courier-federation.

Notes from Below (2019). About. *Notes from Below*. At https://notesfrombelow.org/about.

Rebel Roo, The (2016). Rebel Roo Bulletin. *Notes from Below*. At https://notesfrombelow.org/article/rebel-roo-bulletin.

Robertson, M. (2017). The Great British Housing Crisis. *Capital & Class* 41, 195–215.

Silver, B.J. (2003). *Forces of Labour: Workers Movements and Globalization Since 1870*. Cambridge: Cambridge University Press.

The Spoons Striker (2018). Spread the Spoons Strike. *Notes from Below* (September 27). At https://notesfrombelow.org/article/spread-spoons-strike.

Tilly, C. (1978) *From Mobilization to Revolution*. Reading, MA: Addison-Wesley Pub. Co.

Uetricht, M. and Eidlin, B. (2019). US Union Revitalization and the Missing "Militant Minority." *Labor Studies Journal* 44, 36–59.

Upadhya, R.K. (2018). Disrupting Disruption: On Intervening Against Technological Restructuring. *Notes from Below* (March 30). At https://notesfrombelow.org/article/disrupting-disruption.

Upadhya, R.K. (2019). Looking Back. *Notes from Below* (June 8). At https://notesfrombelow.org/article/looking-back.

Waters, F. and Woodcock, J. (2017). Far from Seamless: A Workers' Inquiry at Deliveroo. *Viewpoint Magazine* (September 20). At www.viewpointmag.com/2017/09/20/far-seamless-workers-inquiry-deliveroo.

Woodcock, J. (2014). Precarious Work in London: New Forms of Organisation and the City. *City: Analysis of Urban Trends, Culture, Theory, Policy, Action* 18(6), 776–88.

Woodcock, J. (2016). #Slaveroo: Deliveroo Drivers Organising in the "Gig Economy". *Novara Media* (August 12). At http://novaramedia.com/2016/08/12/slaveroo-deliveroo-drivers-organising-in-the-gig-economy.

Woodcock, J. (2017). *Working the Phones: Control and Resistance in Call Centres*. London: Pluto.

Woodcock, J. (2019). *Marx at the Arcade: Consoles, Controllers, and Class Struggle*. Chicago: Haymarket Books.

Woodcock, J. and Declan (2018). Prospects for Organising the Videogames Industry: Interview with Game Workers Unite UK. *Notes from Below* (August 16). At https://notesfrombelow.org/article/prospects-for-organising-the-videogames-industry.

Woodcock, J. and Englert, S. (2018). Looking Back in Anger: The UCU Strikes. *Notes from Below* (August 30). At https://notesfrombelow.org/article/looking-back-anger-ucu-strikes.

Woodcock, J. and Hughes, L. (2018). The View from the Picket Line: Reports from the Food Platform Strike on October 4th. *Notes from Below* (October 11). At https://notesfrombelow.org/article/view-picket-line-reports-food-platform-strike-octo.

Wright, E.O. (2000). Working-Class Power, Capitalist-Class Interests and Class Compromise. *American Journal of Sociology* 105(4), 957–1002.

Part III

Manufacturing and Mining

7

Worker Organizing in China: Challenges and Opportunities

Jenny Chan

Since the late 1970s, China's integration into the global economy has greatly transformed migration patterns, labor relations, and worker self-organizing. Under the auspices of the state, China's market reform has restructured the working class and reshaped the law and labor policy. Aggrieved workers have used both legal and extra-legal strategies to make economic and political demands. Despite some modest labor gains in wages and social insurance benefits, workers' ability to organize remains severely restricted by employers and by the government. In times of crisis, workers have sought to establish self-help groups and reached out to labor activists for support. This chapter, in part based on the author's participation in cross-border labor rights groups in Hong Kong and the mainland, will assess the changing relationship between the Chinese state, labor, and capital over the past four decades. In this way, it could be said to be a workers' inquiry from above into the evolving technical composition of capital and workers' self-organized efforts to recompose their power in China.

Repression and relaxation oscillate in political governance. Chinese authoritarianism is strong and resilient despite widespread instabilities. The authorities have suppressed autonomous worker organizations while also opening some spaces for material concessions and policy improvements, thereby preserving the one-party rule even after the Soviet Union and Eastern Europe communist regimes had collapsed (Selden and Perry 2010; Lee 2014; Wedeman 2019; Howell and Pringle 2019). So far most worker-led actions have been short-lived and eventually broken up. However, a transformation of worker leaders and their followers has also been taking place that has fueled the demand for more inclusive rights such as the right to unionize.

This chapter begins by exploring workers' attempts to organize independent unions amid the broader pro-democracy student movement and its brutal crackdown in spring 1989. During the 1990s and 2000s, in the face of moral condemnation, the reform-minded leadership deepened enterprise restructuring by shedding tens of millions of state sector jobs. Affected workers and pensioners, driven by a feeling that Chinese socialism was betrayed, staged waves of anti-privatization protests and demonstrations but were largely defeated. At the same time, rural migrants, who have become the mainstay of the export-oriented industry, have risen to resist systemic abuses and class exploitation. In restoring industrial harmony and boosting its legitimacy, the state has expanded legal rights protection and grievance redress mechanisms for hundreds of millions of workers. Important pro-labor measures aside, the central problem of worker representation has remained unresolved. Accordingly, in the absence of union leadership, workers organized to bargain collectively with employers. With the tightening grip of the Xi administration on civil society since 2013, worker organizing, including non-governmental organizations (NGO) and student activism, have been greatly controlled. The chapter concludes by reflecting on the challenges and opportunities for the development of a labor movement in a globalized China.

CONTENTIOUS POLITICS AND INDEPENDENT UNIONISM IN 1989

In the course of China's capitalist transition, economic livelihood was a major concern among working-class people. Between 1986 and 1988, ordinary residents in Beijing and in many other Chinese cities shouldered the rising costs of living resulting from bureaucratic corruption and runaway inflation. In the workplace, factory directors pitted workers against each other to increase output and labor productivity. Grievances accumulated over unequal pay and unfair work practices, among other specific disputes centering on job responsibilities, labor discipline, and women workers' rights. The rising discontent was expressed by a shoe factory worker who told a journalist, "I cannot afford a decent life so naturally there is anger in me ... When I hear our leaders speak of 'reform', I know that means the price of food is about to increase ... [Inflation and corruption make] rich men of party cadres and leave the masses behind" (cited in Walder 1989: 34). The balance of power has indeed been shifting from the working masses to the management.

In the spring of 1989, emboldened by the university students' call for democracy and liberty, workers demanded the resignation of their dictator-like directors. In their workplaces and residential quarters, they aggregated demands through face-to-face meetings and coordinated protest actions. At a larger scale, the Beijing Workers' Autonomous Federation, an independent worker-led organization, called for price stabilization, opposition to political oligarchy, and freedom of association (Walder and Gong 1993). While workers had been excluded from student organizations during the early stages of the movement, the emerging unity between workers and student activists clearly presented a threat to the regime. In the eyes of the government, the "political turmoil" was the largest since the birth of the People's Republic of China in 1949 (Saich 1990: 199).

Following the bloody crackdown on the popular movement on June 4, 1989 in Tiananmen Square, the Beijing leaders took both repressive and conciliatory approaches to put things in order. Prominent worker organizers and student leaders were arrested and imprisoned, while a few others were forced into exile. State surveillance at the workplace and in local neighborhoods was strengthened with military backing, thereby consolidating the topmost leadership (Lee and Hsing 2010). At the same time, the reformers established new mechanisms to guarantee workers' basic rights to redress grievances while speeding up economic reform to attract investment and secure export markets to boost growth. The broad direction was to liberalize the economy by encouraging competition and raising income for the majority, so much so that inefficient firms were shut down on a massive scale. This state-guided economic restructuring process resulted in contradictory outcomes, including job losses for many.

WORKERS' PLIGHTS, PROTESTS, AND STRIKES

By 2002, over 60 million urban workers had been laid off as a result of the privatization and reorganization of state firms. This amounted to "a 44 percent reduction of the 1993 state sector workforce within a 10-year period" (Hurst 2009: 16). Official statistics also showed that state sector jobs as a share of urban employment fell sharply from "76 percent in 1995 to 41 percent in 2000 to only 27 percent in 2005" (Park and Cai 2011: 17). Simultaneously, state bank loans and subsidies were provided to new private investors and foreign enterprises, alongside large state firms. Labor relations have become more unstable with the end of job tenure for state sector workers and the intensified competition for profits between firms.

During this period, disgruntled workers engaged in anti-privatization campaigns to fight for their rights and interests. Government statistics showed that the number of "mass incidents," which covered strikes, protests, riots, demonstrations, collective petitions, and other forms of civil unrest, were on the rise. The cases of mass incidents stood at 8,700 in 1993, increased to 32,000 in 1999, and surpassed 58,000 in 2003 (Tanner 2005: 2). In 2005, the number reached 87,000, an average of 240 incidents each day (Xinhua 2006). These documented mass incidents were carried out by workers *and* many others over a wide range of issues, ranging from unpaid wages to land seizures and environmental degradation. These rapidly rising numbers indicate that social conflicts and class inequalities were getting more serious.

Not only state workers but also rural migrants had taken collective action in intolerable situations, although they had *not* united to form a common front. In other words, they did not succeed in recomposing their class power to successfully advance their claims and respond to the newly emerging technical composition of capital. Intra-class fragmentation and intra-group divisions were not overcome. The rights entitlement of urban workers varied widely according to their financial standing, the organizational capacities of their work organizations, and their own rank and seniority. While some workers would accept the compensation agreements, others rejected them (Lee 2007; Philion 2009). In the absence of strong leadership and mobilization, mutual support and cohesion between workers became weaker and weaker, exposing them to divide and rule strategies (Chen 2017). From the early to mid-2000s, as the new government launched job retraining programs and other social assistance projects for the most adversely affected workers and their families, large-scale resistance subsided (Solinger 2009). In short, the introduction of social welfare programs managed to defeat existing forms of worker organization.

Chinese migrants from the countryside, however, had long been deprived of access to public healthcare services or other social support in the city. They often experienced discrimination and social exclusion as second-class citizens. They were placed in dangerous, dirty, and difficult jobs with low wages. From factories to offices and construction sites, as Anita Chan (2001) meticulously detailed in *China's Workers under Assault*, nonpayment or underpayment of wages and benefits, illegal dismissals, and occupational injuries and diseases were rampant. A despotic factory regime characterized the accumulation of capital in the fast-expanding special economic zones across China. Rural migrant workers relied heavily on their family and kinship ties, as well as local and social networks spun in the workplace, for daily support. Many of them lived, and still live, in shared dormitories or small rental apartments to make ends meet. Today, in megacities like Beijing (21.7 million people) and Shanghai (24.2 million), internal migrants make up about 40 percent of those residing in the city (Hurst and Sorace 2019: 349). Nationwide, the rural migrant laborers reach some 288 million, making up one fifth of the total Chinese population (National Bureau of Statistics 2019).

Chinese workers have potentially strong *workplace bargaining power* in a densely integrated production system at the heart of the globalized economy; that is, they have the power to "cause costly disruptions via direct action at the point of production" (Silver 2014: 52). If the first generation of migrants were silent in their workplaces out of fear of the consequences of speaking up, the second cohort of the post-1980 generation—who arguably possess a stronger organizing capacity with a better mastery of mobile communications technologies than their predecessors—have stood up to voice their grievances and make two kinds of demands or claims (Elfstrom and Kuruvilla 2014). Defensive claims refer to workers' demands for the basic standards set forth in the labor laws, such as the statutory minimum wage, to be met. By contrast, offensive or more progressive claims refer to workers' fight for higher wages and better benefits *above* the legal limit.

In China, the official count of strikes is not publicly available. As early as 1975, the provision for the "right to strike" was incorporated into the amended Constitution of the People's Republic of China. The Constitution enacted in 1978 also stipulates that citizens have the "freedom of strike" and other civil rights. The "freedom of strike" stipulation, however, was removed from the 1982 Constitution, as the Chinese state tightened its rule in response to democratic protests happening in Beijing and former Eastern Europe at that time (Chang and Cooke 2015). The revocation of the legal right did not end labor strikes, however.

The Hong-Kong-based China Labour Bulletin (CLB)'s Strike Map, with reference to reports of labor strikes collected from online news archives and other digital sources, recorded a total of 10,948 cases from January 1, 2011 to December 31, 2018. Still, the available data captured only a small subset of the population in light of the state's ubiquitous censorship. Geoffrey Crothall, Communications Director of CLB, has distilled the partially available government statistics to estimate that the Strike Map at best "accounts for about 5 to 10% of all incidents of workers' collective action in China" during the first five years of President Xi Jinping's rule, that is, between 2013 and 2017 (Crothall 2018: 28). In addition to strikes and protests, aggrieved workers had taken their bosses to court in an attempt to use labor law to press their demands and seek redress.

ARBITRATION AND LITIGATION OF LABOR DISPUTES

Local officials recognize the growing tensions and complexity of labor relations due to the diversification of ownership and the contractualization (rather than regularization) of employment. In 1993, as rural to urban migration accelerated, the central government extended institutional access to the resolution of labor disputes to rural migrant employees. The regulations laid down a three-stage process of mediation, arbitration, and litigation to give workers and employers "an avenue to enforce legal rights directly through formal proceedings" (Ho 2003: 3). Grievances would first be handled by workplace-based labor dispute mediation committees before proceeding to government-administered arbitration and, if necessary, a civil suit. The consequence was that mediation sessions from within the enterprise were rendered less and less effective in settling critical labor conflicts.

Officials seek to divert open protests and massive strikes into the judicial system by streamlining the legal procedures. The first national labor law was promulgated in 1994 and came into force on January 1, 1995. In 1996, 48,121 labor disputes—including individual *and* collective cases that involved 189,120 persons in total—were accepted for arbitration. The number of arbitrated labor disputes continued growing rapidly. In 2008, at the start of the global economic crisis when tens of millions of workers were laid off, the number of cases skyrocketed to 693,465—nearly double from one year previously—involving more than 1.2 million laborers across the country. Following a brief decline, since 2011 the number of labor dispute cases has shot up annually, reaching an unprecedented 828,410 cases in 2016. This was a seventeen-fold increase in arbitrated disputes in the two decades between 1996 and 2016. In 2017, while standing at a high level, the number slightly dropped to 785,323 cases, involving 979,016 workers (China Labour Statistical Yearbook 2019).

"Using the law as a weapon" remains burdensome despite impressive legal reforms including the provision of government-operated legal aid services. For working people, particularly low-income rural migrants, access to affordable *and* effective legal representation is still hard to come by. "Since 2007, workers have become less likely to 'totally win' and more likely to only 'partially win' in labor arbitration" (Halegua 2016: 1), indicating that there are institutional barriers of time and cost to using the legal process. When either party is dissatisfied with the arbitration award, the disputant can appeal the case to the lower court. If dissatisfied with that outcome, the litigant can further appeal the verdict to the intermediate court whose ruling is final.

Judges often insist that cases be filed individually while handling collective lawsuits stemming from labor disputes. Feng Chen and Xin

Xu have shown how this individualization of collective labor actions fragments and isolates plaintiffs, thereby robbing workers of their strength in unity. For example, in 2009, a court in Dongguan city turned 39 collective disputes, involving groups ranging from 10 to 988 people, into 4,167 individual cases (Chen and Xu 2012: 94). This judicial intervention weakened the power of organized workers to access the court.

In *Against the Law*, Ching Kwan Lee observed that plaintiffs "do not necessarily see the law or the courts as a neutral or empowering institution in their fight against official corruption and abuse of power." Still, without better alternatives, "many continue working through and around the law and its related trappings in the state apparatus" (2007: 260). Patricia Chen and Mary Gallagher also argue that "the atomizing effects of court procedures and legislation" has partially restrained "the development of a labor movement" in China (2018: 1033). What we have seen is workers oscillating between judicial and extrajudicial tactics for resolving conflicts in order to draw the attention of, and responses from, the government, media, and the concerned public (Chan and Selden 2019).

THE LIMITS OF LABOR LAW REFORM AND TRADE UNION PROTECTION

In China, as in many countries, rights are enshrined by law in such a way that workers are expected to act as "firefighters" who self-enforce their rights by sounding the "fire alarm" at labor departments and courts to force senior officials to uphold labor standards (Gallagher 2017). If workers sound the alarm by filing cases and the government consistently enforces worker protections, employers may anticipate the risk of a dispute and avoid the problem. But if enforcement is lax and punishment is mild, because local governments often prioritize attracting investment rather than enforcing laws and regulations, employers will likely ignore the letter and spirit of the law, and conflict will be prevalent. A persistent pattern is that although desperate workers sound the fire alarm, serious problems such as nonpayment of wages and abuse by management continue and remain unresolved. "At the heart of poor working conditions," Eli Friedman and Ching

Kwan Lee (2010: 514) show, is the fundamental imbalance of power between workers and employers at the point of production.

Under the Chinese Trade Union Law, Article 10 stipulates that all types of enterprises with 25 employees or more are supposed to have "basic-level trade union committees" on the shopfloor (Trade Union Law 2001). However, independent union organizing is illegal. The enterprise union must be approved by the next higher level trade union. In this centralized organizational structure, the All-China Federation of Trade Unions (ACFTU) monopolizes the power of union representation by imposing its authority over any group of organized workers on the shopfloor.

The ACFTU operates under the command of the ruling Communist Party and it primarily serves the state's interests to preserve industrial peace and social stability. From 2003, against the backdrop of enterprise restructuring and the loss of old members, the ACFTU has extended its membership to rural migrant workers, who have been increasingly recruited to both the state and private sectors. However, workers have cause to generally lack confidence in official trade unions. Surveys of enterprise union leaders consistently reveal that the majority are concurrently personnel department heads or senior managers who normally stand with management rather than with workers (Kong 2012).

Chinese officials consistently fail to protect workers' union rights from management retaliation. A typical example is the continued control by the Foxconn trade union. Since 2007, the company union has been led by a senior female manager appointed by Terry Gou, the corporate founder. In the aftermath of a spate of employee suicides in 2010, Foxconn attempted to improve communications with employees through the publication of free company newspapers, the sponsorship of social and entertainment activities, and above all the expansion of its union membership. However, Auret van Heerden, the Fair Labor Association's president and CEO (2003–13) and Apple's commissioned auditor (2012–13), found that "the Foxconn union does hold elections but the candidates are often management-nominated" (2012: 280). In 2015, Foxconn supervisors were widely accused of manipulating the union elections by instructing workers to cast their votes for designated candidates. Out of fear of retaliation, workers followed the instructions. Clearly, the new rounds of "elections" of union leadership at Foxconn have been done as a formality that would leave intact the structure of power of the union. Some workers learned about the very existence of their unions only when they received souvenirs, such as water bottles bearing the union logo, from union staff members (Chan, Selden and Pun 2020).

In the face of growing labor conflicts, the ACFTU is slowly reforming itself to become more responsive to the workers. Trade union officials, along with judges and lawyers, have proactively mediated in negotiations with company executives and worker representatives in an attempt to reach a quick settlement onsite (Su and He 2010; Elfstrom, 2019). For example, the imminent relocation of a Walmart store in Changde city of Hunan province prompted a one-off, union-led closure bargaining in June 2014, winning a severance payment for all the affected workers (Li and Liu 2018). In a few cases, provincial and municipal unions have intervened to facilitate re-elections of workplace union leaders during post-strike negotiations. However, the elected worker representatives and union committee members were invariably harassed or even dismissed by management thereafter (Chan and Hui 2014; Kuruvilla and Zhang 2016).

Much more rare is any recognition of self-organized workers' unions. Remarkably, in 2006, after a strike against gross underpayment of minimum wages and non-provision of labor contracts at an Ole Wolff electronics factory, workers succeeded in setting up a union through elections to take matters into their own hands. They clearly demonstrated workers' subjectivity and trade union consciousness. The birth of the elected workplace trade union marked a new page of grassroots labor struggle (Au 2009). In a broader context, the ACFTU accelerated its unionization drive by officially recognizing the Ole Wolff elected workplace trade union and reaching out to workers at major foreign invested firms (Chan 2015).

Interestingly, the Yantian International Container Terminal trade union "developed a system of annual collective bargaining" after the 2007 strike in Shenzhen city in Guangdong (Pringle and Meng 2018: 1053). Disruptions can negatively affect the upstream and downstream linkages of the entire logistics and maritime and ground transportation chain. One critical factor in the longshore workers' success is the militancy of crane operators—middle-aged male rural migrants with low turnover—who display a high degree of bargaining power at one of the world's busiest ports in the capital intensive sector in South China. The elected workplace union leaders serve dockworkers' interests to negotiate with management on a regular, rather than one-off, basis. Through their participation in the collective bargaining, dockworkers exercise their associational power while accepting the institutional supervision of the union federation across different levels.

Nevertheless, a representative enterprise level union is highly exceptional in the Chinese political economy. Both management and the government guard against organized labor while prioritizing profitability and stability. Workers' participation in trade union decision-making processes remains severely restricted. Consequently, workers frequently bypass unions and seek assistance from non-state organizations when applying for labor arbitration or taking part in strikes.

THE EMERGENCE OF GRASSROOTS LABOR ORGANIZATIONS

Since the 1990s, with the deepening of transnational and transborder social links characteristic of neoliberal globalization, grassroots organizations in Hong Kong and on the Chinese mainland have emerged to cope with the growing needs of worker organizing. Hong Kong-based China Labour Bulletin, founded in 1994 by mainland Chinese activist and independent union organizer Han Dongfang (who was imprisoned for participating in the 1989 Democracy Movement), was among the first NGOs to promote and defend workers' rights on the mainland. Other Hong Kong-registered labor rights NGOs (such as the Chinese Working Women Network and Labour Action China), comprising workers, social workers, academics, movement lawyers, and other concerned individuals, have also played a pioneering role in building a nascent class-based Chinese force through local and global solidarity (Chan 2005; Leung 2015).

Labor NGOs, through their workers' centers or community networks, usually provide social and cultural services, legal consultation, leadership training, and gender rights awareness workshops to male and female workers in major industrial districts (Lee and Shen 2011). Worker activists, some of them injured in workplace accidents or by occupational diseases, have joined these autonomous organizations as volunteers or staff members to emphasize safety and health protection by visiting workers' dormitories and hospitals. They have also disseminated legal knowledge and practical know-how to support workers to win work-related injury compensation and unpaid wages, thus gaining trust and confidence from workers and their families (Chan 2013; Xu 2013).

At the workplace level, some labor NGOs have experimented with partnerships with multinational corporations (such as Reebok and HP) to coordinate corporate social responsibility programs to improve supply chain labor, social, and environmental governance (Chan 2009; Chan 2012). Dialogue between workers and employers at supplier factories is encouraged under this voluntary private self-regulatory framework. On a few occasions, direct trade union elections have taken place in the presence of independent observers and assessors. But the expansion of such corporate-facilitated labor rights programs in the context of transnational production remains uncertain. Commercialization and marketization of the training projects aside, the outcomes of labor participation on the shopfloor will depend heavily on workers' agency and collective resistance, as well as the continuous monitoring and concerted actions of local and international labor organizations.

Beyond the corporate-led governance framework, there have been instances in which NGO activists have directly intervened in labor strikes and protests. Instead of leading or organizing contentious actions, however, they have mostly tried to prevent them from escalating by resolving the labor crises through legitimate, nonviolent means, such as offering constructive suggestions in collective negotiations with employers (Pringle 2018; Franceschini and Lin 2019). Indeed, provincial government officials have facilitated collective bargaining by implementing new labor laws intended to maintain production and social stability in Guangdong, which had long been plagued by big and small labor incidents. However, in response to strong opposition from employers and business associations, the government weakened the major provisions in successive drafts of what became the Regulations on Enterprise Collective Contracts in Guangdong, which came into force on January 1, 2015 (Standing Committee of Guangdong Provincial People's Congress 2014). Article 18 stipulates that over 50 percent of the workforce must endorse the formal call for compulsory talks to take place, a formidable obstacle to worker actions.

In a meeting with the union leadership in Beijing, President Xi reiterated that "trade unions should adhere to the employee-centered working approach; focus on the most pressing, most immediate issues that concern the employees the most; and fulfill the obligation of safeguarding workers' rights and interests and sincerely serving workers and the people" (Xinhua 2018). Facing mounting pressure from above and below, the ACFTU has begun contracting with selected NGOs to deliver social and legal services to marginalized groups, such as women migrant workers, migrant children, youth and the elderly, in order to build a harmonious society (Howell 2015). This is a penetrating and more subtle way to achieve "social management" at the community level. At the same time, movement-minded NGOs have been squeezed and driven underground.

Labor organizers coached workers to take *individual actions*, rather than collective protests, to make their urgent appeals. This strategy is a tactical innovation for rights activists to address the critical threats to organizational survival from repression and cooptation (Fu 2017). In the rights defense process, labor organization leaders offered much needed support to individual workers at the backstage, framed the problems, and formulated media strategies to press for economic compensation for their grievances. In successful cases, worker claimants have demonstrated their class consciousness by transforming themselves into core members to support fellow workers by sharing their own experience.

In massive conflicts, however, labor organizing can hardly be covered up. Conflicts over toxic poisoning, unpaid wages, and illegal firings, to name just a few examples, often involve a large number of workers. The collective nature of labor discontent requires effective online and offline mobilization, making worker leaders more difficult to hide from the authorities. Following the state assault on feminist groups in March 2015 and on human rights lawyers in July, labor activists from several NGOs based in Guangdong were arrested in December (Franceschini and Nesossi 2018). Meng Han, who helped a group of shoe factory workers to recover unpaid social insurance before the factory's planned closure and relocation, was jailed for 21 months, while three other activists of the Panyu Migrant Workers Service Center had their sentences suspended. This heightened control of civil society shows the government's overriding concern is for economic growth and political stability, rather than realizing greater collective rights for its citizens.

CONTENTIOUS STATE–LABOR RELATIONS IN CHINA

Fundamentally, the "representation void" remains unfilled. Workers do not find government-controlled and management-dominated unions a reliable ally (Kuruvilla 2018: 1020). When massive strikes do occur, either employers or government officials require workers to elect representatives, generally limited to five, to engage in talks. Once worker representatives are elected, the company moves to take control of the negotiations. This intervention typically marks the beginning of a fragmentation, cooptation, and crushing of worker power.

To prevent company retaliation, protesting workers have learned through bitter experience to protect each other in a collectivity that presents no visible leaders. In many other cases, however, worker leaders have been quickly identified. Yanhua Deng and Kevin O'Brien (2013) focus on "relational repression" as a strategy for controlling protest. By pressuring the families, relatives, friends, and significant others of target protesters, the authorities manipulate "social ties" and "feelings of affection" to defuse collective protest before escalation. This labor-intensive process of "stability maintenance" involves an irreducible amount of psychological pressure inflicted on those seeking justice (O'Brien and Deng 2017).

Heavy-handed repression is an integral part of Chinese authoritarianism, precisely because the "soft" means of protest absorption and other forms of social containment do not always work. "Dishing out cash payments or other material benefits in exchange for compliance" can only go so far, especially when the principled protesters refuse to back down by taking the money (Lee and Zhang 2013: 1486). Where a resolution cannot be reached, stability-sensitive officials may detain a large number of "trouble making" citizens to deter further action (Chen 2012).

Some veteran activists and organizers remain undeterred, boldly establishing their own organizations after they have been fired or released from prison, a practice that Feng Chen and Xuehui Yang (2017) call "exit with voice." These labor leaders have developed "indigenous" groups to advocate for workers' rights by adapting to the changing economic and political contexts (Chan 2018). In 2016, for example, two former Walmart employees took the lead to mobilize against the corporate implementation of a flexible hour system and a significant wage cut through online strategizing. They moderated an internet-based forum under the banner of the Walmart Chinese Workers' Association, breathing new life into a self-organized network linking Walmart workers across multiple cities in China. While the momentum of the movement died down following a split over worker strategies, coupled with management attacks and government intimidation, the experience was not entirely negative. Walmart workers enthusiastically debated the timing and effectiveness of strikes, among other key questions over fundraising and coordination, demonstrating their active participation, reflexivity, and capacity to devise their own tactics, strategies, and organizations.

A new wave of clampdowns on worker organizing soon followed. In July 2018, the state targeted a core group of workers who organized to form a trade union at the Jasic welding machinery factory in Shenzhen. The police detained 30 individuals, including workers, their families and friends, and one female university student, on July 27 (Amnesty International 2018). On August 24, in yet another coordinated raid, 50 student activists—the backbone of the Jasic Worker Solidarity Group—were interrogated, harassed, and warned to immediately stop taking part in the "illegal activities" or face criminal charges. While the majority of the 80 protesters were later released, four workers were formally arrested (Chan 2019).

During the fall and winter semesters of 2018, national security officials and their university cadres shut down Marxist study groups and related student associations in an effort to remove the institutional support for the Jasic workers and their allies. As Au (2019) has succinctly observed, "though Xi Jinping continues to demand the people learn from Marxism-Leninism and Mao's thought, the state continues to crack down on any independent and collective effort at seriously studying left classics—and to crack down even harder when these efforts carry an aspiration to sympathize with working people."

It was estimated that, between January and May 2019, more than a dozen activists (from eight labor NGOs, social work organizations, community service centers, and a law firm) were detained or arrested, even though they do not appear to be linked to the Jasic labor struggle (Chinese Human Rights Defenders 2019). To nip the emerging alliance between workers and activists in the bud, the Chinese government has clearly cast a wide net to contain and suppress various forms of social and worker organization. Under such conditions, worker self-organization has remained fragmented and limited even though it continues to be widespread.

CONCLUSION

The clashing interests and intentions *within* and *across* the many elements in the Chinese state are complex. Since the 1980s labor market liberalization, state and employer offensives against self-organized workers have simultaneously provoked resistance. Although both government reform initiatives and workers' demands have resulted in expanded workplace rights, many of those rights remain aspirational and go unenforced. Worse, concessions have been accompanied by repression. In recent years, the political environment for those working on labor rights issues in China, notably self-organized workers, NGOs, student activists, social workers, and lawyers, has been much constrained.

Will the government take firmer action to protect workers in a slowing economy? Despite rising levels of workers' struggle and social activism in China, there are reasons to be pessimistic about the outlook for worker organizing, democratically controlled unions, and obtaining and defending workplace rights. The state has turned to deploying significant coercion to combat worker challenges, especially as it appears that workers are attempting to recompose their power.

But the brighter side is that workers—in and through their successive fights—have accumulated organizing experience, leadership skills, and the capacity to make their legitimate claims. Xi's iron fisted suppression of young Marxists has sparked growing anger from leftists on China's political spectrum and in the international community (Pun 2019; Chan 2020). If Chinese labor protest is to transcend localized actions in dispersed sites of resistance to span whole industries, it will be necessary to build a broad-based social movement that wins support both at home and abroad.

ACKNOWLEDGMENTS

The author is very grateful to Robert Ovetz for his intellectual support. She also thanks Immanuel Ness and Zak Cope for their helpful comments on an earlier draft of this chapter. Funding for the research presented here was provided by the Early Career Scheme (2018–20) of the Research Grants Council of Hong Kong (RGC/Gov No.: PolyU256025/17H).

REFERENCES

Amnesty International (2018). China: Thirty People Detained at Factory Worker Protest Must Be Released. (July 31). At www.amnesty.org/en/latest/news/2018/07/china-free-shenzhen-factory-worker-protest.

Au, L.Y. (2009). China: End of a Model … Or the Birth of a New One? *New Politics* XII(3). At https://newpol.org/issue_post/china-end-modelor-birth-new-one.

Au, L.Y. (2019). The Jasic Struggle in China's Political Context. *New Politics* XVII(2). At https://newpol.org/issue_post/the-jasic-struggle-in-chinas-political-context.

Chan, A. (2001). *China's Workers Under Assault: The Exploitation of Labor in a Globalizing Economy.* Armonk, NY: M.E. Sharpe.

Chan, A. (2009). Challenges and Possibilities for Democratic Grassroots Union Elections in China: A Case Study of Two Factory-Level Elections and Their Aftermath. *Labour Studies Journal* 34(3), 293–317.

Chan, A. (ed.) (2015). *Chinese Workers in Comparative Perspective.* Ithaca: Cornell University Press.

Chan, A. (2018). The Relationship Between Labour NGOs and Chinese Workers in an Authoritarian Regime. *Global Labour Journal* 9(1), 1–18. At https://mulpress.mcmaster.ca/globallabour/article/view/3272.

Chan, C.K.-C. (2013). Community-Based Organizations for Migrant Workers' Rights: The Emergence of Labour NGOs in China. *Community Development Journal* 48(1), 6–22.

Chan, C.K.-C. and Hui, E. S.-i. (2014). The Development of Collective Bargaining in China: From "Collective Bargaining By Riot" to "Party State-Led Wage Bargaining." *The China Quarterly* 217 (March), 221–42.

Chan, J. (2005). The Chinese Working Women Network. In Ascoly, N. and Finney, C. (eds.), *Made by Women: Gender, the Global Garment Industry and the Movement for Women Workers' Rights*. The Netherlands: Clean Clothes Campaign, pp. 28–33.

Chan, J. (2012). Labour Rights Training at HP Supplier Factories in China. In Traub-Merz, R. and Ngok, K. (eds.), *Industrial Democracy in China: With Additional Studies on Germany, South-Korea and Vietnam*. Beijing: China Social Sciences Press, pp. 314–27.

Chan, J. (2019). Jasic Workers Fight for Union Rights. *New Politics* XVII(2). At https://newpol.org/issue_post/jasic-workers-fight-for-union-rights.

Chan, J. (2020). A Precarious Worker–Student Alliance in Xi's China. *The China Review: An Interdisciplinary Journal on Greater China* (February).

Chan, J. and Selden, M. (2019). Labor Legislation, Workers, and the Chinese State. In Wright, T. (ed.), *Handbook of Protest and Resistance in China*. Cheltenham: Edward Elgar Publishing, pp. 105–18.

Chan, J., Selden, M., and Pun, N. (2020). *Dying for an iPhone: Apple, Foxconn and the Lives of China's Workers*. Chicago: Haymarket Books, and London: Pluto.

Chang, K. and Cooke, F.L. (2015). Legislating the Right to Strike in China: Historical Development and Prospects. *Journal of Industrial Relations* 57(3), 44–55.

Chen, F. and Xu, X. (2012). "Active Judiciary": Judicial Dismantling of Workers' Collective Action in China. *The China Journal* 67 (January), 87–107.

Chen, F. and Yang, X. (2017). Movement-Oriented Labour NGOs in South China: Exit with Voice and Displaced Unionism. *China Information* 31(2), 155–75.

Chen, P. and Gallagher, M. (2018). Mobilization without Movement: How the Chinese State "Fixed" Labor Insurgency. *ILR Review* 71(5), 1029–52.

Chen, X. (2012). *Social Protest and Contentious Authoritarianism in China*. Cambridge: Cambridge University Press.

Chen, X. (2017). Elitism and Exclusion in Mass Protest: Privatization, Resistance, and State Domination in China. *Comparative Political Studies* 50(7), 908–34.

China Labour Statistical Yearbook 2018 (2019). Beijing: China Statistics Press.

Chinese Human Rights Defenders (2019). China Must Release Detained Labor Rights Advocates. (July 25). At www.nchrd.org/2019/07/china-must-release-detained-labor-rights-advocates.

Crothall, G. (2018). China's Labour Movement in Transition. *Made in China* 3(2), 28–35.

Deng, Y. and O'Brien, K.J. (2013). Relational Repression in China: Using Social Ties to Demobilize Protesters. *The China Quarterly* 215 (September), 533–52.

Elfstrom, M. (2019). Two Steps Forward, One Step Back: Chinese State Reactions to Labour Unrest. *The China Quarterly* 240 (December), 855–79.

Elfstrom, M. and Kuruvilla, S. (2014). The Changing Nature of Labor Unrest in China. *ILR Review* 67(2), 453–80.

Franceschini, I. and Lin, K. (2019). Labour NGOs in China: From Legal Mobilisation to Collective Struggle (and Back?). *China Perspectives* 2019–1, 75–84.

Franceschini, I. and Nesossi, E. (2018). State Repression of Chinese Labor NGOs: A Chilling Effect? *The China Journal* 80 (July), 111–29.

Friedman, E. and Lee, C.K. (2010). Remaking the World of Chinese Labour: A 30-Year Retrospective. *British Journal of Industrial Relations* 48(3), 507–33.

Fu, D. (2017). Disguised Collective Action in China. *Comparative Political Studies* 50(4), 499–527.

Gallagher, M.E. (2017). *Authoritarian Legality in China: Law, Workers, and the State.* Cambridge: Cambridge University Press.

Halegua, A. (2016). *Who Will Represent China's Workers? Lawyers, Legal Aid, and the Enforcement of Labor Rights.* US Asia Law Institute, New York University School of Law.

Ho, V.H. (2003). *Labor Dispute Resolution in China: Implications for Labor Rights and Legal Reform.* China Research Monograph 59. Berkeley: Institute of East Asian Studies, University of California.

Howell, J. (2015). Shall We Dance? Welfarist Incorporation and the Politics of State–Labour NGO Relations. *The China Quarterly* 223 (September), 702–23.

Howell, J. and Pringle, T. (2019). Shades of Authoritarianism and State–Labour Relations in China. *British Journal of Industrial Relations* 57(2), 223–46.

Hurst, W. (2009). *The Chinese Worker After Socialism.* Cambridge: Cambridge University Press.

Hurst, W. and Sorace, C. (2019). Urban China: Changes and Challenges. In Joseph, W.A. (ed.), *Politics in China.* 3rd Edition. Oxford: Oxford University Press, pp. 347–70.

Kong, X. (2012). Capacity-Building and Reform of Chinese Trade Unions: Using Legal and Democratic Means to Resolve the Conflict of Roles of Trade Union Chairs. In Traub-Merz, R. and Ngok, K. (eds.), *Industrial Democracy in China: With Additional Studies on Germany, South-Korea and Vietnam.* Beijing: China Social Sciences Press.

Kuruvilla, S. (2018). Editorial Essay—From Cautious Optimism to Renewed Pessimism: Labor Voice and Labor Scholarship in China. *ILR Review* 71(5), 1013–28.

Kuruvilla, S. and Zhang, H. (2016). Labor Unrest and Incipient Collective Bargaining in China. *Management and Organization Review* 12(1), 159–87.

Lee, C.K. (2007). *Against the Law: Labor Protests in China's Rustbelt and Sunbelt.* Berkeley: University of California Press.

Lee, C.K. (2014). State and Social Protest. *Daedalus: The Journal of the American Academy of Arts and Sciences* 143(2), 124–34.

Lee, C.K. and Hsing, Y.-t. (2010). Social Activism in China: Agency and Possibility. In Lee, C.K. and Hsing, Y.-t. (eds.), *Reclaiming Chinese Society: The New Social Activism*. London: Routledge, pp. 1–13.

Lee, C.K. and Shen, Y. (2011). The Anti-Solidarity Machine?: Labor Nongovernmental Organizations in China. In Kuruvilla, S., Lee, C.K., and Gallagher, M.E. (eds.), *From Iron Rice Bowl to Informalization: Markets, Workers, and the State in a Changing China*. Ithaca: Cornell University Press, pp. 173–87.

Lee, C.K. and Zhang, Y. (2013). The Power of Instability: Unraveling the Microfoundations of Bargained Authoritarianism in China. *American Journal of Sociology* 118(6), 1475–508.

Leung, P.P. (2015). *Labor Activists and the New Working Class in China*. New York: Palgrave Macmillan.

Li, C. and Liu, M. (2018). Overcoming Collective Action Problems Facing Chinese Workers: Lessons from Four Protests Against Walmart. *ILR Review* 71(5), 1078–105.

National Bureau of Statistics of the People's Republic of China (2019). *Investigative Report on the Monitoring of Chinese Rural Migrant Workers in 2018*. (In Chinese). At www.stats.gov.cn/tjsj/zxfb/201904/t20190429_1662268.html.

O'Brien, K.J. and Deng, Y. (2017). Preventing Protest One Person At a Time: Psychological Coercion and Relational Repression in China. *The China Review* 17(2), 179–201.

Park, A. and Cai, F. (2011). The Informalization of the Chinese Labor Market. In Kuruvilla, S., Lee, C.K., and Gallagher, M.E. (eds.), *From Iron Rice Bowl to Informalization: Markets, Workers, and the State in a Changing China*. Ithaca: Cornell University Press, pp. 17–35.

Philion, S.E. (2009). *Workers' Democracy in China's Transition from State Socialism*. New York: Routledge.

Pringle, T. (2018). A Solidarity Machine? Hong Kong Labour NGOs in Guangdong. *Critical Sociology* 44(4–5), 661–75.

Pringle, T. and Meng, Q. (2018). Taming Labor: Workers' Struggles, Workplace Unionism, and Collective Bargaining on a Chinese Waterfront. *ILR Review* 71(5), 1053–77.

Pun, N. (2019). The New Chinese Working Class in Struggle. *Dialectical Anthropology*. At https://link.springer.com/article/10.1007/s10624-019-09559-0.

Saich, T. (1990). The Rise and Fall of the Beijing People's Movement. *The Australian Journal of Chinese Affairs* 24, 181–208.

Selden, M. and Perry, E.J. (2010). Introduction: Reform, Conflict and Resistance in Contemporary China. In Perry, E.J. and Selden, M. (eds.), *Chinese Society: Change, Conflict and Resistance*. 3rd Edition. London: Routledge, pp. 1–30.

Silver, B.J. (2014). Theorising the Working Class in Twenty-First Century Global Capitalism. In Atzeni, M. (ed.), *Workers and Labour in a Globalised Capitalism:*

Contemporary Themes and Theoretical Issues. Basingstoke: Palgrave Macmillan, pp. 46–69.

Solinger, D.J. (2009). *States' Gains, Labor's Losses: China, France, and Mexico Choose Global Liaisons, 1980–2000.* Ithaca: Cornell University Press.

Standing Committee of Guangdong Provincial People's Congress (2014). *Regulations on Enterprise Collective Contracts in Guangdong.* (In Chinese). At www.gdrd.cn/gdrdfb/ggtz/201409/t20140928_142698.html.

Su, Y. and He, X. (2010). Street as Courtroom: State Accommodation of Labor Protest in South China. *Law and Society Review* 44(1): 157–84.

Tanner, M.S. (2005). *Chinese Government Responses to Rising Social Unrest.* The RAND Corporation. At www.rand.org/content/dam/rand/pubs/testimonies/2005/RAND_CT240.pdf.

Trade Union Law of the People's Republic of China (2001). At www.gov.cn/english/laws/2005–10/11/content_75948.htm.

van Heerden, A. (2012). FLA Investigation of Foxconn in China. *Global Labour Journal* 3(2), 278–81. At https://mulpress.mcmaster.ca/globallabour/article/view/1125.

Walder, A.G. (1989). The Political Sociology of the Beijing Upheaval of 1989. *Problems of Communism* (September–October), 30–40.

Walder, A.G. and Gong, X. (1993). Workers in the Tiananmen Protests: The Politics of the Beijing Workers' Autonomous Federation. *The Australian Journal of Chinese Affairs* 29, 1–29.

Wedeman, A. (2019). Unrest and Regime Survival. In Wright, T. (ed.), *Handbook of Protest and Resistance in China.* Cheltenham: Edward Elgar Publishing, pp. 12–26.

Xinhua (2006). China Strives to Handle Mass Incidents. (December 9). At www.chinadaily.com.cn/china/2006–12/09/content_754796.htm.

Xinhua (2018). Xi Urges Breaking New Ground in Workers' Movement, Trade Unions' Work. (October 29). At www.xinhuanet.com/english/2018–10/29/c_137567374.htm.

Xu, Y. (2013). Labor Non-Governmental Organizations in China: Mobilizing Rural Migrant Workers. *Journal of Industrial Relations* 55(2), 243–59.

8

Self-Organizing is Breathing Life into Workers' Struggles in South Africa

Shawn Hattingh and Dr. Dale T. McKinley

Over the last decade, workers in a number of sectors have undertaken radical actions in South Africa to try and win gains at the point of production. They have used innovative tactics in the context of post-apartheid South Africa which have involved going outside the labor relations framework and embarking on wildcat strikes and, at times, sit-ins. In the vast majority of these circumstances, such actions were organized outside and even against trade unions by the workers themselves through mass meetings, worker committees, and worker forums/councils.

This chapter traces the history of some of these struggles with a specific focus on the worker committees that arose in the platinum belt in South Africa during the 2009 to 2013 period and more recently with the experiments of the Simunye Workers' Forum (SWF)—which is supported by the Casual Workers' Advice Office (CWAO)—in the industrial areas east of Johannesburg. The chapter begins by outlining the context in which these initiatives and actions have arisen focusing on the political decline of trade unions, why they have taken place outside of trade unions, and some of the challenges they have faced. Although some of these new forms of organization and innovative actions are on the decline, since 2015 the SWF/CWAO have been using workers' forums in attempts to build and sustain new forms of organizing.

In order to trace the above developments, the chapter examines how the composition of the working class was structured during the heyday of trade unionism in the country in the late 1970s, how it was decomposed by neoliberalism, and the implications this has had for organizing. Indeed, capital in South Africa under neoliberalism introduced new technologies (including automation) and moved towards reducing the size of the permanent workforce through retrenchments and embarking on the use of contract, casual, and labor broker workers. It thus deconstructed and fragmented the working class, and trade unions in South Africa have been unable to effectively respond to this. But this decomposed working class, now consisting of a greater number of precarious, contract, casual, and labor broker workers, has begun to self-organize to address the challenges it faces and rebuild its power. This chapter traces the story of this self-organizing from the perspective of the working class.

THE TRADITION OF REVOLUTIONARY TRADE UNIONS IN SOUTH AFRICA

Historically there has never been just one form of trade unionism. Unions have varied in the way they have organized and the tactics they have used. Some have been revolutionary, others reformist, and some even conservative or right-wing. Unfortunately, today, the vast majority of unions in South Africa are highly bureaucratized, patriarchal, and often deeply embedded in capitalism through the investment companies they own (Moussouris 2017). They tend to largely recruit permanent workers, mostly within the state sector, as members. Workers that are employed through labor brokers, and contract workers, casual workers, outsourced workers, or those unemployed are, for the most part, ignored by trade unions. In many cases shop stewards no longer work alongside their members but are full-time officials paid by the companies that they have members in, and they often attempt explicitly to implement amiable relations between workers and employers. The workers in the worker committees and forums that have arisen since 2009 have been organizing outside of these types of trade unions.

To understand why thousands of workers have embarked on new forms of self-organization outside of trade unions we have to understand the forces and processes that have led to the demise of the once militant trade union movement in South Africa, which includes how the working class has been decomposed under neoliberalism.

Internationally, much of the early industrial unionism of the late nineteenth and early twentieth centuries was influenced by revolutionary syndicalism or anarcho-syndicalism. These used direct democracy and radical actions, and aimed for a social revolution in which the working class would eradicate the state and capitalism, replacing them with structures of working-class self-governance and a socialized and worker self-managed society (van der Walt 2016).

South Africa too has a history of such unions, notably in the early part of the twentieth century. The first union that targeted black workers in the country, the Industrial Workers' of Africa, was founded along anarcho-syndicalist and revolutionary syndicalist lines in 1918. It used militant and innovative tactics to pressure the state and capital to provide concessions to workers (van der Walt 2011). In the 1970s and early 1980s another form of militant trade unionism arose in South Africa. In 1973, black workers in the city of Durban embarked on wildcat strikes that shook the country to its core. At the time, unions for black workers were illegal under the apartheid state's laws. Out of these wildcat strikes independent unions emerged, and in 1979 some of these formed the Federation of South African Trade Unions (FOSATU) (Ulrich 2005).

By the time of FOSATU's formation a large part of the black working class had been urbanized. Migrant labor still defined the mining sector, but most of the black working class lived permanently in townships, which tended to be adjacent to large industrial areas. The bulk of the black working class in South Africa by the 1970s tended to be employed on a permanent basis centered around the manufacturing sector. FOSATU's membership reflected this configuration of the working class.

FOSATU was a left-wing radical grassroots organization. It stood for worker control of unions and was explicitly not aligned to any political party. It built a working-class identity, culture, and counterpower amongst its members. Its fight was not just to defeat apartheid but also to end capitalism. FOSATU, therefore, aimed to use struggles to win reforms and to build on these as steps towards socialism. The socialism that FOSATU envisioned should not be confused with that of the Soviet Union (which in reality was state capitalism)—it rather wanted a redistribution of wealth and power through workers directly controlling workplaces, the economy, and society (Byrne, Ulrich, and van der Walt 2017).

THE POLITICAL REASONS FOR THE DECLINE
OF WORKER-CONTROLLED UNIONS

Before outlining how the working class was decomposed under neo-liberalism and how this has led to the decline of unions in South Africa, it is important to first understand the political forces that led to the decline of FOSATU and ushered in an era of bureaucratic unionism in South Africa.

By 1985, FOSATU had merged with other unions largely influenced either by Black Consciousness or the African National Congress (ANC) to form the Congress of South Africa Trade Unions (COSATU). In 1987, the National Union of Mine Workers (NUM) proposed that COSATU adopt the guiding document of the ANC, the Freedom Charter. After much debate this was accepted by the majority of affiliates and was adopted, marking a distinct point at which the largest trade unions in the country began to openly align with the politics of the ANC and its partner the South African Communist Party (SACP). In 1990, COSATU entered into a formal alliance with the ANC and SACP (Twala and Konpi 2012).

This saw a political shift in which the idea of a two-stage revolution became the guiding policy of unions in COSATU. The idea was that the first stage of the revolution—which came in 1994 in this paradigm—marked a democratic revolution of people winning political rights. In the aftermath, the aim would be to alter the racial structure of capitalism in South Africa. This would involve the state using its power to break up monopolies in the economy and through this open up opportunities to black capitalists to gain access to the top echelons of capitalism. It was also argued that although capitalism would remain, during the first stage the state would provide benefits to the working class. The role of the SACP and trade unions in this thinking would be to contest space within the first stage and push the country into the second stage. In the latter, a system of socialism (but in reality a form of state capitalism similar to the Soviet Union) would be implemented according to its proponents in the SACP such as Joe Slovo (1988). With the adoption of the ideology of the two-stage revolution and the consequent entering into an alliance with the SACP and ANC, the COSATU unions became ever more dogmatic and formulistic, killing political debates that had been the life blood of the unions in the 1970s and early 1980s. It was here that the slide towards bureaucratization began (Moussouris 2017).

The close alignment with the ANC and SACP saw many of the leaders within COSATU joining these parties, which had a detrimental impact on the unions. These included people such as Cyril Ramaphosa, Gwede Mantashe, Sbu Dlamini, Irvin Jim, Sam Shilowa, and John Gomomo, who rose through the ranks of the ANC and became prominent politicians, and in the case of Ramaphosa, the head of state in 2017. The unions, therefore, were transformed into stepping stones for ambitious leaders to embark on political careers in the ANC and SACP from 1990 onwards. This negatively impacted on the unions and began to reverse the traditions of workers' control. Linked to this process, the worst of the ANC and SACP practices, in terms of so-called democratic centralism and at times outright authoritarianism, began to filter into the unions (Moussouris 2017). The consequence was that the unions began a long path towards bureaucratization.

When 1994 dawned and apartheid officially ended with the ANC gaining state power, many of the top leaders of COSATU left the organization and went into the state—either as parliamentarians or as executives in the various state departments. The mass exodus of top leaders saw remaining officials and leaders demanding comparable salaries to parliamentarians. From 1994 onwards, a gulf opened up between what members of the unions earned and what officials earned. Union leaders, including those in COSATU, entered into the middle class and some even moved into exclusive suburbs such as Sandton in Johannesburg. Perhaps the best example to highlight this point was that in 2009—a year when workers in the platinum mining sector began to rebel against the NUM—the NUM General Secretary Frans Baleni was earning R 1.4 million a year when the average salary for a mine worker was between R 48,000 and R 60,000 a year (Good 2014).

Feeding into this was the fact that in the mid to late 1990s some of the largest unions in the country, including the so-called left-leaning National Union of Metalworkers of South Africa (NUMSA), began forming investment companies. These were sold to members on the basis that the profits made by these companies would be used for the benefit of union members and their families. The reality was very different. Union investment companies soon became behemoths that sought, like any other company, to maximize profits. Many, such as the NUM investment company, even provided loans through finance institutions it owned to workers at loan shark rates. Consequently, leadership battles emerged in many unions to gain personal access to the wealth of the investment companies, and all unions with investment arms have been mired in corruption scandals (Mahlakoana 2017).

After 1994, unions also began entering into institutions and initiatives established by the post-apartheid state under the ANC that explicitly promoted so-called social harmony between the state and capital on one side, and the working class on the other. Notably, the National Economic Development and Labour Council (NEDLAC) was established as a forum for the state, big business, and unions to develop labor, trade, and investment policies to supposedly benefit all South Africans. A new layer of bureaucrats was employed by the unions to engage in NEDLAC, which further increased the gap between members and union officials and employees. Even with this, unions were unable to really influence policies within NEDLAC, and business and the state continuously outmaneuvered them. What entering into NEDLAC did do, however, was essentially begin to bring the unions directly into the fold of the state and further bureaucratize them (van der Walt 2010).

While many workers celebrated the introduction of the Labour Relations Act (LRA) and the Basic Conditions of Employment Act (BCEA) by the state after 1994, in practice these acts also negatively impacted the power of unions and fed into why many workers eventually became disillusioned with them. The LRA stipulated that employers only need to recognize unions that are registered with the state. There is no obligation for employers to recognize non-registered unions or other worker organizations.

The state also set out how unions should be structured under the LRA. They must, for instance, have an executive and shop stewards. By doing so, the state ensured that any registered trade union would have a hierarchical structure feeding into the model of bureaucratized unions. The LRA further established lengthy procedures for unions to follow should they want to embark on a protected strike, thus providing ample time for employers to implement plans to limit the impact of strikes. The LRA stipulated that workers could be dismissed for embarking on wildcat strikes—effectively blunting the most successful weapon that the militant unions of the 1970s and early 1980s had to build their unions (Gentle 2012).

In the 1990s and 2000s unions also began concluding multi-year deals with employers. This was promoted by industry-wide bargaining councils in many sectors. Rather than pressure from the shopfloor, it was union officials in boardrooms that began to be the center of wage negotiations. Workers' control of the unions, and even the bargaining process, was largely ended by this practice. As we shall see, this was one of the drivers for many workers breaking with trade unions.

One labor practice of the biggest companies that emerged in the 2000s was the provision that full-time shop stewards would be paid by employers to do union work. What appeared at first as a victory for workers turned into a curse. Full-time shop stewards were drawn out of the shopfloor and given office space. The companies paid their salaries and even provided perks such as company vehicles, which meant they were paid well above the salaries of their members. Not only was there a gulf between members and union officials, but one also developed between shop stewards and workers. Many workers, as we will see in the following section, began to perceive shop stewards as agents of the employers rather than defenders of workers' interests (Gentle 2012).

By the late 1990s and early 2000s the form of politics that unions in South Africa adopted, along with how their structures changed due to outside forces such as NEDLAC and the LRA, saw them becoming highly bureaucratized. Gone were the militant shopfloor-led unions of the 1970s and early 1980s. Mandates now came from above and general secretaries began to wield power. Leadership within unions could and did manipulate congresses and elections through the resources they had at their disposal.

TRADE UNIONS' (NON-)RESPONSE TO THE RESTRUCTURING OF CAPITALISM

As in many other parts of the world, South Africa was severely impacted by the capitalist crisis that began in the 1970s. One of the central responses of South African capitalists was to maintain profits by decomposing the working class and restructuring work, thereby changing the composition of the class by introducing casual and contract labor on a large scale. This made it hard for the restructured class to build unity and to organize collectively due to greater fragmentation—a process that has now been underway for three and a half decades.

With the trade liberalization begun in the late 1980s, and fully entrenched in the 1990s, South Africa's manufacturing sector came under increasing pressure from imports. Capital responded to this in a number of ways. Increasingly, the largest manufacturers, such as those in automotive manufacturing, began to mechanize, thereby reducing the size of their workforces to remain competitive and increase profits. Others shifted from manufacturing to importing and distribution, using precarious workers in the warehouses that have sprung up across South Africa's industrial areas. Alongside such shifts, sections of capital also moved into the service sector, implementing a system of precarious work as they did so.

Another tactic used by capital that remained in manufacturing and mining was to restructure their workforces. By the 1990s, companies in the manufacturing and mining sectors began a process of employing casual, contract, and labor broker workers on a large scale. This was done to maintain and increase profits in the neoliberal era. Such employers could pay casual, contract, and labor broker workers less than permanent workers. They also further reduced labor costs because they did not have to provide such workers with pensions, provident funds (similar to a pension fund but a worker receives a lump sum in full on retirement), or medical coverage, gains that had been won by workers through trade unions in the late 1970s and early 1980s. Using casual and contract labor meant that capital could also fluctuate the size of its workforce more easily according to an increase or a decline in the demand for goods in the market.

Capital also used the threat of replacing permanent workers with casual or contract workers as a way to discipline workers and to keep wages low. Indeed, wages for the restructured working class since the neoliberal era began have stagnated. The result is that the decomposed working class in South Africa has become indebted in order to offset stagnant wages and maintain any semblance of a decent living standard. In the last two decades a plethora of companies, including ones owned by trade unions, has sprung up, pushing loans onto casual, contract and labor broker workers and even South Africa's growing unemployed (Bond 2012).

All of this has resulted in a decline in permanent workers as a percentage of the workforce and the rise of contract, casual, outsourced, and labor broker workers (Kapp 2013). Unions in the country have been totally ineffective at recruiting or organizing these workers. Part of the reason is that the dues from these workers are unreliable and unions feel it does not pay to recruit them. Rather, unions continue to focus on the decreasing number of permanent workers as this offers a steady income stream. They have also shifted to increasingly focusing on permanent workers in the state sector, such as the police, nurses, and teachers, as opposed to the growing number of precarious workers in the private sector. The result is that they have alienated large sections of the restructured working class engaged in casual, contract, outsourced and labor broker employment, as well as the unemployed workforce. The credibility of unions among the South African working class has, therefore, taken a severe dent in the last 15 years and union membership has declined. Indeed, from its peak in 1997 at 45 percent of the workforce, by 2012 union membership had declined to 25 percent (Steyn 2014).

THE CASE OF THE NUM AND WORKER COMMITTEES
IN THE PLATINUM MINES

In 2009, the frustration that workers, and in particular labor broker, contract, and outsourced workers, had been feeling towards unions—and the close relationship many had with corporations—began to break out into open rebellion in the country's platinum mines. That year, workers in a number of mines began self-organizing and embarked on underground sit-in wildcat strikes without formal unions and even at times in the face of open union hostility.

The reasons for these strikes were many and often interrelated. Many workers were unhappy with the multi-year wage agreements their unions—the NUM and the Association of Mineworkers and Construction Union (AMCU)—had signed. They felt that, in particular, the NUM had not heeded their mandates and that the leadership and shop stewards sold them out and sided with the employers by agreeing to cap salary increases. The mandates that were given to the NUM largely involved workers demanding above inflation wage increases and that outsourced and contract workers be made permanent. One militant worker summed up this perspective when he was interviewed in 2012: "as time went on, it became a perception of workers to say the relationship between NUM and management in the mines is too close … they were becoming cosy at the expense of the majority of workers" (Sinwell and Mbata 2016: 90). Many participating in the wildcat strikes and sit-ins also demanded an end to contract work, labor brokering, and outsourcing.

At least six underground sit-ins, occupations and wildcat strikes, collectively involving thousands of mineworkers, occurred in the platinum mining sector between 2009 and 2011. These included sit-ins at Eastern Platinum's Crocodile River Mine (De Bruyn 2009a); Aquarius Platinum's Kroondal Mine (De Bruyn 2009b); Impala Platinum's Rustenburg Mine (Hattingh 2010a); Anooraq Resources' Bokoni Mine (Hattingh 2012); African Rainbow Mineral and Impala Platinum's Two Rivers Mine (Pringle 2009); and Australia Platinum's Limpopo mine (Hattingh 2010b). In each case, the workers involved were militant and the sit-ins were preceded by wildcat strikes. Many of the workers who undertook these actions also tended (but certainly not exclusively so) to be contract or labor broker workers, and all of the actions were planned and carried out outside of the two main unions, NUM and AMCU, through worker self-organizing. In each and every case, NUM officials distanced themselves from and condemned the actions of workers. What became apparent, however, was that the wildcat strikes and sit-ins were highly effective. They caught the mining companies completely off-guard and in most cases their demands were often won (Hattingh 2010b).

The platinum mine workers' next phase of the struggle began in early 2012 at Impala Platinum. General and mass meetings of workers unhappy with the NUM's multi-year wage agreements started to take place. Through these meetings, workers took the decision to embark on a wildcat strike for a minimum wage of R 9,000 a month. Part of the reason why workers were demanding such an increase was that, due to the restructuring of the class under neoliberalism, the vast majority of them were heavily indebted and under financial pressure as wages had been stagnating (Bond 2012).

The strike began on January 20, 2012 and soon spread to all of Impala's operations. The workers' demands were put in writing, and the strike was organized using direct democracy in mass meetings in which the workers elected a committee of five to negotiate with management if need be. The committee members were mandated by workers to put forward their demands to the company and were directly accountable to the mass meetings. The committee had no decision-making power, only the mass meetings did. The strike was marked by militancy and was met with force by Impala's security guards and the police. The power of the collective actions of workers, however, was evident, and by March 3 the management at the mine conceded to the demands and raised the workers' minimum salary to R 9,000 (Munshi 2017).

The NUM, for its part, condemned the workers' wildcat strike. As a consequence, it lost the vast majority of its members at Impala after 11,000 workers resigned from the union by March 31. In fact, the NUM became despised by workers. While the management had conceded to the demand for R 9,000 a month, they had also attempted to dismiss 17,500 workers during the strike, an action which the NUM had backed. Eventually in the face of pressure, 15,000 workers were reinstated, but 2,500 of those identified as the most militant workers were not. It was clear from the reaction of the NUM that it feared workers self-organizing and saw its power waning as workers went outside of the framework of the LRA and formal bargaining procedures.

The way the Impala Platinum workers had organized outside unions, and the victory they had won, inspired workers at two other companies in the platinum sector, Amplats and Lonmin, to begin meeting in ad hoc committees independently of the unions in April and May of 2012. While there was no link between workers at the two companies, they similarly formed committees and began formulating their demands and planning actions to pressure the companies to concede. At Lonmin, workers demanded a R 12,500 basic monthly salary, while at Amplats they demanded R 16,070 a month, both of which were significantly higher than the R 4,500 to R 5,000 a month, respectively, that the NUM had settled for in multi-year wage agreements for both mines. The workers calculated these demands on the basis of what would be needed to provide decent housing, food, and education for themselves and their families. Independently of each other, the worker committees at both Lonmin and Amplats approached the management on a number of occasions with their demands. Each time they were rejected and the management at both companies insisted the workers approach them through the NUM. The NUM again condemned the self-organizing of workers.

On August 9, 2012, workers at Lonmin Eastern and Western Operations held a mass meeting to decide on a way forward given the continuous rejection of their demands by the management and their refusal to negotiate directly with them as workers. At that meeting, the workers democratically decided to embark on a wildcat strike. The next day, thousands of workers marched to Lonmin's offices at Marikana to once again directly put their demands to management. And yet again they were informed they could only raise such demands through the largest union, the NUM.

On August 11, Lonmin workers—many of them still NUM members—marched to the NUM offices at Marikana hoping to pressure the union to take up their demands with management. NUM officials at the office were not willing to engage and had clearly decided their own members were a threat. The NUM officials had armed themselves and as workers approached their office they opened fire, severely wounding two workers. With this, open hostilities broke out between the union and the workers. Workers armed themselves with spears, sticks, and blades in the aftermath, fearing another attack by the NUM officials. The next day the police attempted to disarm the workers and clashes took place. Over the next few days, eight people were killed (four mine workers, two policemen, and two security guards).

By August 16, Cyril Ramaphosa (then a shareholder in Lonmin, formerly NUM General Secretary in the 1980s, and now President of South Africa) had contacted the police commissioner and told them the strike must be ended. It was clear that the state and Lonmin now intended to violently crush the strike. That day, workers had gathered on a hill near Marikana and were demanding negotiations with management. Management had refused and in the afternoon police moved in with automatic weapons to end the strike. That day is now infamous, as 34 workers were massacred by the police (Ntswana 2014).

The Lonmin workers, however, continued the strike and a workers' committee was elected and mandated to again take their demands to management. On September 18, the Lonmin strike ended with workers agreeing to a 22 percent wage increase. By then, wildcat strikes had spread across the country and as many as 100,000 workers were out on strike.

On September 12, 2012, workers held mass meetings and decided to embark on a wildcat strike at Amplats to force the company to agree to their demand of R 16,070. During this strike, worker self-organizing through democratic mass meetings and mandated worker committees reached its zenith on the platinum belt. There was even an attempt by workers—with the assistance of progressive activists in the Democratic Left Front and Democratic Socialist Movement—to establish a national coordinating strike committee. In fact, the self-organizing at Amplats was particularly powerful, and many workers felt that their committees could become a lasting alternative to trade unions in the platinum sector. This, however, was not to be. After two months on strike the workers won a concession of a slight increase and soon abandoned the committees they had created (Sinwell and Mbatha 2016).

WORKERS DRIVEN BACK INTO TRADE UNIONS

The mass worker meetings and worker committees that defined the wildcat strikes of 2012 were based on a form of direct democracy and held the potential for spreading workers struggles across South Africa. Their strikes were an attempt to recompose the working class by uniting the very active and militant casual, contract, labor broker, and even permanent workers. For this reason, the ruling class (capitalists and top state officials/politicians) unleashed the full might of the police and military against them.

During and after the wildcat strikes on the platinum belt, the military was deployed along with a massive police presence. In Marikana alone, 1,000 troops were stationed in the area after the massacre. Curfews were established and people caught on the streets at night in townships in the platinum belt were fired at with rubber bullets. Workers' houses were raided and collective punishment was meted out to the residents of working-class areas where the miners resided. Numerous worker leaders involved with the committees were tortured by the police, and activists feared for their lives. Fellow workers of the Marikana martyrs were even charged under the apartheid era "common purpose" law, claiming that the striking workers, not the police, had been guilty of murder due to the police shootings. The net result was that many workers decided it was safer to partake in the existing labor relations through the established unions. They feared that if they continued to embark on wildcat strikes through worker committees the state would unleash increasing amounts of violence against them.

At the same time, the companies simply refused to recognize the worker committees. Their position was that to be recognized going forward, worker committees either had to register as unions or workers had to re-join the established unions to be able to negotiate. The AMCU had offered solidarity to the workers at Marikana and, under pressure from the bosses and the state, workers elected to join AMCU in order to be recognized. Essentially, the workers were traumatized by the state's response and retreated back into the union once the wildcat strikes were over. So, while the NUM's membership declined from 300,000 to 185,000 in the aftermath of the 2012 strikes (Modjadji 2018), AMCU's membership grew from 60,000 before Marikana to 150,000 in 2014 (Botiveau 2014). The change was mostly due to mine workers leaving the NUM for the worker committees in 2012 and subsequently joining the AMCU. Some attempts were made to try and maintain the worker committees, but these lost traction as AMCU gained momentum into 2013.

The reality is that AMCU is no different than the NUM. It is a bureaucratic union that has had the same leader since its founding almost two decades ago, and whose members have at times raised issues about a lack of internal democracy (Whittles 2016). AMCU's leadership insisted that the workers' committees needed to be dissolved before the workers could join the union, stating explicitly that the committees were a threat to their authority. Indeed, some workers who raised issues about the lack of internal democracy in the union after joining the AMCU were soon expelled (Sinwell and Mbatha 2016).

In 2013, it looked as though workers' experiments with directly democratic methods of organizing had ended in South Africa in the face of massive state repression and hostility from capitalists and the unions. By the end of 2013 there were no active worker committees left on the platinum belt. Yet, new struggles began to emerge in the industrial heartland of South Africa, Johannesburg. These soon began to organize outside of unions, and, with the assistance of the Casual Workers Advice Office (CWAO), galvanized into the Simunye Workers Forum (SWF) in 2015.

THE CASUAL WORKERS ADVICE OFFICE
AND THE SIMUNYE WORKERS FORUM

The CWAO was founded in 2011 "as a non-profit, independent organisation to provide advice and support to workers, privileging casual, contract, labour broker and other precarious workers." Precisely because "the traditional labour movement appears incapable or unwilling to organize the new kinds of workers created by neoliberalism," CWAO's core focus has been on catalyzing self-organization amongst precarious workers. For CWAO, there is no predetermined organizational "model" or approach. Rather, "new organisational forms ... will be determined by workers through struggle [in order to] ... best defend their rights, improve upon those rights, and connect with broader struggles for social justice and an egalitarian society" (CWAO 2017).

After an initial period of CWAO outreach and consolidation, involving identifying and meeting with precarious workers and providing educational and legal support, a group of the precarious workers formed the Simunye Workers Forum (SWF) as a direct expression of self-organization offering a non-union organizational and mobilizing alternative. Alongside the advice and support from CWAO, it has been through the activities of the SWF that precarious workers have practically taken forward the defense of their labor rights as well as new forms of organizing and struggle in the neoliberal era.

The SWF was formed when labor broker, outsourced and contract workers, who had been holding mass meetings at CWAO every second Saturday, decided to launch an organization to take their struggles forward. Many had been mobilizing for labor broker and contract workers to win the right to permanent work that had been legislated in the wake of the platinum sector strikes in 2012 and 2013 through an amendment to the LRA.

In the run up to forming the SWF, workers held mass meetings to discuss their struggles, address issues faced at work, and plan how to fight for permanent status. The meetings were characterized by a form of direct democracy where anyone could speak and where there were no formal leaders. Workers debated forming a union, but decided instead to try a new way of organizing as a Forum, launching SWF in 2015.

Hundreds of workplaces on Johannesburg's East Rand now participate in SWF by sending delegates to its mass meetings held at CWAO's office. There are no paid officials or organizers—rather workers organize themselves. SWF-aligned workers have established workplace councils and committees through which workers engage, negotiate, and defend each other against their employers and organize new workers into SWF.

At each central meeting of the SWF at CWAO, workers make voluntary contributions of any amount towards a strike fund and any legal costs that may be incurred. Should there be a strike, all participants at the SWF meeting vote on how much of the fund should be distributed to the strikers (Dor 2017). The SWF has adopted a constitution which in some ways echoes the the militancy and politics of South African workers in the 1970s and early 1980s. It states: "The purpose of the Simuye Workers Forum is to build unity and solidarity amongst workers across all workplaces. It is a democratic organisation that values openness, accountability, respect, study/education and cultural life, non-racialism and non-sexism" (Dor 2017: 9).

In the last few years the SWF has been engaged in a number of new battles. A prime example has been the CWAO/SWF "Big New Rights Campaign," which was instituted after the Constitutional Court ruled in July 2018 that labor broker workers should become the workers of only the client company after three months and must be treated "not less favourably" than the client's other permanent workers. When worker groups engaged in coordinated pamphleteering in Johannesburg's industrial areas, it "led to 117 new workplaces approaching the CWAO and SWF between August 2018 and February 2019" (Schroeder 2019: 1). As the CWAO has noted, such a response suggests

> that workers are now moving beyond just being hostile to trade unions and are now actively organising themselves outside of these dying organisations. We see this in the number of workplaces that are organising themselves, in how they are organising other workplaces within their companies, and in the growth nationally of worker initiatives outside of the trade unions. (Schroeder 2019: 1)

The CWAO/SWF model of worker self-organization has spread to other parts of the country. Examples of such growth include the Workers Assembly in Harrismith, the Thoyandou Unemployed Teachers Forum, and the Mossel Bay Independent Workers Advice Centre. Numerous community health workers forums have sprung up around the country, such as the Gauteng Health Workers Forum

(GHWF), "a provincial based forum with a flat leadership structure that avoids having union-like bureaucratic structures" (Hlatshwayo 2017: 755).

Further confirmation of the uptick in worker self-organization and coordination of struggles is evident in the case of labor broker workers at the Sedibeng brewery of the Dutch beer conglomerate Heineken. Having been effectively abandoned by the dominant union, the Food and Allied Workers Union (FAWU), the workers formed an independent Heineken Workers Council demanding that they be employed directly by Heineken. With legal and procedural assistance from the CWAO, the workers were able to win the right to a protected strike and have now taken up their ongoing struggle in the national and international media and labor arena (Brandt 2018).

Another example of how precarious workers, both through and with the CWAO and SWF, have taken the lead in forging new and creative forms of solidarity and organizing can be found in the case of workers from two different Pioneer Foods workplaces. After approaching the CWAO in 2018, the group of workers joined SWF and "decided to coordinate the struggles at the two workplaces through a WhatsApp group" and to then use this new collective to reach out to organize fellow workers at other Pioneer Foods plants (Hlungwani 2019).

These efforts are all the more significant given the current class composition characterized by the systemic insecurity, impermanency, and vulnerability faced by precarious workers. As SWF members have clearly pointed out, the very nature of precarious work sets workers against each other. The cumulative result is that workers are constantly kept guessing whether or not they will have a job, for how long, and if so under what conditions. This in turn creates a permanent instability and presents a significant obstacle to organizing and mobilizing all the workers (Schroeder 2018). The fact that many manufacturers operate on a 24-hour basis also complicates matters and makes organizing difficult. When there are three eight-hour shifts in such workplaces, workers on different shifts find it hard or even impossible to attend the same organizing meeting for any length of time and there is always a group that cannot attend. These are the very practical challenges the decomposed working class faces under neoliberalism.

Additionally, workers relate how this fragmentation sets workers against each other. For example, when precarious workers do start to organize they are often faced with "leaders" selling them out when the employers offer them a permanent position. The consequent challenges in bringing workers together are made all the more difficult because of the common perception that "the unions are f**ked up … they come to get our monies but then when we need them to represent us they are not there." According to a SWF activist, "when we were struggling to become permanents (at Simba Chips) FAWU [Food and Allied Workers Union] never helped us but now that we are permanent workers (thanks to CWAO) they come to us and say that we must join FAWU … if you can see how unions are working right now, it is all about the money" (SWF members 2018).

In light of these realities, precarious workers have filled the "gap," leaving behind old organizational forms and methods that no longer serve their individual or collective interests. "Now that we are organised ourselves (with the help of CWAO) we do not have to rely on shop stewards to go and negotiate with management, we can go negotiate for ourselves … we know the other workers and what they are going through" (SWF members 2018).

As a result of the collective coming together of workers through the "vehicles" of the CWAO and SWF on the basis of practical workplace needs and struggles, there is an added impetus and desire to go out and get others to join the collective, to be part of non-union forms of self-organizing. This allows workers to lead struggles and new forms of organization that do not revolve around rigidly defined legal, organizational, political and/or ideological status, identity, or affiliation.

For SWF members, the road so far travelled is representative of a simple yet profoundly different approach focused on the majority of contemporary workers—i.e. precarious workers—and their struggles in the workplace. Their forms of organization and struggle can be seen by other workers in other workplaces and then reproduced and expanded.

In this, there is a very distinct recognition that the role of the CWAO and the SWF has been to catalyze more confident workers who now not only have the ability to represent, organize, and advocate on their own but also have the possibility of building something larger. The CWAO/SWF are the incipient "homes" for bigger battles and for the forging of a national workers' movement that can engage in larger-scale complementary struggles on a more class-wide basis. Indeed, SWF's experiment with a new form of organizing is an attempt to recompose working-class power in order for contract, casual, and labor broker workers to find their own collective ways to organize and confront the challenges they face in the neoliberal period.

CONCLUSION

Since 2009, sections of the restructured working class in South Africa have begun to self-organize at the point of production through mass meetings, worker committees, and now worker forums and councils. The reason for this is the workers' dissatisfaction with the bureaucratic form unions have taken in the country. Workers started breaking with trade unions they perceived as being too close to the ANC ruling party, the state, and corporations.

These new forms of workers' self-organization have also been a reaction to the failure of unions to deal with the fragmentation of workers' power and the rise of precarious work, which have been part and parcel of the changing composition of the working class under neoliberalism. What the experiments with forums, committees, and councils by mostly casual, contract, labor broker, and outsourced workers show is that workers themselves can effectively self-organize against neoliberalism, rebuild their own power, and even win gains.

The task now is to spread alternative, new, and directly democratic ways of organizing in South Africa. Indeed, the decomposed and restructured working class under neoliberalism needs such new ways of organizing in order to collectively forge unity and deal with the challenges it faces at the hands of capitalists and the state. In doing so, workers will also need to be willing to go outside of the LRA. Strategies for effective self-defense against the inevitable onslaught of the state and ruling class will also have to be developed to avoid the trauma that the platinum workers were subjected to. If the experiments with formations such as SWF can be built on, spread, and maintained, a better world based on working-class power can be won by the working class itself.

REFERENCES

Bond, P. (2012). Debt, Uneven Development and the Capitalist Crisis in South Africa. At http://ccs.ukzn.ac.za/files/Bond%20Berlin%20paper%20on%20debt%20and%20 uneven%20development%20in%20contemporary%20South%20Africa.pdf.

Botiveau, R. (2014). Marikana and South Africa's Changing Labour Relations. *African Affairs* 13(150), 128–37.

Brandt, F. (2018). No Access to the Right to Strike for Workers at Heineken Sedibeng. *Daily Maverick* (September 9). At https://www.dailymaverick.co.za/article/2018-09-19-no-access-to-the-right-to-strike-for-workers-at-heineken-sedibeng.

Byrne, S., Ulrich, N., and van der Walt, L. (2017). Red, Black and Gold: FOSATU, South African "Workerism," "Syndicalism" and the Nation. In Webster, E. and Pampillas, K. (eds.), *The Unresolved National Question in South Africa: Left Thinking Under Apartheid*. Johannesburg: Wits University Press, pp. 254–73.

CWAO (2017). About page. At www.cwao.org.za/about.asp

De Bruyn, C. (2009a). Hostage Drama Slows Production at Eastplats' Crocodile River Mine. *Mining Weekly* (July 10). At www.miningweekly.com /print-version/ contract-miners-hold-crocodile-river-supervisors-hostage-2009-07-10.

De Bruyn, C. (2009b). Aquarius' Kroondal Mine Reopened After Protest Action. *Mining Weekly* (November 23). At http://www.miningweekly.com/article/ aquarius-kroondal-mine-reopened-after-protest-action-2009-11-23.

Dor, L. (2017). Simunye Workers Forum. *Workers World News* 107(9).

Gentle, L. (2012). The Strike Wave and New Workers' Organisations: Breaking Out of Old Compromises. South African Civil Society Information Service (November 12). At https://sacsis.org.za/site/article/1487.

Good, K. (2014). *Trust in the Capacities of the People, Distrust in Elites*. London: Lexington Books.

Hattingh, S. (2010a). Mineworkers Direct Action: Occupations and Sit-Ins in South Africa. *WorkingUSA* 13(3), 243–50.

Hattingh, S. (2010b). Mine Occupations in South Africa. *Z-Magazine* At https:// saasha.net/2014/06/24/hattingh-mine-occupations-in-south-africa-z-mag.

Hattingh, S. (2012). What Marikana Tells Us. At http://ccs.ukzn.ac.za/files/What%20 Marikana%20tells%20us.pdf.

Hlatshwayo, M. (2017). Responses of Precarious Workers to Their Conditions in South Africa's Public Sector. *Journal of Public Administration* 52(4), 741–60.

Hlungwani, P. (2019). Mobilising Pioneers. *The New Worker* 8.

Kapp, L. (2013). *The Responses of Trade Unions to the Effects of Neoliberalism in South Africa: The Case of COSATU and its Affiliated Unions*. MA thesis, University of South Africa.

Mahlakoana, T. (2017). Internal Revolt Threatens NUMSA Over Financial Disarray. *Business Day* (July 28). At https://www.businesslive.co.za/bd/national/labour/2017-07-28-exclusive-internal-revolt-threatens-numsa-over-financial-disarray.

Modjadli, N. (2018). Marikana Proves Costly for Once Mighty NUM. *Sowetan* (June 21). At https://www.sowetanlive.co.za/news/south-africa/2018-06-21-marikana-proves-costly-for-once-mighty-num.

Moussouris, M. (2017). SAFTU: The Tragedy and (Hopefully Not) the Farce. *Pambazuka* (June 15). At https://www.pambazuka.org/human-security/saftu-tragedy-and-hopefully-not-farce.

Munshi, N. (2017). *Platinum Politics: The Rise, and Rise, of the Association of Mineworkers and Construction Union (AMCU)*. MA thesis, Wits University.

Ntswana, N. (2014). *The Politics of Workers Control in South Africa's Platinum Mines: Do Workers' Committees in the Platinum Mining Industry Represent a Practice of Renewing Worker Control?* MA thesis, Wits University.

Pringle, C. (2009). Illegal Sit-In Halts Production at SA Platinum Mine. *Mining Weekly* (October 19). At www.miningweekly.com/.../illegal-sit-in-halts-production-at-two-rivers-2009-10-19.

Schroeder, I. (2018). Interviewed by D. McKinley (November 1).

Schroeder, I. (2019). Big New Rights Campaign Update. *The New Worker* 8.

Sinwell, L. and Mbatha, S. (2016). *The Spirit of Marikana: The Rise of Insurgent Trade Unionism in South Africa*. Johannesburg: Wits University Press.

Slovo, J. (1988). The South African Working Class and the National Democratic Revolution. At www.marxists.org/subject/africa/slovo/1988/national-democratic-revolution.htm.

Steyn, L. (2014). The Downward Spiral of SA Unions. *Mail and Guardian* (November 13). At https://mg.co.za/article/2014-11-13-the-downward-spiral-of-sa-unions.

SWF members (2018). Interviewed by D. McKinley (October 14).

Twala, C. and Konpi, B. (2012). The Congress of South African Trade Unions and the Tripartite Alliance: A Marriage of (In)convenience. *Journal of Contemporary History* 3, 171–90.

Ulrich, N. (2005). The 1973 Strikes and the Birth of a New Movement in Natal. *Khanya: A Journal for Activists* 8, 6–9.

van der Walt, L. (2010). *The Crisis Hits Home: Strategic Unionism, Anarcho-syndicalism and Rebellion*. Johannesburg: Zabalaza Books.

van der Walt, L. (2011). Anarchism and Syndicalism in an African Port City: The Revolutionary Traditions of Cape Town's Multiracial Working Class, 1904–1931. *Labor History* 52(2), 137–71.

van der Walt, L. (2016). Global Anarchism and Syndicalism: Theory, History, Resistance. *Anarchist Studies* 24(1), 85–106.

Whittles, G. (2016). Joseph Mathunjwa the Dictator? AMCU Leader Accused of Crushing Dissent. *Mail and Guardian* (September 15). At https://mg.co.za/article/2016-09-15-00-joseph-mathunjwa-the-dictator-amcu-leader-accused-of-crushing-dissent.

9

Towards a Global Workers' Inquiry: A Study of Indian Precarious Auto Workers

Lorenza Monaco

This chapter will make the case for retrieving the workers' inquiry as a practice of militant research while extending it beyond its original conceptualization in order to embrace the global nature of today's working class. By building on the debate initially developed by the Italian workerists from the 1960s such as Panzieri, Alquati, and Tronti, it examines the meaning, ideal design, and possible applications of such a practice. To do so, this chapter will reflect on the experience of conducting a workers' inquiry in the Indian automotive cluster surrounding Delhi (National Capital Region) between 2011 and 2019. Ultimately, the chapter also aims to highlight the necessary synergy between research and organizing by reconsidering the role of the militant researcher, or activist scholar, today.

WORKERS' INQUIRY AS A MILITANT PRACTICE

There is a need not only to retrieve but also to stretch the boundaries of the workers' inquiry. This is critically necessary in order to address the character of the global working class. To do so, we must first examine the meaning, ideal design, and possible applications of the workers' inquiry at the global level.

The starting point for the conceptualization of a workers' inquiry is the centrality the early workerists attribute to the struggle for the production of revolutionary knowledge, which in turn is needed to plan organized actions. This is the case because, according to Tronti (2006,

2009), "knowledge is tied to struggle"—political theory and practice become strictly intertwined and research per se comes to represent a totally functional exercise to inform militant practices. This requires reconsidering our three points above—meaning, design, application—and is directly linked to the role of the militant intellectual.

Understanding the original meaning and the function of a workers' inquiry requires reconnecting to the debate of the early workerists on the issue of method. Panzieri (1976, 1994), for example, considered the possible formalization of a workers' inquiry by applying the research methods used in a sociological survey to materials directly produced by the workers themselves and to the participant observation of processes of industrial restructuring and productive organization (Tronti 2009; Monaco 2015b).

Another line of workers' inquiry, one closer to the common critique of bourgeois science and more allergic to the standardization of an inquiry, was articulated by Alquati (1975), who remained faithful to the idea of research as a political tool, expressly intended to support the design of revolutionary actions. In this sense, Alquati kept his "radical genius" in the theorization of a workers' inquiry as a pure instrument of struggle (Monaco 2018). In doing so, he strongly defended the idea of a correspondence between the "subject" and the "object" of the study, whether they be the interviewer and the interviewee or the militant researcher and the worker engaged in the struggle. His idea of workers' inquiry was strictly linked to that of *co-research* (see also Centro Riforma Stato 2011), as an attempt to bring the sociology of work and the study of labor straight into workers' struggles as a proper organizing tool. The idea of co-research theorized a disappearance of the distance between the activist scholar, the militant, and the worker in an overall commonality of objectives and tactics (Monaco 2015a). This was actually occurring in Italy in the 1960s. The experiences of inquiry and co-research had multiplied from the FIAT factories in Turin, to the dockworkers' struggles in Genoa, to Porto Marghera—Italy was an expansive political laboratory where militant researchers and struggling workers came together (Monaco 2018; Wright 2002).

The idea of co-research brings together a discussion of the ideal design of a workers' inquiry and of the use one can make of it. As a political practice based on the co-production of knowledge, its design and objectives should not only rest on a collective discussion of the needs and the aims of the struggle in question, but should actually be formulated on the basis of what can be *most useful* for the advancement of a struggle.

For example, besides the Indian inquiry discussed later in this chapter, I also had two very interesting and constructive experiences in the UK and in South Africa, where the actual workers' inquiries were conducted as a team, bearing in mind the interests and the timings of the ongoing struggles. The group in the UK were a group of peers, all precarious teachers, scholars, and activists engaged in an anti-casualization campaign. In South Africa we worked together in a small, mixed group of eight to nine researchers and workers—the researchers were also activists and the workers became workers-researchers, administering and presenting the research results themselves. Overall, while the initial need was expressed by organizers involved in a campaign for permanency with the Casual Workers Advice Office (Johannesburg), the subsequent stages (development of the idea, design, test of the survey, distribution, analysis, and presentation of findings to the broader workers' forum) were all shared as a group (Monaco 2019d). In a sense, the South Africa workers' inquiry closely resembled the early workerist practice of identifying a *collective worker*: a single, vocal, politicized individual, with deep knowledge of the struggle, who could embody and represent the experience of a mass of workers engaged in the struggle. The collective worker would be actively involved in both the struggle and the inquiry, acting as a collective voice and a channel to transmit the contents of the inquiry to the workers who could use it in their struggle (Monaco 2018).

However, while co-research practices are ideal in the design and the administration of an inquiry, the idea of inquiry as a political instrument meant to serve objectives of struggle brings along a rejection of excessive formalization and standardization. Once again, the distinction between *political practice* and *method* comes up. Here, we embrace the former, whereby the intrinsic political use of the inquiry itself calls for flexibility and adaptation, far from a rigid definition of tools, procedures, and aims. For example, Woodcock (2016) distinguishes between two possible types of inquiry, which can take shape according to the political circumstances, the kind of workplace investigated, the level of possible exposure of the workers, and the positionality of the researcher, among other factors. One type is an inquiry "from below," and the other an inquiry "from above." The first is closer to the co-research idea, and responds to the needs of the workers themselves; the second follows a direction initiated by the militant researcher rather than the workers engaged in struggle. In practice, each inquiry might pursue different patterns and draw on different tools. For example, the need to conduct an inquiry may arise from the workers as well as from their organizers when they become aware that they need more information in order to organize more effectively (something similar to what we faced in South Africa). Likewise, the best research tools may depend on what is more feasible, considering for example whether workers can freely meet, the level of corporate repression at the time, the intensity of the conflict at that stage, the assumed targets (e.g. ideal outreach), etc.

The last point in defining a workers' inquiry concerns its use and possible applications. Seeing an inquiry as a *tool for struggle* (Tronti 2009) recalls an instrumental use in directly contributing to building a militant intervention. In practice, this link might not be that straightforward or easy to build. For example, it may not be self-evident that the research could be used to strengthen the struggle. In South Africa, this realization emerged during a few lengthy group discussions. It may frequently occur, however, that workers, especially if engaged at the peak of a struggle, may consider the time needed for the research excessive or its objective superfluous. In addition, they might be "rightly" suspicious of researchers who often bring their own individual or vested interests, power, and privileges. There has been a strong and interesting debate in South Africa on this very question of the role of academics in social movements (Mdlalose 2014; Bond 2015; Walsh 2015).

Indeed, this debate is centrally connected to the role of the militant researcher today, who, if an academic, will be under the pressure of neoliberal academia, where research times are squeezed, the possibility of conducting "non-marketable," independent research is very limited, and the "publish or perish" mantra dominates, restricting the space for collaborations, collective authorship, and political critique. This all makes the relationship between research, working-class struggle, and organizing harder to build, and requires strong individual resistance to the marketization of knowledge production and research.

THE CASE FOR EXPANDING THE WORKERS' INQUIRY TO THE GLOBAL WORKING CLASS

Having outlined the main features of an ideal workers' inquiry, we may conclude that it should not only be reconsidered as a still valid tool for an analysis of class composition and the dynamics of struggle, but should also be applied to a wider global extent. Of course, while acknowledging that the workers' inquiry emerged as the expression of a specific period and political experience (Italy during the industrial boom from the late 1950s to the early 1970s), retrieving and expanding it today will imply two different operations.

The first operation will require overcoming a rigid historical determinism, often common on the left, according to which an experience cannot be repeated if it is abstracted from a prior political "golden age." The second will involve the search for a balance between sound political principles in design and implementation, and the need for flexibility around political practices in order to adapt research tools to a changing global working class. This will entail, above all, a constant attempt to establish relationships of trust between activist scholars and workers, securing workers' ownership of the process and defending them from self-interested academics. The role of the militant intellectual in both operations must be seen as evolving and fluid, embracing the changing setting of an era characterized by global mobility and the interconnectedness of both production and struggles.

For a global workers' inquiry to be established, two main directions will have to be followed. Although some very interesting cases already exist, more can be done to lay a stronger foundation and enhance global political strategies. Firstly, a workers' inquiry today must embody the nature of global production, that is, the global connection between production, non-production (e.g. manufacturing-related services, logistics, etc.), and financial nodes within the same value chain. This means, on the one hand, going beyond a traditional factoryism in order to embrace non-production workers as part of the same economic platform. On the other hand, it means maintaining a connection with production workers even if located outside of the now mostly deindustrialized capitalist core. In turn, this will require abandoning exclusively Northern/Western-centric perspectives and more strongly affirming experiences of militant research coming from the Global South, while valorizing the evolving role of the activist scholar. The workers' inquiry conducted in the Delhi auto cluster, which will be discussed in the next section, represents an attempt to move in these two directions.

There have already been several critical steps taken to move in these directions. Firstly, for the past few decades we have seen some very interesting initiatives combining research and labor activism in relation to non-production workers in the Global North. One of the most valuable of these initiatives is the work done by the *Notes from Below* group in the UK (see Chapter 6 in this volume). In the wake of Ed Emery's (1995) call "no politics without inquiry," they have seriously relaunched the idea of the workers' inquiry as a ground for political action to be applied to today's categories of vulnerable workers. Brilliant work has been done on call center workers, the gig economy, delivery and logistics workers, supermarkets, and recently on the videogame industry. This work has also been collected in two books by Woodcock, *Working the Phones* (2016), on call center workers, and *Marx at the Arcade* (2019), on the videogames industry, and another by Cant, *Riding for Deliveroo* (2019), on Deliveroo platform workers in the UK. Both Woodcock and Cant worked in the workplace/work networks they describe, the former as an "undercover researcher" given the ruthlessness of employers in that sector, and became directly involved in worker organizing. They provide direct accounts of the oppressive work rhythms, poor working conditions, and the difficulty of organizing a workers' struggle.

Outside of the UK, there is also a growing body of political research on knowledge workers, logistics, and the gig economy. Bologna (2013, 2014a, 2014b), for example, traces the evolution of Italian workerism from the Fordist to a Post-Fordist society, highlighting how the legacy of the early workerism provided the lenses and the approach to understand the new categories of workers that have emerged outside the large factory. He not only analyzes the proliferation of self-employed and knowledge workers, but also clearly elucidates the structure and working conditions in the Italian logistics sector. Recently, interesting work on the gig or platform economy has also emerged, such as the study of workplace solidarity and organizing of food courier workers in Italy and the UK conducted by Tassinari and Maccarone (2019).

While many interesting debates and initiatives of militant research have been conducted in the Global South, these often do not enjoy the same attention as cases of scholarly activism in the North. With this in mind, the militant research reported in this chapter tries to shed light on the Indian experience, not only exporting the practice of a workers' inquiry, but also underlining the need to further explore the Indian labor market and to value the richness of Indian political activism. Beginning in 2006, brilliant work was carried out by the collective publishing project *Gurgaon Workers News* (*Gurgaon Workers News* 2006–15) concerning the same industrial area surveyed here, the National Capital Region (NCR) industrial zone surrounding Delhi. Strongly inspired by a workerist approach, the group collected and reported excellent material about workers' lives and working experiences in the area, voicing their struggles, and actively denouncing the corporate exploitation in the zone. Brave and valuable labor activists, like those involved with the Workers Solidarity Centre in Gurgaon of the NCR, continue supporting precarious and vulnerable workers and their strikes, despite the fierce state and corporate repression they have been subjected to since the Maruti unrest in 2011–12.

In South Africa, as noted above, the debate around the connection between research and activism, and the direct engagement of academic researchers in social movements and labor struggles, has also been rich. A very interesting contribution was made by Dawson and Sinwell (2012) who discuss the ethical and political challenges potentially arising from the direct involvement of researchers in social struggles. While acknowledging dilemmas, they also underline how strengthening the link between theory and action can contribute both to the production of critical knowledge and to the advancement of social movements. In practice, besides the cases treated by Dawson and Sinwell, the aforementioned work conducted around the Casual Workers Advice Office (CWAO) in Germiston, Johannesburg, represents a very good combination of research, legal support, and political struggle for the regularization of labor broker workers, the right to strike, and the right to a living wage (see, for example, Chapter 7 in this volume). The CWAO has already supported several surveys and reports on the conditions of labor broker workers, including one in 2018 based on a co-research project in which I participated, on the coverage of minimum wage agreements.

In China, the group around gongchao.org has also produced brilliant workers' inquiries. From 2012 to 2015, Hao Ren et al. (2012–15) published the magazine *Factory Stories,* on working conditions and struggles in Chinese workplaces. Also influenced by Italian workerism, they explored factory work in Shenzen, discussing critical issues around labor shortages, short-term working arrangements, overtime, life in the workers' dorms, etc. The strength of this project was not only the nature of the investigation within sensitive industrial areas and under an oppressive labor regime, but also its significant effort to share workers' stories by translating them into multiple languages. Edited by the same author who launched *Factory Stories,* the book *China on Strike: Narratives of Workers' Resistance* (Hao Ren, Friedman, and Li 2016) also represented one of the first notable attempts to share stories of struggles in multinational companies with factories in China, such as Apple, HP, Nike etc. Another important contribution is the recent volume by Shigang (2018), which analyses the formation of a new industrial working class in China's south-eastern export processing zones over the past 35 years. It particularly focuses on the condition of Chinese migrant labor coming from the hinterland, and their participation in màss protests. Again, these extremely important contributions, reporting on the conditions of industrial workers in today's global production hub, still have a very insufficient coverage, and should be given a much wider outreach.

While the work towards a global workers' inquiry still requires deeper connections and exchanges, stronger solidarity, and an internationalism of struggles in order to reflect the current interconnectedness of productive platforms and the global nature of work, some good initiatives exist, and they should be put into dialogue across sectors between Global North and South. The path is not simple, but this chapter constitutes a humble contribution to this effort.

THE CASE OF INDIAN CONTRACT WORKERS
IN THE NCR AUTO CLUSTER

Amongst the legacies of Italian Workerism, Corradi (2011) rightly highlighted, beyond the use of workers' inquiry and co-research as political tools, the commitment to the analysis of class composition and the attempt to constantly report a sort of historiography of workers' struggles (see also Wright 2002, 2007). The inquiry recounted in this chapter was inspired by such objectives. In addition, it was informed by an experience of co-research conducted around the FIAT Pomigliano plant in Italy (see Centro per la Riforma dello Stato 2011; Monaco 2015a), and by my first meeting with Tronti (Monaco 2011), which involved an enlightening discussion on the centrality of conflict in revealing the relations of production and the contradictions of capitalist development.

The Indian automotive sector was selected for comparing the evolution of traditional industries in emerging economies and newly industrialized areas. More specifically, the Indian NCR was chosen as a privileged field due to the presence of an intense industrial conflict, which saw its peak during the Maruti-Suzuki strikes in 2011–12. The idea was to focus on two main objectives: mapping the labor composition in the area, and understanding the dynamics of the ongoing struggle. Unlike traditional workers' inquiries that aim to map class composition, the present inquiry started from a prior stage and took a more "cautious" approach. Given the greenfield area in Manesar (recent industrial formation, no previous unionization, and first manifestations of struggle) and the young composition of the workforce, its objectives were to map the working and living conditions in the industrial cluster (to better understand workers' material demands) and to analyze the motivations and dynamics of the struggle in order to ultimately assess *whether* a process of class formation occurred and how.

The research methods were chosen in relation to the actual dynamics of the conflict and in collaboration with the actors involved (unionists, labor activists, and rank-and-file workers), who bounced ideas back and forth in order to indicate what was most doable. The inquiry involved a first round of meetings with local unions and labor activists to understand the issues at stake, plus focus groups with Maruti, Suzuki, and Honda workers who explained the issues of contention. Following the focus groups, a questionnaire was designed based on the problems they raised, and then translated into Hindi and checked and distributed by the workers. During this phase, given the acute tension around the ongoing conflict—heavy politicization of the Gurgaon-Manesar area, a curfew which targeted even minor gatherings in the aftermath of the first strikes, coupled with the easy visibility of the researcher (a white, foreign woman in a male-dominated industrial area)—precautions had to be taken. For example, the factory plants could not be accessed and meetings took place outside, mostly with the assistance and mediation of local trade unions active in the Gurgaon area. The access to more autonomous workers was possible only through independent labor activists.

Later on, other rounds of in-depth interviews followed which tracked the dynamics of the conflict in the short and long run. The inquiry began in 2009, and was largely developed while the Maruti strikes were going on in 2011 and 2012. Follow-up interviews were conducted in 2017 and 2019 with the objective of understanding the evolution of the industrial relations system in the Gurgaon-Manesar area. These interviews also delved into the legacy of the last round of struggle, including the repression that followed, the legal case, the backlash against the workers, and the lessons learnt by the workers from the Maruti dispute (see Monaco 2020, forthcoming).

Overall, it can be said that the inquiry entailed an "extensive" and an "intensive" phase. The first extensive phase involved the questionnaire survey of 146 workers from six Original Equipment Manufacturers (OEMs or large assembly companies) and 13 auto component suppliers. This allowed an assessment of the existing socio-political composition of the workers by constructing a map of working and living conditions in the area, profiling the workers, and gauging levels of unionization. The second intensive phase allowed the inquiry to gauge the social and political factors that could explain a process of class formation and the demands advanced through the struggle. This phase consisted of long interviews, focus groups, the collection of some life histories of workers, visits to the industrial areas and the workers' villages, and participation in workers' sit-ins and protests (where possible, considering the high level of repression and police surveillance at the time). Such methods were intended to allow for a more direct observation of and involvement in the protests, and an overall analysis of the struggle's dynamics and the power relations permeating the conflict.

The mapping exercise disclosed characteristics of a greenfield site in the Gurgaon-Manesar area, and a site of older industrial formation in Faridabad. Overall, the NCR area is dominated by three Maruti-Suzuki plants which have implemented the Japanese production and management system (see also Jha and Chakraborty 2014). While the Faridabad/Noida area is older, the Maruti Manesar plant was the last one opened by the Indo-Japanese group in 2006. The opening of the plant in a new industrial area (Industrial Model Township/IMT) provided an opportunity to test a greenfield site with no established trade unions and with the availability of an educated workforce drawn straight from technical schools in the Delhi region (Monaco 2015a, 2020 forthcoming).

In Manesar, in fact, the inquiry uncovered a young, educated workforce, often in their first paid job, coming from many different Indian states, often leaving their families back home, and generally engaged in their first political experience of class struggle. The survey also confirmed a significant level of casualization, with workers either employed on a contract basis or as apprentices, and a wide disparity between the wages of permanent and casual workers. In relation to working conditions on the factory floor and the technical composition of the workforce (and the actual application of the Japanese lean model), the questionnaires reported a very high speed on the assembly line, extremely short breaks, missing or overcrowded facilities, and frequent accidents. In Figures 9.1 and 9.2, and Table 9.1 below, we can observe the composition of the surveyed workers per education levels, duration of employment, and the overall increase in contract workers in Indian organized manufacturing (Chandrasekhar and Gosh 2014).

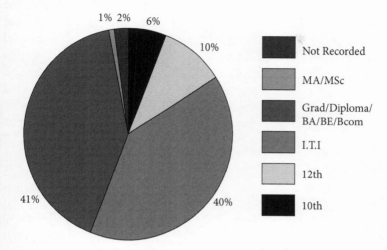

Figure 9.1   Composition of NCR Workers per Education Level
Source: author's inquiry, 2012.

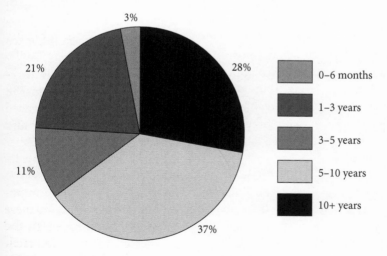

Figure 9.2   Composition of Workers per Duration of Employment
Source: author's survey, 2012.

Table 9.1   Contract Workers in Indian Organized Manufacturing
Source: Chandrasekhar and Ghosh 2014: 2.

What emerged from the sample of surveyed workers was a confirmation of the young age of workers (87 percent below the age of 30), with relatively high levels of education (82 percent with technical school diplomas or post-secondary education), mainly employed at the time the Maruti Manesar opened or soon thereafter. In terms of the percentage of workers employed on a casual or contract basis, the inquiry revealed up to one third of the sample had been hired on non-permanent terms. In reality, and today, this is much higher. Firstly, the inquiry had a possible bias towards permanent workers, who were accessible through unions and risked less when filling the questionnaire. Second, the percentage will have increased following recent strikes (with the constant substitution of permanent workers with casual ones) and largely vary per company (with many companies now employing a majority of precarious workers, up to 90–95 percent of the total).

Despite a slight improvement in contract workers' wages following the Maruti dispute, the salary gap between permanent and casual workers remains large (Monaco 2017, 2019a, 2019b). Overall, what the general analysis of the social and technical composition of the NCR workforce showed was a young, educated labor force, often employed right out of school, that saw their expectations clashing with the reality of dehumanizing work on the line (see also Peoples

Union for Democratic Rights 2013). Such a mismatch, together with the extreme exploitation of the casual workforce, the contradiction of corporate rhetoric with the actual possibilities of consumption and social reproduction, and the violent repression jointly perpetuated by state and capital, are seen as the factors contributing to a process of working-class recomposition in the newly industrialized area (Monaco 2015b).

Alongside the questionnaire survey, the multiple rounds of interviews, focus groups, and meetings helped to grasp motivations, modalities, and outcomes of the Maruti strikes and of the generalized wave of protests and strikes that followed in the Gurgaon-Manesar area. The main demands of the Maruti strike, which came up repeatedly in other protests and strikes in the same region, were the registration of an independent union (management in many plants did not allow a union to exist or imposed a yellow/management-friendly union without regular elections) and the regularization of contract workers. Indeed, one of the peculiarities of the Maruti strikes, which also came up in more recent protests, was the large participation of contract/casual workers, struggling together with the permanent workers, in an unprecedented display of solidarity. While management abuses and anti-union behaviors functioned as a common ground for all categories of workers, the frequent violations of the Contract Labour Act (which defines areas and tasks in which the employment of casual workers is not allowed), and the arbitrary distinctions created between permanent and casual workers, only increased the involvement of the most vulnerable workers (Monaco 2019c).

With regard to political practices and the dynamics of struggle, the Maruti strike was one of the most prolonged that has affected the NCR in the last ten years, lasting almost one year, and including two factory occupations, a 33-day factory lock out, and repeated toolsdown strikes (Monaco 2015b, 2017; Peoples Union for Democratic Rights 2013). The strike also inaugurated a period of fierce repression starting with a supposed accident on July 18, 2012, followed by a fire in the Manesar plant in which a human resources manager died. This resulted in the arrest of hundreds of workers and the dismissal of the rest. About 80 workers arrested without trial were not bailed out until March 2015, while the remaining 13 workers, including former worker leaders and the heads of the newly formed independent union (Maruti Suzuki Employees Union, MSEU, then Maruti Suzuki Workers Union, MSWU), remained high in the public profile thanks to a "Free the 13 Maruti workers" campaign organized on their behalf. Protests that followed after the Maruti strike also saw a heavy police presence, mass arrests, increasing difficulties for independent unions to register, and authoritarian managerial practices (International Commission for Labor Rights 2013). As a positive outcome, the strike taught local workers important lessons and represented an impressive turn in the politicization of casual workers. While the alliance of permanent and casual workers during the Maruti protests was unexpected and marked an unprecedented degree of solidarity, the political involvement of casual workers in strikes and protests has become increasingly frequent, even outside the legal protection of existing trade unions.

Overall, the inquiry revealed the contradictions and the brutality of a labor regime characterized by high levels of casualization and aggressive anti-union repression. However, it also disclosed an ongoing process of political sensitization and class formation developed around a common awareness of exploitation and deluded expectations. In practice, it allowed the workers to grasp the material reality that led to their strike demands, affecting the dynamics of their struggle over the following years through the subsequent rounds of research conducted in 2017 and 2019 (for a more detailed account of this story, see Monaco 2020, forthcoming).

CONCLUDING REMARKS: USING AN INQUIRY TO UNDERSTAND GLOBAL STRUGGLES

A workers' inquiry intentionally designed as a political tool can connect research and organizing to allow for a deeper understanding of class composition and the dynamics of struggle. However, it needs to be extended into a Global Workers' Inquiry which is able to investigate the interconnectedness of production and work within global value chains, as well as the continuities and differences in corporate strategies and labor responses emerging within the same industrial sectors or multinational companies across the world.

For a Global Workers' Inquiry to be carried out, two main issues will have to be considered. Firstly, understanding the meaning, design, and application of such an inquiry is critically needed in order not only to learn from the original workerist debates but also to incorporate the fluidity of current processes of production and struggle together with a consideration of the evolving role of the militant researcher. Secondly, only an extension of the inquiry across production and non-production sectors and to the Global South will allow for a complete picture of the changing world of work and for the establishment of stronger political strategies based on global solidarity.

In practice, while the need for an inquiry will always have to emerge from specific struggles or groups of workers, researchers may have to act as bridges and support the formation of global solidarity networks. They may have to serve workers' struggles by sharing stories, writing, translating, and encouraging the use of media connecting different parts of the globe. In this sense, a militant researcher coming from abroad, and reporting on struggles happening on the other side of the world, will have to be seen as a useful channel rather than automatically an outsider.

At the same time, translating workers' experiences and stories of struggle in order to create a sort of global depository should become a shared practice (see what www.gongchao.org is attempting to do). Finally, facilitating the use of media and social media would be a useful contribution. This could be done, for example, by recording and sharing videos, live-streaming events, or even just training workers on how to use WhatsApp or similar apps to create political groups, like CWAO does.

In concrete terms, merging country-focused platforms and websites into a global platform which may serve as an international reference would be useful. Grouping reports of struggles by productive sectors and multinational companies would be another important step. Harmonizing objectives and practices (but not necessarily methods—see the discussion above about how the excessive standardization and formalization of tools fails to respect the fluidity of specific struggles) could also prove to be helpful. For example, workplace and sector mapping could be a starting exercise (see Brooks, Singh and Winslow

2017; Englert 2018), to be followed by surveys about working and living conditions in and across workplaces (Monaco 2015b). Finally, a strong effort in terms of translation into multiple languages in order to guarantee the accessibility of the platforms used will have to be a constant concern (in this regard, *Notes from Below*'s work as described above in Chapter 6 is a very good example).

Overall, though, research and international organizing practices will always have to be sensible and respect contextual variations in terms of language, identity, levels of repression and conflict, etc. Once again, militant researchers will have to cautiously enter terrains of conflict, where workers will lead and highlight research needs building on their own knowledge of the struggle and on their organizing necessities.

This chapter has provided a practical example of a workers' inquiry into a traditional production sector but one located in an emerging economy. The case of the Indian auto workers showed the possibility of conducting an inquiry by adapting research methods to the political context and circumstances in order to explore the labor composition, the processes of working-class formation, and the dynamics of class struggle. The methods of inquiry were particularly essential to mapping the material conditions that led to grievances and strikes, disclosing the features and the vulnerabilities of a labor regime built on high levels of casualization, and analyzing a system based on strong anti-union behaviors, police violence, and state repression.

However, as already noted, while the inquiry disclosed important information that can contribute to a deeper understanding of casualization in India and can serve as a comparison with the working conditions and the struggles of auto workers in different economies, for a Global Workers' Inquiry more has to be done. Indeed, an additional task for militant research to embrace will be that of constantly sharing such stories and political experiences. In order for global solidarity and stronger international strategies to be built, connecting struggles, building bridges, and shedding light on struggles that often receive very little attention (especially in the Global South) is and will continue to be of the utmost importance. This chapter is an attempt, or the beginning of a project, in such a direction.

REFERENCES

Alquati, R. (1975). *Sulla FIAT e altri scritti*. Milan: Feltrinelli.

Barnes, T., Lal Das, K.S., and Pratap, S. (2015). Labour Contractors and Global Production Networks: The Case of India's Auto Supply Chain. *The Journal of Development Studies* 51(4), 355–69.

Bellofiore, R. (2006). Between Panzieri and Negri: Mario Tronti and the Workerism of the 1960s and 1970s. At http://libcom.org/library/between-panzieri-negri-mario-tronti-workerism-1960s-1970s.

Bologna, S. (2013). Workerism: An Inside View. From the Mass-Worker to Self-Employed Labour. In van der Linden, M. and Roth, K.H. (eds.), *Beyond Marx: Confronting Labour-History and the Concept of Labour with the Global Labour-Relations of the Twenty-First Century*. Leiden: Brill, pp. 121–44.

Bologna, S. (2014a). Workerism Beyond Fordism: On the Lineage of Italian Workerism. *Viewpoint* (December 15). At https://viewpointmag.com/2014/12/15/workerism-beyond-fordism-on-the-lineage-of-italian-workerism.

Bologna, S. (2014b). Inside Logistics: Organization, Work, Distinctions. *Viewpoint* (October 29). At http://viewpointmag.com/2014/10/29/inside-logistics-organization-work-distinctions.

Bond, P. (2015). The Intellectual Meets the South African Social Movement: A Code of Conduct is Overdue, When Researching Such a Conflict-Rich Society. *Politikon* 42(1), 117–22.

Brooks, C., Singh, S., and Winslow, S. (2017). *Trainer's Guide: Secrets of a Successful Organizer*. New York: Labor Notes. At https://uale.org/document-table/resources/resources-for-activism/543-secrets-trainers-guide-labor-notes/file.

Cant, C. (2019). *Riding for Deliveroo: Resistance in the New Economy*. Cambridge: Polity Press.

Centro per la Riforma dello Stato (CRS) (Gruppo Lavoro) (2011). *Nuova Panda schiavi in mano—La strategia FIAT di distruzione della forza operaia*. Rome: DeriveApprodi.

Chandrashekhar, C.P. and Ghosh, Jayati (2014). Contract Workers in Manufacturing. *Business Line* (April 28). At www.researchgate.net/profile/Jayati_Ghosh2/publication/315768208_Contract_Workers_in_Manufacturing/links/58e36480a6fdcc385932468d/Contract-Workers-in-Manufacturing.pdf.

Corradi, C. (2011), Panzieri, Tronti, Negri: le diverse eredità dell'Operaismo Italiano, in Poggio, P.P. (ed.), *L'Altronovecento. Comunismo Eretico e Pensiero Critico, Vol. 2: Il Sistema e i Movimenti (Europa 1945–1989)*. Milan: Fondazione Micheletti-Jaca.

Dawson, M.C. and Sinwell, L. (2012). Ethical and Political Challenges of Participatory Action Research in the Academy: Reflections on Social Movements and Knowledge Production in South Africa. *Social Movement Studies* 11(2), 177–91.

Emery, E. (1995). No Politics Without Inquiry: A Proposal for a Class Composition Inquiry Project 1996–7. *Common Sense* 18 (December), 1–11. At https://notesfrombelow.org/article/no-politics-without-inquiry.

Englert, T. (2018). *Precarious Workers, Their Power and the Ways to Realise It: The Struggle of Heineken Labour Broker Workers*. MA thesis, Wits University.

Gurgaon Workers News (GWN) (2006–2015). Workers News from the Special Exploitation Zone (blog), Issues 41, 44, and 61. At https://gurgaonworkersnews.wordpress.com.

Hao Ren et al. (2012–15). *Factory Stories: On the Conditions and Struggles in Chinese Workplaces*. At www.gongchao.org.

Hao Ren, Friedman, E., and Li, Z. (eds) (2016). *China on Strike: Narratives of Workers' Resistance*. Chicago: Haymarket Books.

International Commission for Labor Rights (ICLR) (2013). *Merchants of Menace: Repressing Workers in India's New Industrial Belt. Violation of Workers' and Trade Union Rights at Maruti Suzuki India Ltd*. New York: ICLR.

Jha, P. and Chakraborty, A. (2014). Post-Fordism, Global Production Networks and Implications for Labour: Some Case Studies from National Capital Region, India. Institute for Studies in Industrial Development working paper 2014/172. At http://isid.org.in/pdf/WP172.pdf.

Mdlalose, B. (2014). The Rise and Fall of Abahlali baseMjondolo, a South African Social Movement. *Politikon* 41(3), 345–53.

Monaco L. (2011). Interview with Mario Tronti. October 18.

Monaco, L. (2015a). Nuova Panda schiavi in mano: Workers' Inquiry as a Tool to Unveil Fiat's Strategy of Labour Control. *Historical Materialism* 23(1), 221–42.

Monaco, L. (2015b). *Bringing Operaismo to Gurgaon: A Study of Labour Composition and Resistance Practices in the Indian Auto Industry*. Doctoral thesis, SOAS, University of London.

Monaco, L. (2017). Where Lean May Shake: Challenges to Casualisation in the Indian Auto Industry. *Global Labour Journal* 8(2). At https://mulpress.mcmaster.ca/globallabour/article/view/3040.

Monaco, L. (2018). Interview with Mario Tronti, September 14.

Monaco, L. (2019a). Focus group with Mark Exhaust Systems Ltd workers, January 16.

Monaco, L. (2019b). Interview with labor activists from Workers Solidarity Center, Gurgaon, January 24.

Monaco, L. (2019c). Emerging Insecurities: Precarization of Employment Relations in the Indian and South African Auto Industries. *Labour, Capital and Society* 49(1).

Monaco, L. (2019d). Between Research and Organising: Some Reflections from Workers' Inquiries in UK, India and South Africa. *Notes from Below* (November 27). At https://notesfrombelow.org/article/between-research-and-organising forthcoming.

Monaco, L. (2020, forthcoming). *An Autonomous Conflict? Workers' Inquiry, Casualisation and Labour Agency in the Indian Auto Industry*. London: Routledge.

Panzieri, R. (1976). *Lotte operaie nello sviluppo capitalistico*. Turin: Piccola Biblioteca Einaudi.

Panzieri, R. (1994). Socialist Uses of Workers' Inquiry. In Merli, S. (ed.), *Spontaneità e organizzazione. Gli anni dei Quaderni Rossi 1959–1964*. Pisa: BSF Edizioni. At http://libcom.org/library/socialist-uses-workers-inquiry.

Peoples Union for Democratic Rights (PUDR) (2013). *Labour Struggles and Violation of Rights in Maruti Suzuki India Limited*. New Delhi: PUDR.

Shigang, F. (2018). *Striking to Survive: Workers' Resistance to Factory Relocations in China*. Chicago: Haymarket Books.

Tassinari, A. and Maccarrone, V. (2019). Riders on the Storm: Workplace Solidarity among Gig Economy Couriers in Italy and the UK. *Work, Employment and Society*. At https://doi.org/10.1177/0950017019862954.

Tronti, M. (2006). *Operai e capitale*. 3rd edition. Rome: DeriveApprodi.

Tronti, M. (2009). *Noi operaisti*. Rome: DeriveApprodi.

Tronti, M. (2010). Workerism and Politics. *Historical Materialism* 18(3), 186–9.

Walsh, S. (2015). The Philosopher and His Poor: The Poor-Black as Object for Political Desire in South Africa. *Politikon* 42(1), 123–7.

Woodcock, J. (2016). *Working the Phones*. London: Pluto.

Woodcock, J. (2019). *Marx at the Arcade: Consoles, Controllers, and Class Struggle*. London: Haymarket Books.

Wright, S. (2002). *Storming Heaven: Class Composition and Struggle in Italian Autonomist Marxism*. London: Pluto.

Wright, S. (2007). Back to the Future: Italian Workerists Reflect Upon the Operaista Project. *ephemera: theory & politics in organization* 7, 270–81. At https://libcom.org/files/7-1wright-libre.pdf.

About the Authors

Alpkan Birelma is an assistant professor in the Department of Humanities and Social Sciences at Özyeğin University. As a sociologist, his research focuses on labor movements, working-class subjectivity, and the sociology of work. As an activist, he has volunteered in various labor unions and associations in Turkey since he was an undergraduate. He is a member of Labor Studies Collective, which has been publishing annual reports on working-class protests in Turkey since 2015 at www.emekcalisma.org. He recently published a chapter entitled, "Subcontracted Employment and the Labor Movement's Response in Turkey" in a book edited by P. Durrenberger, and a report for Friedrich Ebert Stiftung entitled *Trade Unions in Turkey 2018*. His latest piece, on working-class entrepreneurialism, will appear in the next issue of New Perspectives on Turkey. Email him at: alpkan.birelma@ozyegin.edu.tr

Dario Bursztyn is a journalist and sociologist born in Buenos Aires, Argentina. He graduated from the Universidad de Buenos Aires (UBA). Dario has collaborated with cultural and political magazines including *Clásica*, *Dirigencia*, and *Crisis*, the National Broadcasting Radio Argentina, and was the author of Chapter 8 in *New Forms of Workers Organization* edited by Immanuel Ness (PM Press, 2014). Dario is the editor of the web magazine *Cuadernos de Crisis* found at www.purochamuyo.com, and editor of books published by Colectivo Editorial Crisis. He has translated books and articles by Franco Bifo Berardi, Miguel Benasayag, Aziz Choudry, Saskia Sassen, Radha D'Souza, Alessandro De Giorgi, Moshe Zimmermann, Bryan W. Van Norden, Jack Shenker, and Luis Fernando Novoa Garzon.

Callum Cant is the author of *Riding for Deliveroo* (Polity Press, 2019). He is a PhD student at the University of West London.

Jenny Chan is an assistant professor of sociology at The Hong Kong Polytechnic University and a vice president of the International Sociological Association's Research Committee on Labor Movements (2018–22). *Dying for an iPhone: Apple, Foxconn and the Lives of China's Workers* is her first book (coauthored with Mark Selden and Pun Ngai, 2020). Jenny Chan can be contacted at HJ433, Department of Applied Social Sciences, The Hong Kong Polytechnic University, Hong Kong. Email: jenny.wl.chan@polyu.edu.hk

Patrick Cuninghame is a sociologist and social historian at the Universidad Autonoma Metropolitana in Mexico City. His most recent publications are "#Yo soy132 and the 'Mexican Spring' of 2012: Between Electoral Engagement and Democratisation," published in 2017 in the *Bulletin of Latin American Research* 36(2), and "Self-Management, Workers' Control and Resistance Against Crisis and Neoliberal Counter-Reforms in Mexico," in *An Alternative Labour History: Worker Control and Workplace Democracy*, published in 2015.

Anna Curcio is a militant scholar in the field of autonomous Marxism. She has published internationally on the conflicts and transformations of labor in relationship with race and gender. Among her publications in English are *Challenging Italian Racism* (ed. with Miguel Mellino), Darkmatter journal special issue 2010; "The Common and the Forms of the Commune" (with Ceren Özselçuk), *Rethinking Marxism* 22(3), 2010; "Practicing Militant Inquiry: Composition, Strike and Betting in the Logistics Workers struggles in Italy," *ephemera* 14(3), 2014; "Paths of Racism, Flows of Labor: Nation-State Formation, Capitalism and the Metamorphosis of Racism in Italy," *Viewpoint* (2014); "The Revolution in Logistics," in Azzelini, D. and Kraft M. (eds.), *New Forms of Workers Organization and Struggles: Autonomous Labor Responses in Time of Crisis* (Brill, 2015); "Logistics is the Logic of Capital" (with Gigi Roggero), *Viewpoint* (2018).

Sai Englert is a researcher.

Shawn Hattingh is based in Cape Town, South Africa. He works as a research and education officer at the International Labour Research and Information Group (ILRIG). Hattingh has written numerous articles for South African and international activist websites and publications, covering issues such as the capitalist crisis, new forms of worker organizing, and anarchism. He has also been involved in a number of activist organizations in South Africa. For more information on ILRIG visit: www.ilrigsa.org.za

Lydia Hughes is a trade union organizer.

Wendy Liu is a software developer and (reformed) startup founder. She is an economics editor for *New Socialist* and is working on a book for Repeater called *Abolish Silicon Valley*, out in 2020.

Dr. Dale T. McKinley is based in Johannesburg, South Africa. He is an independent writer, researcher, and lecturer as well as research and education officer for the International Labour, Research and Information Group. He holds a PhD in International Political Economy/African Studies and is a veteran political activist who has been involved in social movement, community, and liberation organizations and struggles for over three decades. The author of four books, McKinley has written and published widely on various aspects of South African, regional, and global political, social, and economic issues and struggles. He is also a regular speaker at various civil society and academic, social, and political conferences and events and a contributor in the print media as well as a commentator on radio and television.

Achille Marotta is a member of the London IWW.

Lorenza Monaco is currently a senior lecturer in the School of Economics, University of Johannesburg. She holds an MA in International Development from the University of Naples, L'Orientale, and a PhD in Development Studies from the School of Oriental and African Studies, University of London. Lorenza's main research interests include the political economy of development, industrial development in emerging economies, and labor in global production. She has conducted extensive research in India, South Africa, and recently in Thailand, with a particular focus on labor casualization in the global auto industry and on the relationship between casual workers' movements and trade unions. She has been politically active in Italy, the UK and South Africa, especially in anti-casualization campaigns. Since 2010–11, she has been working on issues related to workers' inquiries and co-research, trying to connect Italian workerist practices to the study of labor in the Global South.

Robert Ovetz is a contingent lecturer in political science at San José State University in California and a member of the California Faculty Association. He is the author of *When Workers Shot Back: Class Conflict from 1877 to 1921* (Brill 2018 and Haymarket 2019). He is a member of the editorial board of *The Journal of Labor and Society*. Post information about your strike threat at https://strikethreats.org and follow him at @OvetzRobert.

Seth Wheeler is a PhD student at the University of Royal Holloway.

Jamie Woodcock is a researcher.

Index

Index

Thanks to our Patreon Subscribers:

Abdul Alkalimat
Andrew Perry

Who have shown their generosity and comradeship in difficult times.

The Pluto Press Newsletter

Hello friend of Pluto!

Want to stay on top of the best radical books
we publish?

Then sign up to be the first to hear about our
new books, as well as special events,
podcasts and videos.

You'll also get 50% off your first order with us
when you sign up.

Come and join us!

Go to bit.ly/PlutoNewsletter

Institutions of care   conflict resolution
          - developed   mutual aid
          outside family
              unit

educational institutions

cultural institutions

production